MANAGING TECHNOLOGY

MANAGING TECHNOLOGY

Competing through New Ventures, Innovation, and Corporate Research

FREDERICK BETZ

National Science Foundation

PRENTICE-HALL, INC., Englewood Cliffs, New Jersey 07632

Library of Congress Cataloging-in-Publication Data

BETZ, FREDERICK.
    Managing technology.

    Bibliography: p. 249
    Includes index.
    1. Technological innovations—Management.
2. Research, Industrial—Management.   I. Title.
HD45.B43 1987   658.5'14   86-5084
ISBN   0-13-550849-5

Cover design: Ben Santora
Manufacturing buyer: Ed O'Dougherty

Printed in the United States of America

10 9 8 7 6 5 4 3 2

ISBN 0-13-550849-5   01

Prentice-Hall International (UK) Limited, *London*
Prentice-Hall of Australia Pty. Limited, *Sydney*
Prentice-Hall Canada Inc., *Toronto*
Prentice-Hall Hispanoamericana, S.A., *Mexico*
Prentice-Hall of India Private Limited, *New Delhi*
Prentice-Hall of Japan, Inc., *Tokyo*
Prentice-Hall of Southeast Asia Pte. Ltd., *Singapore*
Editora Prentice-Hall do Brasil, Ltda., *Rio de Janeiro*

For Nancy,
Sara, Fred, and Franz David

CONTENTS

PART III   MANAGING RESEARCH

PART IV   R&D INFRASTRUCTURE

23   NATIONAL R&D SYSTEMS   221

24   TECHNOLOGY REVOLUTIONS   231

PREFACE

Technology underpins business, providing the technical knowledge for the goods and services that a firm produces. Technological innovation is new technology creating new products and services—hence new business opportunities. This is the basic importance of innovation and the reason innovation is fundamental to economic development, the creation of business opportunities.

Managing technology means to use new technology to create competitive advantages. It is a difficult problem to manage, partly due to the differing cultures in a corporation. Technology is often thought to be solely the domain of the scientific and engineering personnel of an organization. Yet successful business use of technology requires strategic decisions about technology by personnel in other functional areas, such as production, marketing, sales, finance, and so on. The focus of this book is on bridging these two cultures: technical and functional. We will examine how management can integrate technological strategy into business strategy.

The issues in managing technological innovation have been organized under four topics: (1) innovation, (2) new ventures, (3) corporate research, and (4) R&D infrastructure. Innovation is the most general concept, covering the process from the invention of technical knowledge to the commercialization of products and processes based on that knowledge. New ventures focus on the organizational dynamics which are required to manage innovation into successful business ventures. Corporate research is the business function that must be well managed and integrated with other functions if an organization is to be innovative over the long term of the corporate future. The larger knowledge context for corporate research is the R&D infrastructure of a nation. Accordingly, three different but related literatures have been distilled in this book: those on innovation, on R&D administration, and specifically, on new ventures and entrepreneurship. The value of covering these areas together is that they enlighten one another. For example, what is mysterious in the innovation literature is how to create new technical knowledge. This is focused on in the R&D administration literature. Yet the eternal problem in the R&D administration literature is how to translate technical success into business success. And this is the focus of the venturing and entrepreneural literature.

For the general reader, this book intends to provide an overview of the role of technological change in the corporation. It is also intended to be useful in management and business schools as an introductory course (at either a graduate or undergraduate level) on the management of technology. This is a topic that is beginning to be covered more and more in curricula—as the importance of the strategic role of technological change in business planning becomes appreciated. Accordingly, this book's emphasis is on breadth and inclusiveness of ideas in managing technological change.

Some management schools have begun to offer graduate specializations in the management of technology in their M.B.A. programs. Such a specialization is often of particular interest to students who had previously obtained technical degrees. In addition to an overview course (at the level of this book), other courses in such a program might profitably spend a semester each on the innovation process and upon ventures/entrepreneurship—both topics of R&D management and of technology and society also deserve two more semesters in their own right. A course in marketing new technological products could also be offered, as well as a course in manufacturing strategy.

Stylistically, theoretical topics are generally preceded by an actual example of a corporation dealing with technological change. The examples were chosen to be prototypical of the issues discussed in the theory of the chapter. They provide a concreteness for the abstractness of the ideas. Since they are real cases, they do not strictly limit themselves to the point at hand, but they do show that the issues being discussed are real and often vitally important to business success.

Technology played a vital role in the original industrial revolution of the eighteenth and nineteenth centuries. Technological innovation continues to play an important role in industrial competitiveness and in the globalization of markets and industry that is occurring in the twentieth century and into the twenty-first.

FREDERICK BETZ

CHAPTER ONE
INNOVATION AND COMPETITION

CENTRAL IDEAS

1. Technological change and competitive advantage
2. Transformation of inventions into products
3. Types of innovation
4. Impact of innovation on markets and competition
5. Transilience of innovation

Example: Timing Innovation—The Osborne Computer

Managing technology is the timely creation and improvement of the products and productive capability of the corporation. Innovation processes, research, and new ventures are the tools of the innovative manager.

Correct timing of innovation can create business success; conversely, incorrect timing can create failure. In the early 1980s, the rise and fall of Osborne Computer illustrated the strength and ruthlessness of timing innovation. In July 1981, as a brand new company, Osborne shipped its first computers. In two months, it had its first $1 million in sales; by the second year, net revenues were over $100 million. Yet six months later, it was bankrupt.

The personal computer market had begun in the middle 1970s, and Adam Osborne wrote and published books about programming and microcomputers. By the summer of 1980, Osborne was working for McGraw-Hill, to whom he had sold his computer book publishing company. He decided then to create his own computer, because he saw an awkwardness in the marketing of personal computers. They were being sold as components—computer, disk drive, monitor, printer, software. Osborne decided to package them together as a portable computer and to sell the package cheaper than competitors' equivalent component sets (Osborne and Dvorak, 1984).

1

Osborne incorporated a new company and hired Lee Felsenstein to design the electronics for the computer. Then he presented his ideas for the new venture to Jack Melchor, a venture capitalist. Melchor invested $40,000. It was an instant success. By the end of the first year, sales of the Osborne personal computer soared to one-third of the then leader in personal computers. Osborne had created a new market niche.

Quickly, competitors entered the new market (notably Kaypro), focusing on the Osborne's visibly weak features—small screen and narrow column width. The screen was 5 inches diagonally—very small, showing tiny characters. Also, its display showed only 52 characters across rather than the normal 80-character width on a typed page. Kaypro corrected this product mistake of display, with a larger screen showing 80 characters. This small difference in features made a big difference in the application of the personal computer as a word processor. Kaypro sales soared. Osborne sales plunged.

This is a general lesson for technology management. A new product concept creates new markets or alters old markets. Competitors enter the new market, focusing on obviously weak features of the innovative product.

The reason Osborne had chosen a 5-inch display was to keep the computer as compact as possible and to minimize interferring radio noise inside the computer. Product design always requires trade-offs on desirable features. He later planned to enlarge the screen, but delayed the introduction of a new, larger-screen model too long. This was the first problem.

The second problem was also an unfortunate delay—in the generation of additional capital through a public offering. Osborne had planned it for the summer of 1982 but put it off until early 1983. Then, at that time, the brokerage firm decided not to make the offer yet, because of the sales slump which began that last summer. What had happened was that potential Osborne customers had decided to wait for Osborne to offer a new model with a larger screen, like the Kaypro screen. Thus after the summer of 1982, Osborne's sales decline had created a financial crisis.

November and December passed, without significant sales. January, February, March, and April passed, without sales. The Osborne Company was going through a cash-flow hemorrhage. Bank loans could not be increased, and the public offering had not occurred. Osborne made several attempts to raise new capital privately, but there still was not enough cash to carry the company. In September 1983, the Osborne Company declared insolvency under Chapter 11 of the bankruptcy law. All the millions of equity on paper only a year before had vanished. The company failed under one of the basic tenets of technology management. All products have finite lifetimes, and timely product innovation should be a part of every management's technology strategy.

All through the 1980s, the market for portable computers continued to grow, even in the year the Osborne Company failed. Kaypro, its competitor, had in that same year one of its most profitable years. Andrew F. Kay and his family (who owned Kaypro) offered 5 million shares to the public in 1983, realizing $9 million from the sale of part of their equity.

And for Osborne Computer Corp—a happy ending, sort of. A reorganized company emerged from Chapter 11 in 1984, offering a new version of the computer with a 7-inch screen. But Adam Osborne was not part of the reorganized firm; he had gone on to form the Paperback Software Company. You can't keep an American entrepreneur down for long.

TIMING AND INNOVATION

The timing of technological innovation can be the critical factor in both business success and failure. In this example, a new company was started by a novel product that developed a market. New ventures can begin in this way, but they do not stop there. The example showed further that the company failed at the first challenge of competition. At first, everything went together right; but later, everything went wrong at the same time. This often happens in new ventures, everything seeming either to go right or wrong at the same time. Successful new ventures must cope both with rapid growth and increasing competition. In Chapter 4 we will return to this example to explain in more detail the problems of newly growing companies (when we can explore the reasons, using theoretical concepts called industrial systems dynamics).

For now, we should understand that the example illustrated two of the three types of timing in innovation:

1. New product introduction
2. Product improvement
3. Cost reduction through process innovation

Managers should create competitive lead time with innovative new products, since this provides market positioning. They should continue to introduce timely product improvement to keep the product technologically competitive. They must also continually improve production processes to lower product cost, keeping the product price competitive. In the management of technology, doors in time open and close; and business opportunities appear and disappear.

TECHNOLOGY AND COMPETITION—ABOUT WHICH WE WILL BE THINKING

We digress for a moment to point toward where we are going. Timing is only one of the factors important in managing technology. Although technological competitiveness is necessary for corporate survival, it is not sufficient. The reason it is necessary is that a corporation with inferior technology cannot compete at the same price level with a corporation superior in technology. The reason superior technology alone is not sufficient is that business is a system, and there are many other factors that determine business success. Accordingly, to use technology as a competitive edge, management must manage it as a part of the business system.

That is what we are to do in this book—show how technological innovation can be integrated with production, marketing, finance, and personnel into a balanced business system. The topics of the book have been chosen to show the coupling of technology with other aspects of business. These topics have been grouped under four central concepts in managing technology: new ventures, innovation, research, and research infrastructure.

The first concept discussed is the new venture, since one important result of technological innovation is new business. Although new ventures centered on new technology are an important class of new businesses, new high-tech ventures are difficult because they involve two major risks: developing new products and creating new markets. Ideas central to new ventures are entrepreneurial management, the business plan, and the dynamics of organizational growth.

Innovation is discussed next because it is the overarching concept, denoting the whole span of activity from creating new technological knowledge to implementing it in new businesses. Ideas central to innovation are the concepts of the types of innovation, processes of innovation, the technology S-curve, technology life cycle, economic long cycles, sources of innovation, business opportunities in a technological system, marketing and new technology, corporate diversification through new ventures, and technology in manufacturing strategies.

The third concept discussed is corporate research. Technological change is new knowledge about what things to produce and how to produce them; and in the corporation, new knowledge often comes from corporate research. The corporate laboratory is charged with looking forward to the future productivity of the corporation. Managing and integrating corporate research with other management functions and strategies is essential to technology management. Central ideas in research management include the organization of research, project management, research personnel, and corporate research strategy.

The fourth concept discussed is the R&D infrastructure. The technologies of a corporation do not exist in a vacuum but are part of a larger technological context, first of the industry, then of the nation, and then of the world. This larger context is a research and development infrastructure, and it has an important influence on the competitive conditions in a country. With the expansion and increase of intensity of international competition, the R&D infrastructure of a nation can play a critical role in economic competition.

Our focus, therefore, is understanding how to manage technological change in the corporation. Some have called this a kind of "high-tech strategy." For example, Rosenbloom and Abernathy critiqued the role of technology strategy in the consumer electronics industry:

> The successful innovators in the home videocasette recorder turned out to be, then, consumer electronics companies that had long pursued a global "high technology" strategy toward their business. . . .
> In contrast, the American consumer electronics industry in the late fifties and through the 1960's was captive of a different ideology.
> First, managements responded . . . by focusing on cost cutting.
> Second, the American industry never developed markets abroad.
> Third, American managers tended to look to market research and "objective" analysis to identify latent market opportunities, whereas . . . [others] took risks on novel products and set out to develop the market. (Rosenbloom and Abernathy, 1982, p. 221)

Managing technology is taking risks in novel products and developing new markets.

Example: The Xerox Innovation

To understand these risks, let us next clarify the distinction between innovation and invention, since invention is only the beginning of innovation. The steps required to transform invention into innovation can be illustrated in the famous Xerox story.

In 1935, Chester Carlson was working in the patent office of Mallory Company. His technical background included work as a carbon chemist, printer, and then as a patent lawyer. He became concerned about the errors in copying patents for public dissemination and at the costs involved in copying. Using his chemistry and printing background, he began experimenting with new ways to create a copying process. His basic idea was (1) to project the image of a typed paper onto a blank sheet of paper coated with dry ink, (2) to hold the ink temporarily at spaces of typed letters by static electrical charges induced by the light, and (3) finally to melt the ink into the paper by baking the paper. This would produce a quick, dry reproduction of a typed page; and the process came to be called xerography.

Carlson succeeded in obtaining a crude image, thereby reducing his idea to practice. He filed for a patent. Yet like all new inventions, it was still not commercially efficient, cost-effective, or easily usable. It required development. Development of new technology usually costs a great deal of money, takes time, and requires skilled resources. All inventors face similar problems—first conceiving the invention, reducing it to practice, obtaining a patent, then obtaining support for development and commercialization.

Carlson went from company to company seeking support. He was turned down, again and again. By 1942, he had obtained the valuable patent on the basic process. Then a venturesome group at Battelle Memorial Institute agreed to work on the development in return for a share in potential royalties. Battelle was a nonprofit research and development organization, with a range of advanced technical research capabilities.

Finally, the innovative pieces for Carlson began to fall in place—invention, patents, development, commercialization. In 1945, while Battelle began development of the xerography process, a small company named Haloid learned of Carlson' patents. Joseph Wilson, the president, was a risk taker and was looking for new products. Wilson produced the first copiers, using Carlson's patents and Battelle's developments.

The rest of the story became business history. That company became Xerox, creating a new industry in office copying products. Xerox grew and grew, keeping a technological and marketing dominance over the industry for almost three decades. Interesting questions: How many companies missed out on the xerography patents? Why did it take a R&D outfit like Battelle to see the technical potential in Carlson's invention? What leadership qualities do innovative, risk-taking managers like Joseph Wilson possess?

INNOVATION AND INVENTION

Invention is an idea for a novel product or process. The definition of innovation is the introduction into the market place of new products, processes, or services. Technological innovation is a subset of innovation, the introduction of new products, processes, or services based on new technology.

This technological innovation does begin with invention. The first steps are the idea of the invention and the research to reduce the idea to practice. This often results in a functional prototype, which can be used for filing a patent (if the invention is novel). In the Xerox story, this was Carlson's contribution. The next step is the research and development of the prototype into a commercially designed product. This was the role that Battelle played in the Xerox example. Finally, the product must be produced and sold—the role that Haloid played in creating Xerox.

This distinction between invention and innovation is an important one, for the transformation from ideas into a successful product is actually difficult. This transformation is the heart of the complex process of innovation (which we describe in Chapter 5). The hard fact is that few inventions are successfully innovated, with few inventions developed into new products, and even fewer new products succeed commercially. The problem of managing technology thus divides into two parts: encouraging invention and managing successful innovation. Encouraging invention falls within the topic of corporate research, to which we will devote Part III. Managing successful innovation falls within the topic of the innovation to which we devote Part II.

TYPES OF INNOVATION

Technological innovations can be classified by the degree of innovativeness and by application.

Radical, Systems, and Incremental Innovations

Innovations differ significantly in the radicalness of technological change and coupling with other parts of technology. Accordingly, Donald Marquis identified at least three general types of innovation:

1. Radical, basic, breakthrough innovation which changes or creates whole industries;
2. Systems innovations, such as communications networks, which take many years and millions of dollars to accomplish; and
3. "Nuts and bolt" or incremental innovations, which are small but important improvements to products, processes or services. (Marquis, 1969)

Xerography was a radical innovation. Other examples were the electronic vacuum tube and the transistor, which created and revolutionized the electronics industry. Still other examples were the steam engine and the gasoline engine, each of which also fostered new industries. Radical innovations are rare because they usually are based on new scientific phenomena. The vacuum tube used the new knowledge about conduction of electrons in vacuum; the transistor used the new knowledge about conduction in semiconducting materials.

Radical innovations sometimes also become key components of systems innovations. Systems innovations create a new functionality by assembling parts in new ways. For example, the vacuum tube was first used in the telephone system and then became a part of radio communications and television communications systems and computer systems. The transistor first substituted for vacuum tubes and then went on to foster a wider application of digital technologies in electronics. Similarly, the steam engine was put on wheels to become the train and into sailing ships to become steamships. Gasoline engines were combined with carriage and bicycle technologies to create automobiles and then with gliders to create airplanes.

Incremental innovations continue the technical improvement and extend the applications of radical and system innovations. After each new radical or system innovation, there are many, many technological improvements, many new applications, and many new infrastructure developments to improve the original innovations.

For example, the invention of the vacuum tube required the improved means of creating vacuums before it became a practical and reliable component of telephones. Subsequent developments in the three-component tube (cathode, plate, and grid) added more grids until improved tubes had up to five or six grids. These incremental innovations in the vacuum tube improved the volume, range, and fidelity of amplification and allowed the tubes to perform better other electronic functions (such as oscillation). Similarly, hundreds of innovations have improved the transistors, created integrated circuits, large-scale integrated circuits, and very large scale integrated circuits.

Incremental innovations keep corporations continuously innovative and provide the basis for strategic planning of research and development. Incremental innovations are far greater in number than radical and system innovations and, over time, provide as dramatic an impact on technological change as did the original innovations.

Product, Process, and Service Innovations

Technological innovations also divide as applications into product or process or service innovations. A product innovation is the introduction into the market of a new type of technological product. A process innovation is the introduction into the firm or market of a new type of technological production process. A service innovation is the introduction of a new service based on new technological skills (for example, computer software production). Product or process or service innovations can be either radical, systems, or incremental. For example, both the Xerox and Osborne were product innovations; but the Xerox was radical and the Osborne computer incremental.

Example: Industrial Restructuring—Sewall's Plastic Bottles

Although invention is the beginning of innovation, the bottom line of innovation is the market. The market judges whether an innovation is timely and important by buying or ignoring the innovative product. Radical innovations create new markets or alter older markets. Systems innovations provide many business opportunities in the different parts of the system serving the markets. Incremental innovations strengthen the competitive position of a company in an existing market.

As an example of the impact that an incremental innovation can have on industrial competition, consider the transformation of the Dorsey Corporation from a regional into a national manufacturer. In 1982, John T. Pollock was the chairman of the Dorsey Corporation. He, with his associate Charles K. Sewall, changed what was a small southern company from a regional glass bottle company into a major national competitor in a new plastic bottle business.

In 1975, Dorsey's management recognized that a new technology was emerging that would make obsolete Dorsey's major product line but could provide the opportunity to surprise competitors and enable Dorsey to emerge as the major national manufacturer in a restructured industry. The company then consisted of three divisions: Chattanooga Glass, Sewell Plastics, and Dorsey Trailers. Chattanooga Glass made green Coca-Cola bottles. Sewell Plastics produced plastic containers. Dorsey Trailers made cargo trailers to transport dry freight. The Chattanooga Glass Division accounted for 60% of total sales and dominated Dorsey's business (Boyer, 1983).

New technology in plastics, called polyethylene terphthalate (PET), had been invented in the research laboratories of DuPont. A plastic bottle made of PET was not only lighter than glass bottles but could hold carbonated beverages as well as could glass bottles. A potential materials substitution became possible when an engineer at DuPont made a 2-liter container out of PET.

The fact that both the material and application was invented at DuPont, a chemical firm, for the beverage industry was not unusual—for the chemical industry was research intensive, innovative, and continually seeking new markets for its inventions. DuPont had, by 1977, received government FDA approval to use the 2-liter PET bottle as a beverage container. The machine tool company, Cincinnati Milacron, built a tool that could mass produce the PET bottle. The PET bottle was an incremental product innovation, and the tool to mass produce the PET bottles was an incremental process innovation.

There was an opportunity for Dorsey—a small company with an older technology—yet receptive to technological change. It took foresight and determination by its management. In 1977, most glass companies had been ignoring the potential new plastic technology in bottles. Charles K. Sewell (who then was 45 and had been founder and president of Dorsey's Sewell Plastics Division) saw the importance of the technical revolution and was determined to capitalize on it. Sewell was known as an impatient man—and impatience can be a virtue when coupled with determination to innovate. Sewell understood that if his small division was to beat the giant companies (such as Owen-Illinois, Continental Group, and Amoco) into the new 2-liter PET bottle market, he must act swiftly.

Sewell did. He told the company of the opportunity and the required level of investment. The president and the board approved. Sewell then ordered $4 million in machinery from Cincinnati Milacron, following with a $9 million order. He installed the new machines in each of his plants, which previously had made only plastic containers for milk and chemicals. That allowed Sewell to spread the overhead costs on the new PET products and positioned him to serve local markets better.

Sewell's customers saw him as responsive and timely in helping them solve problems. This increased his business. By 1982, after aggressive investment, Sewell Plastics had rapidly moved into the position of market leader in the $800 million volume of the 2-liter container market. It was a story of a David beating out the giants, with foresight and aggressive change in corporate technology. It is important to note that Sewell's correct business strategy had been based on two sources of understanding: technology and market. Because Sewell Plastics was in the plastic container business, Sewell had the technological background to appreciate the significance of the PET technology. Second, because Sewell's sister division, Chattanooga Glass, was in the soft-drink glass-container business, Sewell also understood the potential market for the new technology.

This illustrates an important lesson—major technological innovations always provide times for restructuring industrial competition. Still, one of the most difficult managerial tricks is the transformation of the basic technology of a company. Such transformation affects all aspects of the organization—capital expenditure, plant and equipment, personnel and skills, markets and sales. Yet when new technology threatens an older technology, it is better to take the risks in a new industry than the certainties of a dying industry: "The alternative is uninviting—a strong position in a flagging industry and no position at all in the successor that's emerging" (Boyer, 1983, p. 176).

TRANSILIENCE OF INNOVATION

Competitive advantage from technological change is a complex process requiring coordination of all parts of the business system. We can see in the example above that, properly implemented, product or process innovations can restructure competitive positions, and that a company need not invent the technological change to implement the innovation and gain the commercial success. This is one of the basic facts about innovation, which we encounter again and again, that makes managing technological change a challenge. Sewall saw the commercial implications of the DuPont invention and conceived the business strategy to use it. Sewall had to persuade his boss and his board to plan a major business change and to commit the investment and organization to change. Sewall's initiative is also an example in entrepreneurial management (a topic we explore in Chapter 2).

Michael Porter, in analyzing competitive strategy, nicely summarized the importance of technology in competition: "Technological change is one of the principal drivers of competition. It plays a major role in industry structural change, as well as in creating new industries. It is also a great equalizer, eroding the competitive advantage of even well-entrenched firms and propelling others to the forefront . . ." (Porter, 1985, p. 164).

Because technological change is such a far-reaching process that extensively affects business functioning, Abernathy and Clark emphasized the "transilient" nature of corporate innovation. By this they meant how the impact of the technology "leaps or passes" from one state of the corporation to another. It is just this "passing-through" aspect of technological change that makes innovation a profound concept for business (Abernathy and Clark, 1985).

For example, to clarify the impact of innovation on the competence of a firm, Abernathy and Clark classified corporate activities into production/technology competencies and market/customer competencies:

1. Under production/technology, they indicated that innovations may alter:
   a. Product design,
   b. Production systems,
   c. Skills and knowledge base,
   d. Materials and capital equipment.
2. Under markets/customers, they indicated that innovations may alter:
   a. Customer bases,
   b. Customer applications,
   c. Channels of distribution and service,
   d. Customer knowledge and modes of communication.
   (Abernathy and Clark, 1985)

On any of these factors, the impact of innovation may range from strengthening existing competencies of the corporation to obsoleting existing competencies. This means, for example, that on the technology/production side, any particular innovation that alters the design of a product may either improve an existing design or obsolete all existing designs. Similarly, an innovation may alter a production process by improving an existing process or it may obsolete the process. The skills of personnel and knowledge base of the organization may be changed by innovation, reinforcing existing skills or obsoleting them. So, too, can capital equipment be affected. On the market/customer side, innovations may also change relationships to customer bases, channels of distribution, customer applications, customer knowledge and communications—either reinforcing existing patterns or radically altering patterns. For example, the PET bottle innovation by Dorsey obsoleted both the product and production processes of glass beverage bottles for larger-sized containers. The innovation had transilient effects on the products, process, organization, and competitive standing of Dorsey.

To summarize the managerial issues in the concept of "technological innovation," one can assert: *If any new technology creates new functions or distinct performance advantages in a function, that technology will be innovated and will supersede previous technology—the only questions are when, where, by whom, and for what market.*

But these are big questions, on which business success or failure can ride. It is to answer these kinds of questions in more detail that we will examine the topics of new ventures, innovation, and research management. Managing technology thus means understanding and anticipating the transilent nature of technological change on business opportunities.

SUMMARY

The keys to successful technology management are timing, innovation, and matching technology to markets—the technically superior product for the right market at the right time. Technological innovations can be radical, systems, or incremental. Radical, systems, or incremental innovations can be as new products, processes, or services. The transilent nature of innovation on the corporation makes it a profound business concept, with any particular innovation potentially reinforcing or obsoleting business strengths.

REFLECTION

1. Think of an industry, and identify a radical, systems, and incremental innovation in the industry. Who made them, and what impacts did they have for the innovating firms and on the industry? When did these innovations occur—early or late in the history of the industry?

FOR FURTHER READING

HILL, CHRISTOPHER T., and JAMES M. UTTERBACK, eds., *Technological Innovation for a Dynamic Economy*. Elmsford, N.Y.: Pergamon Press, 1979.

CHAPTER TWO
ENTREPRENEURSHIP

CENTRAL IDEAS

1. Entrepreneurs and innovation
2. Entrepreneurs and stewardship
3. Role of the entrepreneur
4. Entrepreneurship in large organizations
5. Forms of venturing in large organizations
6. Organizational barriers to innovation
5. Venture teams

Example: Entrepreneurs and Heroes—Nolan Bushnell

The key management style in new ventures and innovation is entrepreneurial, and in the studies of entrepreneurship, three broad themes have emerged:

1. There is an emotional theme. The entrepreneur is a kind of business hero; and like all heroes, they have qualities to be admired: initiative, daring, courage, commitment. These virtues are especially admired in turbulent business conditions, when initiative is required for survival.
2. In many of the stories of successful entrepreneurs, problems of change of leadership occur, particularly after the organization has grown large and requires rationalization. Then the notion of the professional manager, or steward, is sought to take over after the entrepreneur.
3. Within an organization, some entrepreneurship should always be encouraged, supported, and rewarded if the organization is to be innovative. Yet balancing the rewards for entrepreneurship against rewards for stewardship in a large organization is a difficult problem.

An example of an entrepreneur whose career illustrated all these themes is Nolan Bushnell. In the 1970s, Bushnell innovated the first commercially successful video game. Then he started two companies based on games, Atari and Pizza Time Theatre. Both blasted off—as in a video game—flying high, for a while, then exploded.

One of the first widely used computer game was "Spacewar," invented by an MIT student in 1962. In the next decades, many computer games were passed around and filed surreptiously in large computers at universities and research laboratories. Intellectuals like intellectual fun. In the late 1960s, Bushnell was an engineering student at the University of Utah, where he played the games on their computers and also worked in an amusement park during vacations (Coll, 1984).

By 1971, Bushnell was working as a research engineer in the Silicon Valley of California. He wrote his first game, which he called Computer Space. He couldn't sell it. At that time, the only commercial outlet for video games were coin-operated machines, the classic pinball games. Bushnell next developed a simple but visually quick game called Pong. He formed a company which he called Atari and produced Pong. The game changed the coin-operated game business. Competitors rushed in; by 1974, the industry produced 100,000 Pong-type video games, but Atari had produced only 10% of them. Atari was too small to compete strongly.

Bushnell then decided to build an inexpensive attachment hooked up to a home TV set that would play Pong. Although a little earlier, in 1972, Magnavox had introduced the first home video game, called Odyssey, it had not caught fire. But Bushnell's video game flashed! It was a hit! He introduced it in 1975, and it was sold out before it reached the stores. Sears, Roebuck had agreed to buy all that Atari could produce that year, about 100,000 games.

Busnell knew he had a big thing—home video games—but he needed capital for rapid expansion. He decided to look for a large buyer. He had always admired Disney and approached them, but they did not buy. Warner Communications bought for $28 million. Busnell was then 33 years old, and his share was $15 million.

Bushnell bought a Lear jet and a yacht (which he named Pong). He bought a 16-acre northern California estate, with old stone walls and riding stables, a swimming pool, and tennis courts. He also bought homes in Aspen, Colorado, and in Paris. Entrepreneurs have a sense of adventure and fun. And money is fun. Yet for an entrepreneur, the real fun is starting companies. Bushnell decided to start an entertainment empire (Coll, 1984).

At first after Warner purchased Atari, Bushnell had stayed, developing a new video game system. In 1977, Warner had invested an additional $120 million to develop and market the system. Sales began in late 1977, but sales did not grow through 1978. A Warner executive proposed a reorganization of Atari. Bushnell argued that the unit had been priced too high. In December 1978, Bushnell resigned from Atari.

Atari went on to big times, for a while, under a new president, Raymond Kassar. From 1979 through 1981, video games and home video game attachments made up the hottest game in town. In 1980, Atari sold $415 million, clearing an operating income of $77 million. Meanwhile, the personal computer industry boomed. Atari developed home computers (models 800 and 400) to compete with Apple. In 1981, it looked like nothing could go wrong for Atari, but everything did.

By 1982, the home video game market had become saturated, and Atari was stuck with a huge inventory. Simultaneously, in 1982, Atari's home computers were undercut in price by Commodore. Atari bled from both sides, games and computers. Raymond Kassar resigned. Warner brought in a new president, experienced in marketing cigarettes. To no avail, for Atari did not have a marketing problem; it had a product problem. Commodore, led by Jack Tramiel, had introduced a lower-priced computer, and Atari could not meet the price. Irony—Tramiel contributed to the decline of Atari; but after Tramiel left Commodore, Warner sold Atari to Tramiel. Tramiel then shaped a new Atari to attack his old Commodore.

The sorrows of Atari illustrated the classic problem—entrepreneurship versus stewardship. The entrepreneur with vision was Bushnell. He needed capital for rapid growth and sold to a big firm. The firm decided the company needed stewardship and brought in management to organize the growth in a stable way. Initially, the stewardship worked but lacked long-range vision—the kind of vision of the entrepreneur. Things were all right for the steward until the market and competitors changed the conditions of competition. Entrepreneurs have vision.

ENTREPRENEURS AND INNOVATION

Innovation and new ventures require leadership—entrepreneurship. New ideas are tried and new ways implemented. What constitutes the makeup of an entrepreneur—part innovator, part capitalist, part risktaker, part visionary? Can entrepreneurship be encouraged in the large corporation? How can entrepreneurship in the beginning of a new firm be transformed into strong management for the growth and stability of a firm?

Let us first turn to the relationship between innovation and entrepreneurship. Innovation, in general, is any kind of change in industrial practice which improves productivity, competitiveness, or service of markets. Peter Drucker listed several sources of opportunity for innovation:

1. Unexpected occurrences,
2. Incongruities,
3. Process needs,
4. Industry and market changes,
5. Demographic changes,
6. Changes in perception,
7. New knowledge.
   (Drucker, 1985b, p. 68)

Unexpected occurrences include events such as finding new markets for existing products; incongruities include adapting existing products to new functions when discrepancies exist between expectations and results for existing operations. Process needs are opportunities for improvement in existing processes. Industry and market changes and demographic changes provide business opportunities as industries, markets, or demographic changes create new needs or balances of needs. Changes in perceptions, such as life-style, may also create new market opportunities. The last source of innovative opportunities is new knowledge. It has been this source on which we have focused—technological innovation.

The concept of entrepreneurship, however, encompasses all sources of innovation. The entrepreneur is the kind of manager who creates business change. Howard Stevenson and David Gumpert compared managers along two dimensions: (1) desire for future change, and (2) perceived ability to create change. The entrepreneur is the kind of manager desiring future change and perceiving the ability to create such change. Furthermore, the entrepreneur asks:

> Where is the opportunity?
> How do I capitalize on it?
> What resources do I need?
> How do I gain control over them?
> What structure is best?
> (Stevenson and Gumpert, 1985, p. 87)

In contrast, managers who are more concerned with stability than change, ask the following kinds of questions:

> What resources do I control?
> What structure determines our organization's relationship to its market?
> How can I minimize the impact of others on my ability to perform?
> What opportunity is appropriate?
> (Stevenson and Gumpert, 1985, p. 86)

The latter type of manager, concerned with stability, is what we have called "stewardship." In a new, growing organization, entrepreneurship should predominate. In a mature organization, entrepreneurship and stewardship should be properly balanced—for change and efficient operation of existing businesses to be coordinated properly.

THE MAKEUP, OR ROLE, OF THE ENTREPRENEUR

Many have studied the psychology of entrepreneurs, hoping to learn why some people are more likely than others to become successful entrepreneurs. Researchers have listed several attitudes and values they found typical of the entrepreneur. The list includes desires to dominate and surpass, need for achievement, desire to take personal responsibility for decisions, preference for decisions with some risk, interest in concrete results from decisions, tending to think ahead, and desiring to be their own boss (Vesper, 1980, p. 9).

A different approach to understanding the entrepreneur has been sociological. James Quinn, for example, viewed the entrepreneur as a kind of role encouraged by an "individual entrepreneural system"—which is to say a capitalistic system that encourages and supports individual initiative. Quinn identified several characteristics of an entrepreneurial system that encourages technological innovation:

1. Fanaticism and commitment,
2. Chaos acceptance,
3. Low early costs,
4. No detailed controls,
5. Incentives and risks,
6. Long time horizons,
7. Flexible financial support,
8. Multiple competing approaches, and
9. Need orientation.
   (Quinn, 1979, 1985)

Quinn saw the single-minded dedication of the entrepreneur as a kind of fanaticism, and an economic or organizational system must tolerate the kind of ruthless, dedicated purpose required of an entrepreneur. The context of such single-mindedness will appear chaotic and disorganized, because the entrepreneur is fixed on the goal and will use whatever means or expediency which proceeds toward that goal. The economic and organizational system should tolerate this kind of apparent chaos, which includes little detailed control in the early phase of a new venture. The origin of new ventures operate in an opportunistic, cost-cutting, shortcutting way to a single-minded, clear-cut goal.

Quinn also argued that the economic or organizational system wishing to foster entrepreneurship should provide appropriate rewards for the risks taken in entrepreneurship. Moreover, these rewards must be structured for long-term horizons. It takes time for anything really new to become a success. At some point when a new thing takes off, observers often think how quickly and rapidly the successful innovation grew, not appreciating the long, painful starts, false starts, and buildup to the takeoff stage.

Because of the experimentation and learning that goes into new ventures, it is also important for the system to provide flexibility in financing from many sources and for multiple and competing approaches. In the early days of any radical innovation, new ways are being tried out and only down the line will an optimal configuration emerge for a standard design of a new technology. Need orientation should always be the goal of entrepreneurship. Systems that encourage the fulfillment of needs of a marketplace stimulate innovation which lasts and is economically important. Thus for entrepreneurship, the psychological attitudes and the economic and organizational environment are all important—the values of the entrepreneur (such as risk taking, vision, ambition) and a system that encourages entrepreneurship (committed, risk-taking, long-term, need-oriented environments).

Example: Entrepreneurship and Stewardship in Pizza Time Theater

The problem in entrepreneurship after the initial success of a company lies in balancing subsequent entrepreneurial management style with stewardship style. Bushnell had been well out of Atari. He went on to a second great adventure, building an entertainment restaurant for kids—pizza with video games. In 1977, Bushnell opened his first Chuck E. Cheese Pizza Time Theater in San Jose, California. When he left Atari in 1979, he had purchased full rights to Pizza Time for $500,000. The idea was a kind of dining room in a theater. Large animal robots performed on a stage, rooms were filled with coin-operated video games, and pizza was served to families. At first kids loved it. It was part of the video game craze of the time. From 1979 through 1981 the number of restaurants grew from 7 to 88. In April 1981, Pizza Time went public at $15 each for the 1.1 million shares (Coll, 1984).

Bushnell was now chairman of Pizza Time's board of directors and owned 19% of the company. In 1981, Bushnell was one of the richest men in Silicon Valley. But Bushnell was ever the entrepreneur; he was interested in new businesses. Since Pizza Time was launched, he turned his attention elsewhere. This time it was robots. With a group of ex-Atari engineers, Bushnell formed Androbot Inc.

It was one part of his vision. Bushnell formed a kind of holding company to start new companies—Catalyst Technologies. Silicon Valley in the

1970s and 1980s was a hotbed of new companies. Catalyst would provide a range of services to nurture new companies (capital, office space, accounting, business planning). Androbot was the first Catalyst company. In the meantime, Bushnell's noncompete agreement with Warner's in video games was due to expire in October 1983. He had planned a new video game company, Sente, which would be the second Catalyst company.

Then, as happens in Greek tragedies, fate caught up with the hero. First, Bushnell's main enterprise was caught in the same market change as was Atari's video games—saturation of the market. While still liking the games, kids were becoming bored with their similarity; they were all pretty much the same chase and shoot'em, gobble'em, blow'em-up games. Attendance at Pizza Time restaurants began leveling off in late 1982, dropping in 1983. Pizza Time Theater turned out not to be in the theater business after all, but in the restaurant business: "While fashioning a plan to make Pizza Time Theaters the center of the family-entertainment empire, Bushnell had forgotten about one thing—pizza. By the spring of 1983, it was apparent that the company's 'cardboard' pizza, as a former top Pizza Time executive described it, was turning customers away. So was the accelerating national decline in enthusiasm for video games . . ." (Coll, 1984, p. 94).

Meanwhile, at Androbot, Bushnell had decided to create four different new robot products simultaneously. For a new venture, delivering one product on time and within cost is difficult enough, but four new products would strain the resources of any new company. Androbot's resources were quickly strained. Androbot was spending at the rate of $700,000 a month. A public offering for Androbot, was scheduled for the first week of August 1983, but that week, Merrill Lynch withdrew the offering. Androbot was running out of money, with 105 employees and four products in development.

Meanwhile, at Sente, Bushnell's new video games company, a new game had been developed called Snakepit. It was introduced on December 9, 1983, but by then the game market had cooled off. Snakepit was another version of the generic chase-and-kill game. It was not a flop but not a great success.

Troubles. Meanwhile, back at Pizza Time, the company lost more than $75 million between September and December 1983. The collapse of Bushnell's empire began. By January 1984, most of Androbot's founders had gone, and its first product, Androman, was negotiated for sale to Atari, but the deal never went through. Sente was sold to Bally Manufacturing. On March 28, 1984, Pizza Time Theaters filed for protection from creditors under Chapter 11. It owed 5000 creditors more than $100 million. There were Atari, Pizza Time Theaters, Sente, Androbot—there and gone.

What were the lessons that Bushnell saw: "It was a good, serious lesson in spreading yourself too thin. I think that Pizza Time experience was very valuable to me. I think it's important to really understand time budgeting a little bit better, and to find some ways to monitor and to intercede at earlier times. I really think that, looking back, I basically delegated too much responsibility in Pizza Time at too soon a period" (Coll, 1984, p. 97).

Bushnell's personal solvency survived, and he continued to form new companies. In 1984, a new Catalyst company called Etak, Inc. was working on a computer navigation system for automobiles. Entrepreneurial adventure is institutional change—creating and growing new organizations.

Entrepreneurs have vision, like adventure, take chances, and start new ventures. In contrast, stewards pay attention to balance, to organization, to efficiency, to stable growth. Which is better? Neither—any company must have both entrepreneurial leadership and efficient stewardship. Companies fail when either kind of leadership is missing. In this illustration, Bushnell had provided his new companies with entrepreneurial vision. But two initially successful companies failed to keep entrepreneurial vision balanced with organizational stewardship, after Bushnell turned his attention to other new ventures.

ENTREPRENEURSHIP IN CORPORATIONS— INTRAPRENEURSHIP

"Intrapreneurship" was coined to emphasize the problems of fostering entrepreneurship in large organizations. In a large corporation, creating an entrepreneural system that encourages the entrepreneurial role while managing current operations with good stewardship is difficult to accomplish.

Several researchers have studied the conditions for successful new ventures in large corporations. For example, in a study of corporate ventures drawn from the top 200 companies in the Fortune 500, Ralph Biggadike found that most ventures suffered severe losses through the first four years of operation, with an average loss of return on investment of −40% in the first two years and −14% in the second two years. Of this sample of 68 ventures, only 12 reported a profit in the first two years. Biggadike concluded that new corporate ventures require on the average eight years before they attain profitability (Biggadike, 1979).

He also examined the question of which entry strategy was best for corporate new ventures: (1) enter small and plan to grow, or (2) enter big, aiming at an initial large share of the market. His conclusion was that the second strategy—large-scale entry—was best. In his sample, after two years, the average return of investment of the small-scale new venture entries was −41% compared to a −24% of the large-scale entries. Moreover, the small-scale entries at that time had captured only 1% of the market share, while the large-scale entries captured 64% (while losing less money). Corporate ventures are very risky—taking a long time toward profitability, with the risk being compounded by the desirability for entering on a large scale (Biggadike, 1979).

Given this somber news, why do corporations pursue new ventures? Edward Roberts listed several factors that encourage new ventures:

1. When traditional markets become saturated, it becomes difficult to find unmet needs that can provide growth.
2. As technological sophistication diffuses throughout the world, competitive advantage turns even more importantly upon innovative R&D.
3. As foreign markets are becoming even more developed, domestic competitors in these countries are becoming more technologically sophisticated (e.g., Korea).
4. When interest rates are high and price/earnings ratios are low, it is difficult to provide corporate growth through acquisition of other major companies. (Roberts, 1980)

The conclusion is that despite the risks of corporate ventures, the need is so great that the risks must be taken, for over the long term, corporate survival depends on new ventures. All products have finite lifetimes; and the older a technology, the more competition will crowd that market, lowering prices and profit margins.

ORGANIZATIONAL BARRIERS TO INNOVATION

James Brian Quinn listed several factors that impede innovation in an organization:

> Top management isolation.
> Intolerance of fanatics.
> Short time horizons.
> Accounting practices.
> Excessive rationalism.
> Excessive bureaucracy.
> Inappropriate incentives.
> (Quinn, 1985, pp. 76–77)

Organizations that encourage the isolation of top management from contact with the customers or with the factory floor impede innovation. Quinn pointed out that the perception of risk depends on the familiarity and experience with a situation. The less familiar and experienced a decision maker, the less capability he or she has of properly judging risk. Since entrepreneurship requires strong commitment, a company that discourages commitment as a kind of fanatism discourages entrepreneurial behavior.

Short time horizons and accounting practices that penalize long-term

and creative activities also discourage entrepreneurial activity in an organization. So do excessive rationalism and excessive bureaucracy that criticize
and delay project activity as too unplanned and requiring too many approv-
als. Inappropriate incentives that discourage any risk taking and reward only
stable continuity also discourage entrepreneurship.

NEW VENTURES IN CORPORATIONS

The problem, then, is how to encourage entrepreneurial activities in large
organizations and launch new business ventures, while appropriately managing efficiently and avoiding disruption of existing businesses. Various organizational experiments have been made in ways to encourage new ventures
in a corporate structure. Edward Roberts summarized a kind of spectrum of
types of corporate venturing, starting from purely internal ventures, to acquisitions of small firms, to joint ventures with other firms, to spinning off
new business ventures as new firms, to purely venture capital operations
(Roberts, 1980).

At one end of the spectrum are pure venture capital operations. Some
companies have tried these forms, but their record has been mixed. For
example, F. Felda Hardymon, Mark J. DeNino, and Malcolm S. Salter
looked at a sample of these units [which they called CVC (corporate venture
capital]: General Electric Venture Capital Corporation, Exxon Enterprises,
and Sutter Hill Ventures. They found that although these operations may be
successful as venture capital, they had not provided paths for corporate
diversification. The reasons for not providing corporate diversification were
several:

1. Conflicts in investment portfolios intended to optimize return-on-investment
    and to provide diversification opportunities;
2. Difficulties in acquiring companies in which investments were made due to
    conflicts-of-interest in the acquiring corporation as both buyer and seller;
3. Difficulties in making companies which were good investments as later fits into
    corporate structure.
    (Hardymon, DeNino, and Salter, 1983)

Another observer, Norman D. Fast, also commented on the problems of
corporate venture capital units: "It thus appears that corporate venturing
begins with two strikes against it. First, corporations have difficulty maintaining the long-term commitment to venturing . . . . Second, the individual
ventures themselves seem to be constrained and hampered in a corporate
environment . . ." (Fast, 1981, p. 23).

The conclusion is that entrepreneurship in large corporations is probably best structured as a part of normal business activities, which span both the maintenance of ongoing businesses and the starting of new businesses.

THE VENTURE TEAM

To carry out venturing in the large organization within the context of existing businesses, the best solution seems to be to form venture teams. Moreover, the venture team appears to be a universal tool for starting both large and small businesses. For example, in the many interviews of venture capitalists, one of the most frequently cited criteria for deciding to fund a new venture is "management." They look for a balanced "management team."

A venture team requires several roles, each of which brings a different management strength to the team: entrepreneural leadership, technical strength in research and manufacturing, marketing strength, financial strength, and production strength. The entrepreneurial role provides the integrating factor for the team. D. A. Schon coined the term "product champion" for the entrepreneural role in the large corporation. Schon argued that all new products initially meet resistance and that to overcome resistance, vigorous promotion was required: "No ordinary involvement with a new idea provides the energy required to cope with the indifference and resistance that major technical change provokes. . . . Champions of new inventions . . . display persistence and courage of heroic quality" (Schon, 1963, p. 84).

Vision, commitment, and risk taking are essential to the entrepreneural role, and the product champion provides the integrating strength for the venture team. The vision of the product champion must include some of the technical aspects, the market aspects, and financial aspects. Yet no one person can provide sufficient in-depth skills in all these areas or have the time to do all the work required to accomplish a new venture. Therefore, the product champion is the leader of the team, and like any leader, nuturing the team to its best efforts is essential.

The technical role in a venture team displays leadership over technical matters. Many studies of technological innovation have talked about the role of the "technological gatekeeper," that is, the individual with the technical understanding and technical vision required to create a technological innovation at the cutting edge of new technical and scientific knowledge. The marketing and production roles in a venture team provide skills and depth in sales and production. The financial role in the venture team provides skills and depth in finances.

Some companies have even reinforced the closeness of a venture team by locating them separately, in spaces called "skunkworks": "To develop products, companies are increasingly setting up their designers in skunkworks, small offices away from corporate headquarters. Matt Sanders [for example] was exiled to a former credit-union building in Sunnyvale, California, to design and build Convergent Technologies' newest product . . ." (Fraker, 1984, p. 68).

Successful new ventures are created by teams. The entrepreneur is the integrating leader—the hero. As with all heroes, they get the lion's share of the publicity. But one of the reasons they are heroes is that they encourage loyalty, hard work, and excellence in their venture team.

Example: Xerox Product Development Approach

The functional necessity for the venture team arises from the focusing and risk reduction that a team supplies in the movement of an R&D project from research into development, production, and product launch. There are always trade-offs between increased technical performance, product flexibility, and the cost of producing the product. Such trade-offs are often the critical factor in the success or failure of a new product. The technical performance should be as high as possible, but not so high as to price it out of the target market. The technical flexibility of the product should be as great as possible, but not so great as to make learning and use of the product too complicated or burdensome for the target market.

The early phase of new product development emphasizes the technical feasibility of the idea of the product. At this point, manufacturing cost is only estimated. Next, the parts of the product are drawn, and the manufacturing engineers figure out how to produce the product. At this point, problems are how to make the parts on company machinery and with materials so that the manufactured product works and can be produced at low cost. Once manufacturing prototypes are created, it may be found that the manufactured parts do not fit, due to variability in manufacture, or that the product does not perform well or reliably or safely. Then redesign occurs and perhaps repricing. Thus product development is sequential, from technical feasibility to production design and manufacturability and testing.

To minimize the problems caused by this sequentiality, product teams in companies try to integrate the research, marketing, engineering, manufacturability as early as possible in the product development. For example, Wayland Hicks, president of the Reprographic Business Group in Xerox in 1984, described Xerox's emphasis: "At Xerox, as well as at some other major manufacturing companies, a new approach is being established. . . . Key elements include the designing-in of quality and manufacturability right from the start of the program, the elimination of overdesign, and the commonality of parts across product lines. . . . If there is one word that sums up this approach to product development, it is integration . . ." (Hicks, 1984).

To create this integration, the organization moves product authority down the organization hierarchy which integrates skills: "A major element of this new approach is the delegation of decision making as far down . . . as possible. An especially important aspect of our approach is the inclusion of manufacturing engineers in the earliest stage of development. . . . Teams . . . help assure that manufacturability at optimal cost is given as much weight in developing a product as its features and performance" (Hicks, 1984, p. 12).

Venture teams—operating in a corporate, organizational environment that encourages entrepreneurship aimed at market needs—are an important tool for successful innovation in large corporations.

SUMMARY

Innovation and new ventures require leadership—entrepreneurship. The entrepreneur is a kind of business hero. The different stages of a firm provide different situations in which entrepreneurship is more or less important, and even situations in which it is disfunctional. Stewardship is the complementary role to entrepreneurship. Within an organization, some entrepreneurship should always be encouraged, supported and rewarded if the organization is to be innovative. Balancing the rewards for entrepreneurship against rewards for stewardship is a delicate but important problem in large corporations.

Attitudes and values typical of the entrepreneur include desires to dominate and surpass, need for achievement, desire to take personal responsibility for decisions, preference for decisions with some risk, interest in concrete results from decisions, tending to think ahead, and a desire to be his or her own boss. Economic and organizational systems must also support entrepreneurship.

Corporate ventures are risky—taking a long time toward profitability, with the risk being compounded by the desirability for entering on a large scale. The venture team is an important organizational tool for improving the chances for successful new ventures. A venture team requires several roles, each of which brings a different management strength to the team— entrepreneural leadership, technical strength in research and manufacturing, marketing strength, financial strength, and production strength.

REFLECTION

1. **Find a history of an organization or a biography of a person who started a new company. What were the conditions for success, technologically, personally, organizationally, or industrially, that brought about the successful new venture?**

FOR FURTHER READING

DRUCKER, PETER F., *Innovation and Entrepreneurship: Practice and Principles.* New York: Harper & Row, 1985.

CHAPTER THREE
BUSINESS PLANS FOR
NEW VENTURES

CENTRAL IDEAS

1. The format of the business plan
2. Use of the business plan
3. Writing a business plan that sells
4. Conditions for successful new product innovation

Example: Cypress Semiconductor—The Third Wave

New ventures consist of launching of new businesses, which can be a new firm or a new division within a firm. The introduction of a new product model or even of a new product line does not constitute a new venture if the firm already does business in that product market. It is the introduction of a new product line into a new market that constitutes a new venture. Thus the opportunities in new ventures come from both new products and new markets. In 1982, an example of a new venture startup company was the Cypress Semiconductor Corp. It was one of several new firms begun in the "third wave" of new semiconductor ventures, spanning the 30 years from 1952 to 1982.

T. J. Rodgers was employed in 1982 as an R&D executive at a large semiconductor manufacturer, Advanced Micro Devices Inc. In October he had received an unexpected telephone call from a venture capitalist, Stanford Fingerhood. Fingerhood had called to ask Rodgers about references for two of his former subordinates who were planning to launch a new company. Rodgers thought about it, but instead of giving references suggested that if Fingerhood wished to finance a new company, would he instead consider one Rodgers could start? Beneath the shirt of many an executive, there beats the heart of an entrepreneur (Kotkin, 1984).

Fingerhood's response was: sure, he would listen to a good proposal.

Rodgers and Fingerhood met for lunch at Manhattan's 21 Club. They discussed business strategy. Rodgers suggested that there were business opportunities in the new VLSI technology—semicustom chips. The next day, Fingerhood arranged a meeting with Benjamin Rosen, a venture capitalist in the electronics and computer industry and once a vice president of Morgan Stanley & Co. Rosen liked Rodger's perception of the technological and market opportunities in semicustom chips. He sent Rodgers on a plane to Dallas for a meeting with Rosen's venture partner, L. J. Sevin, a former chairman of Mostek Corp. The Mostek Corporation had begun in the second wave of semiconductor firm startups in the late 1960s.

On the plane to Dallas, Rodgers drafted a plan for a company that would become the Cypress Semiconductor Corporation. Rodgers had a technical background, with a Ph.D. degree from Stanford University. Now he had to write a business plan.

The next day in Dallas, Rodgers met with Sevin. Sevin studied Rodgers' figures, focusing on the return on investment. He was skeptical but intrigued. Rodgers returned home. During the next month, Sevin called frequently, questioning Rodgers' assumptions in his plan. Sevin flew from Dallas to California and called Rodgers to visit him there. When Rodgers arrived, Sevin offered to pay Rodgers' salary and expenses in order to draw up a formal business plan. Sevin would back the new venture if he could get other investors to share the risk. If, however, others would not come aboard, Rodgers would be left without a job: " 'What could I say?' the blond, 35-year-old Rodgers recalls. . . . 'I shook his hand and quit my job' " (Kotkin, 1984, p. 58).

Four months later, Rodgers was ready with the business plan. It planned a market-oriented, semicustom chip manufacturer utilizing the new VLSI chip technology. Rodgers' strategy was to focus on a segment of the market the Japanese had not yet dominated, high-speed CMOS (complementary metal-oxide semiconductors). The Japanese were strong in low-speed CMOS chips. Cypress's new products were targeted for the sophisticated computer and scientific instrumentation market, a field dominated by U.S. giants such as Hewlett-Packard, Digital Equipment, and Data General. Rodgers had projected that Cypress's sales would grow to $3 million by 1984 and to $110 million by 1987.

Technological innovation in transistorized electronics had created three waves of business startups: (1) when the transistor was invented in 1948 and the semiconductor invented in 1958, (2) when large-scale integration technology (LSI) was introduced in the 1960s, and (3) when very large scale integration technology (VLSI) was introduced in the 1980s. The first wave created many major semiconductor manufacturers: Texas Instruments, Motorola, and Fairchild in the United States, and Ferranti and Plessely in Europe.

The second wave saw the startup of new American firms such as Mostek. But the second wave had also brought in the vertically integrated Japanese electronic firms: Hitachi, Fujitsu, and Sony. They increased the competition to the then-dominant U.S. semiconductor firms from the first wave and to the new firms of the second wave. The Japanese strength was in manufacturing productivity, producing standard circuits of high quality at low cost.

This background had influenced Sevin when he considered financing Cypress's startup. He had had good and bad experiences. Sevin founded Mostek in the second wave, when the future looked bright. At first, Mostek had grown dramatically, but by September 1979, Sevin's Mostek Corporation had been hurt by the Japanese competition. Mostek's profits had slipped; its stock dropped. It became the target of a takeover battle. Sevin sold Mostek to United Technologies for $345 million: " 'I started seeing the handwriting on the wall back in 1975,' the craggy-faced entrepreneur recalls. 'In 1976, I started to scream about it, but by 1979 I stopped screaming and gave up. The war was over, and the Japanese had won' " (Kotkin, 1984, p. 60).

But in the early 1980s, new technical innovation (VLSI) in the electronics industry had opened up new business opportunities again. When Rodgers met Sevin with his vision of the new opportunities, Sevin had both the technical background and market experience to share that vision. They both correctly saw that the next level of advance, VLSI, would alter the semiconductor market.

And it did. In 1984, customized VLSI semiconductors specialized for specific applications was one of the fastest-growing sectors of the semiconductor industry. It was a new ballgame again for Sevin: " 'The game has changed suddenly. . . . The technologies are exploding and driving the markets here. When it was a question of selling chips by the bagful, it was playing to their [Japan's] strength. Now that there are so many new niches, it's become a marketing game, and that gives the smaller U.S. firms the advantage' " (Kotkin, 1984, p. 62).

This lesson is general. Whenever a major technological advance occurs, an altering of the market will follow; and opportunities for new businesses and market restructuring occur. It is the best time to start new firms.

HIGH-TECH NEW VENTURES

A high-tech new venture is new both in technology and in entering or creating markets. This complicates and increases the risk of the venture. So great are the risks, the fact is that many new ventures do not, unfortunately, succeed. However, the likelihood of success for new high-technology firms compared to new older-technology firms is twice as high—as indicated by studies of the survival rates of new firms in different industries (Vesper, 1980, p. 29).

The basic ingredients for starting any new firm, based on technological innovation are:

1. The idea for a technological innovation
2. A potential market
3. Teamwork in both technical and business expertise

In the example, Rodgers was successful in starting his new venture because he had the technical foresight and the marketing focus to take advantage of the changing technology. In obtaining initial funding, it also helped that the venture capitalist, Sevin, had had both technical and business experience in the earlier wave of semiconductor innovation. New high-tech ventures should have this nice kind of balance between technological vision and market focus.

THE BUSINESS PLAN

The first thing Rodgers had to do to obtain capital for his new venture was to write a business plan. This is the first business step in any new venture. The business plan is a strategic summary of the new venture. Its purposes are (1) to focus strategy to ensure that important points necessary to the success of any business venture have been considered, and (2) to persuade financial investors to capitalize the new venture.

Topics that should be covered in a new venture business plan should include the following:

A. Current business status
    1. Business objectives
    2. Management and organization
B. Products or Services
    3. Product description
    4. Technological background
    5. Competition
C. Benefits to customers
    6. Market
    7. Marketing strategy
D. Capitalization
    8. Capital requirements
    9. Financial forecasts
    10. Benefits to investors

A. Current Business Status

1. Business objectives   The business objectives should generally define the kind of company the new venture intends to become, delineating businesses and markets it intends to provide and serve. In the case of Cypress Semiconductor Corporation, Rodgers' objective was to be the leader in the new custom VLSI chip industry.

2. Management and organization   The management and organization section should describe the management team who will begin and grow the new venture. Experience and balance in management are important. The team should include technical competence, production and marketing competence, and financial and control expertise. Rodgers' background, including technical competence and managerial experience in the semiconductor field, was the major selling point for Rosen and Sevin's willingness to listen to and take a financial gamble on Rodgers.

B. Products or Services

3. Product description   The product section describes the immediate product line the new venture intends to develop, manufacture, and market. For Cypress Semiconductor, the product line was a service, custom chip design and production of high-speed CMOS chips.

4. Technological background   The technological background summarizes the directions of technological change which provide the innovative entry of the new venture and which will provide continuing possibilities for technological improvement. In the case of Cypress Semiconductor, the technological change was the next level of density in circuit reduction, VLSI, which created the possibility for whole circuits on a single chip. This implied the possibility of custom chips replacing standardized chips.

5. Competition   The section on competition should describe current or potential competitors, including analyses of strengths, weaknesses, and reaction time. The critical factor is a judgment of "competitive edge." How will the new venture be able to meet competition, new and anticipated, on the basis of technological leadership, pricing, marketing strength, and responsiveness? For example, Cypress focused on high-speed CMOS chips to avoid head-on competition with Japanese strength in low-speed CMOS chips.

C. Benefits to Customers

6. Market   The market section should focus on a market sector, (1) listing customers by class or name, and (2) targeting ranges of price and performance. It should spell out the benefits of the product to the customers. For example, if the product were industrial equipment, how would the equipment benefit the industrial customer, and how long would it take for the equipment to pay for itself? Rodgers' market, for example, comprised sophisticated computer and scientific instrumentation makers, such as Hewlett-Packard, Digital Equipment, and so on.

7. Marketing strategy   The marketing section should describe the means of distributing the product and communicating with the customers. Rodgers had chosen an industrial clientele, which simplified the marketing problems. Selling large volumes of a product to a small number of technically sophisticated industrial clients requires only a small, but technically competent, sales force.

D. Capitalization

8. Capital requirements   The capital requirements section should state the additional capital required and the use of the working capital. Specifically, any product R&D costs should be spelled out, together with production and inventory costs and marketing costs. The tasks and time scale to production should be described and the equipment and facilities required to produce the product. Cypress Semiconductor required the development of chip design techniques, hiring of VLSI chip designers, and purchase of chip fabrication equipment and facilities.

9. Financial forecasts   Financial projections should detail the expected sales, costs, and profits of the company through the break-even time to profitability. The projection should cover the next five years of operation. The first two years of operation should be projected in monthly detail, the remaining three in yearly detail. Since the failure of new ventures is always a cash-flow crisis, the financial projection must carefully analyze capital requirements until significant cash flow is created.

10. Benefits to investors   The returns to investors should be projected in terms of royalties, dividends, or liquidity of capital. Since most new ventures seldom pay out dividends, requiring profits for growth, it is important to plan liquidity in terms of taking the company public or anticipating acquisition by a larger firm.

USING THE BUSINESS PLAN TO ACHIEVE GOALS

The business plan has two principal uses: a tool to promote careful new venture planning and a tool to raise capital. The business plan should not be lengthy, but it should be comprehensive. In action, there are usually only a few ways to succeed but many ways to fail. Thinking through the many steps and aspects of a new venture is important for success. The business plan should lay out the assumptions being made for the success of the new venture. Incorrect or incomplete assumptions kill new ventures.

Of course, nothing ever goes exactly according to plan. But without good planning, few new ventures go at all. A survey of 1000 readers of *Venture* magazine in 1985 elicited the response that 89% of small companies used their business plans to set goals and establish rewards: " 'Even if I get lazy; says respondent John Roy, owner of Bargain News, a Stratford, Conn., publishing company, 'the employees and managers force me to follow through' " (Madlin, 1985).

In terms of achieving their planned goals, 10% of *Venture* readers said that they met their goals and 45% said they nearly met their goals. Furthermore, those with longer-range plans (five years or more) met their goals more often—30% compared to 10% who only did two to five year plans and compared to 8% who only did less than two year plans (Madlin, 1985). Plans do not make one more accurate, but those who carefully think out plans tend to be less surprized about business outcomes.

Example: The Fast Track of Initial Success

In 1984, Cypress Semiconductor Corp was so hot a company that Rodgers literally had venture capitalists chasing him. This was a switch, since most entrepreneurs chase after venture capitalists. The story is told about Susan Harman of Robertson, Colman & Stephens (San Francisco investment bankers) wishing to invest in Cypress Semiconductor—but Rodgers was too busy to meet with her. After several calls, he said that even lunch was out because he ran at lunch. Ms. Harman, however, was a marathon runner. Good enough. She would run with him. Soon thereafter, one rainy afternoon, she ran 6 miles with Rodgers, making her investment pitch: "When the run was over, Mr. Rodgers had changed his mind, and Robertson, Colman now owns a small piece of Cypress Semiconductor Corp. of San Jose, Calif., one of the most highly regarded new companies in Silicon Valley" (*Wall Street Journal,* 1984, p. 1).

In 1983, at least 10 more new semiconductor companies were founded, including VISIC Inc., Micro Linear Corp., Vitelic Corp., Quasel Inc., Modular Semiconductor Inc., Integrated Power Semiconductors, Logic Devices, Sierra Semiconductor, Xilink, and Dallas Semiconductor Corp.

A BUSINESS PLAN THAT SELLS

The second use of the business plan is to raise capital. Careful, comprehensive strategy, as shown in the business plan, is often an important factor in persuading investors to provide capital for the venture. Adequate capitalization is a critical factor in starting and growing new ventures, and it is often one of the most difficult factors to achieve. A good business plan not only helps plan the venture but raises capital.

S. Rich and D. Gumpert listed several lessons drawn from the experiences of entrepreneurs trying to sell their business plans to investors. Their major point was to emphasize that a "winning business plan" must accurately reflect the viewpoints of three constituencies:

1. The market, including both existing and prospective clients, customers, and users of the planned product or service.
2. The investors, whether of financial or other resources.
3. The producer, whether the entrepreneur or the inventor.
   (Rich and Gumpert, 1985b, p. 156)

Since the entrepreneur writes the business plan and sees the world from his or her eyes, the most frequent failing in business plans is to present the plan without the interests of the customers or investors in mind. The customers will only want products they can afford and that will meet their needs better than any others and provide benefits strong enough to persuade them to buy the product. The investors want investments that provide high, quick returns.

Accordingly, Rich and Gumpert's advice suggested that the winning business plan shows the product user's benefit. For example, in the equipment business, equipment that will pay for itself in the first year almost always sells. When the payback period is two years, some will sell; but when the payback period is beyond three years the product is very, very hard to sell. Investors are therefore reluctant to back products in industrial markets that have long payback periods. Rich and Gumpert also suggest that the business plan should document claims in the plan. For example, evidence that the customers need or want the product should be documented, as well as data on the size and location of markets.

For new and growing private companies, many investors will often be wealthy individuals or professional venture capitalists. Their goals usually look toward investments that anticipate annualized returns in the range 35 to 60%, compounded and adjusted for inflation. Business plans should explicitly project the investors' returns, with plans for liquidity of the returns. The hope of many investors is to cash-out in three to seven years after the investment.

For example, suppose that after five years the company has before-tax earnings of $8 million on $40 million sales, and a larger firm offers to acquire the firm for 10 times pretax earnings, or $80 million. If the investors held 40% of the company, their return is $32 million. An investment of $6 million in the first year would then have provided them an annual return of about 50% per year. This sort of thing is the bottom line for the investor. Therefore, in raising capital, the percentage of the company that the entrepreneur negotiates with investors depends on both the projected value of the company and time of liquidity.

Rich and Gumpert also emphasized a minor but important aspect of the business plan—"packaging is important." The business plan should be no more than 40 pages in length, and the "binding and printing must not be sloppy; neither should the presentation be too lavish." The cover shows title, addresses, dates, and number of copy. An executive summary of two-page length should follow the title page: "The two pages immediately following the title page should concisely explain the company's current status, its products or services, the benefits to customers, the financial forecasts, the venture's objectives in three to seven years, the amount of financing needed, and how investors will benefit" (Rich and Gumpert, 1985b, p. 162).

SUCCESSFUL PRODUCT INNOVATION

New ventures introduce new products into the market, but they are also frought with problems, perils, and dangers. No single factor guarantees success, but several conditions help: good technology, good marketing, good organization, and adequate capitalization. Maidique and Zirger, for example, examined success and failure in product innovation in the U.S. electronics industry and compared their findings to earlier studies (such as the English study of the 1970s, project Sappho). They concluded that the following circumstances helped improve the chances of success:

1. The developing organization, through in-depth understanding of the customers and the marketplace, introduces a high performance-to-cost ratio.
2. The developing organization is proficient in marketing and commits a significant amount of its resources to selling and promoting the product.
3. The product provides a high contribution margin to the firm.
4. The R&D process is well planned and executed.
5. The create, make and market functions are well interfaced and coordinated.
6. The product is introduced into the market early.
7. The markets and technologies of the new product benefit significantly from the existing strengths of the developing business unit.
8. There is a high level of management support for the product through its launch to the market place.
    (Maidique and Zirger, 1984, p. 201).

In high-technology new ventures, it is essential to introduce products with high performance-to-cost ratios—that is the technological competitive edge. But that edge is by no means sufficient. The new venture must be market focused, so that the performance-to-cost ratio is targeted for the right applications for the right market. Proficiency in marketing and commitment of resources to marketing is every bit as important to success as is the technology edge.

It is helpful also to be early into a market to establish recognition, distribution, and market share. High profit margins are also desirable. Yet very high margins, sometimes obtained in the very early days of a new market, are often possible for only a short time. The new venture must also be looking down the line toward timely reduction of production costs and improvement of product models and applications so as to withstand competition.

SOURCES OF VENTURE CAPITAL

A guide to sources of venture capital is published and periodically updated by Pratt (Pratt and Morris, 1984). Funding can be identified in phases: seed, startup, early growth, and expansion. Funding can be in combinations of equity and debt. Eventually, liquidity of investment is obtained through public offerings or acquisition by a larger firm.

SUMMARY

At each major state of technical advance in an industry, there are business opportunities for new firms, since the technological advance will affect the competitive situation. In new ventures, an entrepreneur with both business and technical skills must team with a venture capitalist to set up the new firm.

The first business requirement of a new venture is a business plan. Business plans should be focused and brief, but comprehensive. There are many ways for a venture to fail but only a few ways to succeed. New ventures that introduce new products into the market are also frought with problems, perils, and dangers. No single factor guarantees success, but several conditions help: good technology, good marketing, good organization, and adequate capitalization. Writing a good business plan that accurately reflects the viewpoints of the customers and investors, as well as that of the entrepreneur, is an important tool in raising capital.

REFLECTION

1. Think of an innovative product or service (or chose a recently successful new product) and write a business plan. What is the most difficult information to obtain in writing a business plan? How much of the company would you be willing to give up to obtain financing? Next look at the business plan as an investor. Would you invest in it? How much of the company would you want before you invested?

FOR FURTHER READING

RICH, S. R., and D. E. GUMPERT, *Business Plans That Win $$: Lessons from the MIT Enterprise Forum.* New York: Harper & Row, 1985.
PRATT, STANLEY E., and JANE K. MORRIS, eds., *Pratt's Guide to Venture Capital Sources.* Wellesley Hills, Mass.: Venture Economics, Inc., 1984.

CHAPTER FOUR
GROWTH OF NEW FIRMS

CENTRAL IDEAS

1. Patterns of growth of new firms

2. Corporate systems

3. Dynamic factors affecting corporate growth

Example: Corvus Systems Runs into Trouble

While many ventures create business opportunities, they also create problems due to this interaction of new products and new markets. New firms are difficult to begin, and once begun, are even more difficult to maintain on a smooth growth curve. The reasons for this are many—some due to management, some due to competition, some due to finances, and some due to operations. Corvus Systems is an example of a successful new firm that had problems. In the late 1970s and early 1980s, many new firms were started in the personal computer market. Corvus was one of these.

In 1979, Michael D'Addio and Mark Han created Corvus Systems, selling hard disks for personal computers. These disks were a major advance in the record-keeping ability of personal computers, allowing the storing of 10 million bits of information, far larger than the 100,000 to 400,000 bits of information storable on the floppy disk. Another company, International Memories Inc., helped found Corvus and supplied the drives, to which Corvus added the interface to the computer. Corvus then sold the interfaced Winchester hard disk drives to the retail market (Walthers von Alten, 1984).

Corvus grew fast. For four years it increased each quarter in sales and in profits. It created and sold a complex line of products. In addition to the disk drives, the company also made a microcomputer, a network, and other peripherals. In 1983, Corvus had sales of $47.7 million and made a $4.4 million profit. Not bad for starting from nothing in 1979.

But by March 1984, problems occurred. It lost $1.3 million on $40 million in sales. By June 1984, growth had stopped. Corvus then anticipated a fiscal year 1984 loss and laid off 13% of its 483 workers. Its publically held stock dropped to $4 a share from a high of $21 dollars. These layoffs and loss were the second in six months from January to June 1984. Most fast-growing, initially successful companies run into trouble some time down the line.

What went wrong? *InfoWorld* commented: "Rich Brenner, vice president of finance, blames the loss and layoffs on the delay in releasing Corvus' new line of hard disk drives, increased competition in the disk drive market, and overstaffing. But there's more to the story" (Walthers von Alten, 1984, p. 44).

DYNAMICS OF NEW FIRMS

The story of growth in any new firm is a balance of productive factors in meeting the needs of a market. Concepts in a topic called "industrial systems dynamics" can clarify what can go wrong in new firms with rapid growth. Industrial systems dynamics is a technique that models a firm as a time-dependent operating system. In creating the concept of industrial dynamics, Jay Forrester introduced analytical techniques for examining problems that arise from the differences of timing of activities in a corporation. He characterized a corporation as a system, attending to the relative timing of activities in different parts of the system. He demonstrated that differences in timing of activities in different parts of the corporate system can have a major impact on organizational performance (Forrester, 1961).

Forrester then applied the technique to the startup and growth of new high-tech companies. Figure 4.1 shows four most common patterns that Forrester found happens to new companies. The first curve, A, is an ideal pattern for which all companies hope. Yet patterns B, C, and D are commonly experienced. Pattern B is not so bad. A company may experience a series of problems, slowing growth, but it may learn and continue growing. Pattern C is a company that survives, but finds itself in a market niche with competition it cannot beat. Pattern D is disaster; the first major problem kills the company (Forrester, 1964).

CORPORATE SYSTEMS

A corporate system consists of inputs, outputs, and the transformation function of the system. This is called an open system. Inputs into the system consist of materials and resources and finances; outputs consist of products and profits. The transformation function is the production and marketing by

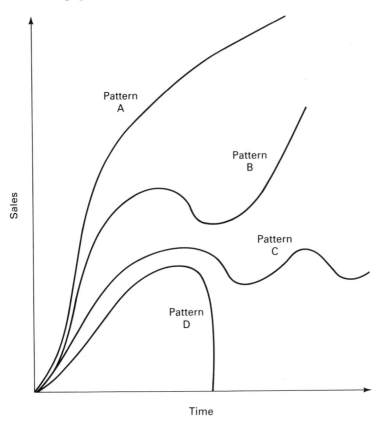

FIGURE 4.1 Growth patterns of initially successful new firms.

the firm—transforming resources into manufactured products (or services) sold in the market. For example, Figure 4.2 depicts the firm as an open system taking resources from the environment and providing products to the market.

So far it seems simple enough. The complications arise when one describes all the activities that go into the transformation. Forrester used rectangular boxes to depict an activity and circles to depict information controlling that activity. Furthermore, Forrester used solid lines to describe the flow of materials from one rectangular activity to another; and he used dashed lines to describe the flow of controlling information. We illustrate this in Figure 10.2b. In this figure, Forrester depicted those activities in the firm which constituted (1) the sales effort, (2) the order backlog, (3) production, (4) product inventory, (5) average revenue, and (6) market.

Connecting these activities is a major loop of flows of finances and materials and products. The sales effort (1) stimulates orders from the mar-

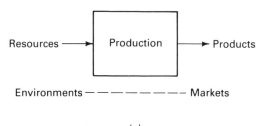

(a)

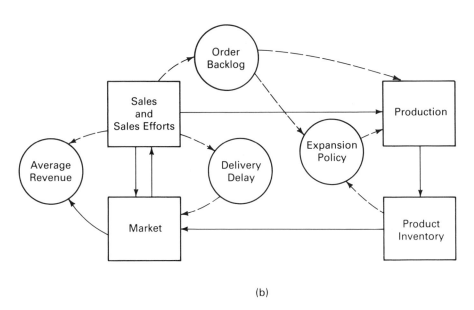

(b)

FIGURE 4.2   (a) Open systems model of a firm: (b) delivery delay and expansion policy in systems model of a firm.

ket (6), which creates an order backlog (2) that determines production (3) in conjunction with the product inventory. Shipment of the product creates revenue at an average revenue rate, some of which finances sales effort. If the world were perfectly steady, everything would balance in this flow and just enough product would be produced to fulfill the order backlog, creating revenues that cover appropriate sales effort. Of course, the world is never— never? well, hardly ever—perfect.

To show some unsteadiness, one can add to this diagram important controlling information in circles—(7) the delivery delay between orders and shipment and (8) the expansion policy of the firm. The reason for including information about the delivery delay is that delay can affect sales.

Figure 4.3 illustrates the general form of the effect of delay in deliver-

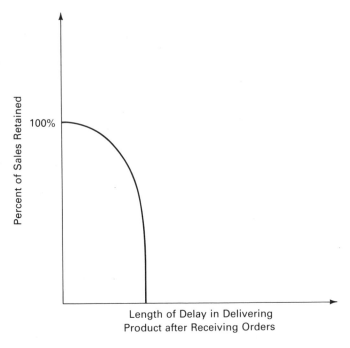

FIGURE 4.3 Impact of delivery delays on sales of a firm.

ing product on sales. If there were no time delay, sales would be unaffected, that is, 100% of potential sales by the firm would be realized as actual sales. However, when the delay lengthens, some impatient customers will cancel their orders and purchase from a competitor. Most customers may tolerate a small delay, but as the delay becomes noticeable to them in affecting their own plans and needs, the toleration drops, even to the point when all sales will be lost.

Accordingly, in a corporate system, there exist relationships which Forrester called "feedback loops." The term comes from electrical engineering, where part of an output signal from a device is fed back into the input signal to influence the output of the device. The feedback loop here is the delay in delivery which affects the sales efforts (losing sales and hence average revenue to the company) (Forrester, 1979).

For a firm in the initial stages of rapid growth, delivery delays are especially important. Therefore, the expansion policy (8) in Figure 10.2b is critical to the growth of the firm. Capital expansion must precede expected sales growth to avoid lengthening of delivery delays, which will cause lost sales to customers. The first crisis for a growing new firm can be a delivery delay either in current product or in the introduction of an improved product.

If the delay problem is not solved in time, lost sales may cause enough of a cash-flow crisis to bankrupt the new company, as in pattern D. This is so because most new companies undergoing rapid expansion are not strongly capitalized. For a pattern B, if the production problem is solved quickly, growth can proceed again. But for a pattern C, if the production problem is solved but too late to beat a competitor, market share may be restricted permanently.

Example: Corvus Systems

We now return to the example of Corvus Systems. The rapidly growing company hit its first crisis in December 1982, three years after it was formed in 1979. Corvus's initial success was due, first, in 1979, to its being a leader in innovating the Winchester hard disk for personal computers; and second, in 1981, in innovating a local-area network for personal computers. Continuing to add more products stretched the R&D capability of the small company, but its confidence soared (Walthers von Alten, 1984).

In 1982, it split into two divisions: the Computing Products Group to develop a microcomputer, and the Network and Mass Storage Division to design peripherals and disk interfaces. It found itself, then, with R&D capability stretched over two separate organizations. In addition, it was manufacturing many products in relatively small quantities, resulting in high manufacturing costs and large inventory costs. Managers in both research and production were spread out in six buildings, some in California and manufacturing in Oregon.

The spread of effort and difficulty in communication contributed to the first problem. Most cash was coming in on the Winchester drive business, which urgently needed a new, improved model to hold off competitors. The new disk drive, called the Omnidrive, was planned for introduction in July 1983. But July passed, August, and on into December 1983—when it became clear that development would not be finished until March 1983. By then sales had slumped and the company posted its first loss, of $2.5 million in the second quarter on revenues of $12.4 million. They laid off 17 people, and upper management took a 10% pay cut and no bonus.

Problems come in bunches. In February someone leaked details of the impending release of the new drive to a computer magazine: "The announcement triggered the 'Osborne effect': Dealers, eager for the new product, stopped ordering the old-line Winchesters. With no new product to ship, sales dropped. Omnidrive finally started shipping in May. . . . But the damage had been done. After virtually monopolizing the disk drive market in 1979, Corvus' lead plummeted to about a 25% market share" (Walthers von Alten, 1984, p. 44).

Corvus had other problems in addition to delivery delay in new products. A second problem related to the targeting of new markets. The microcomputer developed was introduced at a high price $5300 in 1982. To solve these kinds of problems, management cut expenses, reorganized its software developers, started posting weekly sales figures, and began weekly monitoring of product development progress. In addition, they worked at improving communications among managers and with staff. Thus in 1984, Corvus Systems had survived the kind of first crisis that tries corporate souls, and aimed for a pattern B.

DYNAMIC FACTORS AFFECTING GROWTH

New corporate growth requires (1) stimulating sales growth, (2) planning and managing production expansion, (3) improving capitalization, (4) product improvement in a timely manner, (5) product diversification, and (6) continuing organizational refinement. Problems arise from the delay in coordinating any change in one of these factors with another.

Sales Growth

For a new firm, market size and rate of growth are critical to its early success. The larger the size and the faster the growth, the more room there is for new competitors and product variation. An important factor influencing market size and growth is the application and pricing of products. For example, the explosive growth of personal computers in the beginning of the 1980s came from four major applications developed for personal use: accounting, spreadsheets, word processing, and video games. Changes in applications or pricing by the new firm or by its competitors will affect the corporate growth rate.

A new firm must get its products to market, and the distribution mode, distribution size, sales effort, and advertising effort will strongly affect growth rate. The first problem for a new firm is to find customers. Most new high-tech firms choose to be industrial equipment suppliers or original-equipment manufacturers, or try to sell to the Fortune 500 companies, since this lightens the marketing burden to only a few customers (hundreds rather than millions). However, this eventually restricts the size of the firm because of the limited customer population. Moreover, it makes the firm vulnerable to cancellation of orders from a few large customers.

New firms that aim at the consumer market have the most difficult marketing problems; first, in finding distributors and retailers to handle their product, and second, in creating brand recognition among customers. Unless sales climb rapidly enough to afford the massive early investments in marketing, a new firm can have its products pushed off shelf space in retail stores, failing to establish brand recognition. The new firms who have made it big in the consumer market have often been first in creating a market niche.

Production Expansion

In addition to creating a growth market through new applications and stimulating sales through expanding distribution and brand recognition, the new firm must solve the problems of rapid-production-capacity expansion while maintaining product quality. Delays in delivering products provide opportunities for competitors. Problems in quality control early in the life of a new firm can destroy a reputation so much as to be unrecoverable.

Improving Capitalization

While expanding production capacity and inventory buildup, the new firm usually has capital problems. Product expansion for a new firm must anticipate sales expansion or sales will be lost. New firms cannot afford significant sales loss or market-share position will be lost to competitors. When market-share position is lost, small, new firms will never get to be large, old firms.

New firms have small asset size and find bank loans limited. Accordingly, new firms often go for second- and third-round capital funding. If the firm goes for public funding too soon, the final level of capitalization will be too small for sustaining very large growth. Bankruptcy usually occurs when the new firm has a significant drop in sales, being thus caught with large inventory and production costs and without sufficient capital to ride out the losses until problems can be solved and sales growth resumed.

Product Improvement and Diversification

A new firm must upgrade its first-generation products with new products to keep ahead of competition. It must continually lower its cost of production to keep ahead of competition. And it must diversify its product lines to decrease the risk that a single product problem will kill the firm. Often new firms which have had a dramatically successful start encounter major problems during the introduction of next-generation product models and or in product diversification.

Organizational Refinement

Corporate growth will also create new problems of organization. The initially small group of people who started the firm with enthusiasm, hard work, and frequent communication will become a larger, chaotic group of diverse people with poor communication, differing strategies, and underdeveloped managerial and financial controls. Often, the entrepreneurial, free-swinging founders of the company will not have the desire or ability to run the more prosaic and more bureaucratized firm that a larger corporation becomes. In a small firm, coordination is informal. In a large firm, coordination must be more formalized, to ensure that proper communication and coordination occurs among the diverse parts of the firm.

Example: The Osborne Computer Corporation

Let us return to an example we used in Chapter 1, that of the rise and fall of the Osborne Computer Corporation. We are now in a better position to understand how its troubles exemplify the problems in the dynamics of growth of all new high-technology firms.

We recall that Osborne Computer Corporation innovated the portable personal computer in July 1981. Priced at $1795, the Osborne was more conveniently packaged and more completely equipped at a lower price than any other personal computer of the time. Accordingly, its sales soared and its distribution spread rapidly. Only one year later, for 1982, its sales had attained $100 million (Osborn and Dvorak, 1984).

Production expansion   Adam Osborne managed the production expansion by subcontracting for all components. He had planned only to assemble and test units. All components were purchased and all printed-circuit boards constructed by subcontractors. The parts were purchased by PH Components and the boards stuffed and tested by Testology.

There were problems, of course (but management exists to solve problems): "Osborne Computer Corporation quickly ran into problems in August and September of 1981 when Testology was unable to make a logic tester work, and consequently was stuffing and testing many boards but delivering very few. We were nevertheless still committed by contract to pay PH Components and even for those components that Testology could not make work" (Osborne and Dvorak, July 16, 1984, p. 55).

Product improvement   Osborne solved its production problems. Yet product improvement and product diversification created the stumbling point. We recall that the Osborne 1 model had a very small 5-inch screen, making it very hard to read and not providing a standard 80-letter-wide writing space (like the width of standard typewriter paper). Furthermore, in the summer of 1982 a competitor had introduced a similar model but with a 9-inch screen and 80-column width.

This competition and rumors that Osborne was preparing an improved model (then called the Executive model) created a sales crisis in the rapidly growing company. Sales slowed that fall and by the spring of 1983 were very poor. Thus the company experienced the kind of sales turn-off as that shown in pattern D of Figure 10.1.

Improving capitalization and organizational refinement   At that same time, Adam Osborne, the founder and entrepreneur, had been addressing two other problems common to new firms: improved capitalization and organizational refinement. Osborne began planning for a public offering and a new president in the fall of 1982—unfortunately, it all occurred just when the drop in sales began. Robert Jaunich was hired as the new president. He started in January 1983. The Osborne board selected Saloman Brothers as lead underwriter for the public offering, and preliminary meetings between the underwriters and Osborne management also began in January.

Earlier, Osborne had begun with $100,000 in capital, raising $900,000 more in February 1981. Yet by September 1981 (two months after shipping the first products in July 1982), production expansion was requiring more capital. On Friday, September 4, 1981, the Bank of America informed Osborne that the bank would not provide the requested loans without additional equity. Over the weekend, another $1.6 million was raised from venture capital sources.

But financial trouble again appeared in December 1982, just before both the new president and underwriting talks began. That month, the Bank of America had refused to extend the line of credit for the company above $10 million. The troubles grew. The underwriters, after conducting due-diligence interviews, issued an opinion that the time was not right for a public offering. Their reasons were that the transition to new management was incomplete, two new products were to be introduced which might be delayed and the company's future success depended on how well the new products did, and there was continuing instability in financial forecasts.

The losses kept increasing. On April 6, 1983, the president reported to stockholders that the company would report a loss of $1 million for the most recent year, ended February 26, 1983. On April 22, the underwriters were told that the loss was revised to $4 million. On Monday, Osborne said that he was told the loss would be more like $8 to $10 million. An emergency meeting was held on the morning of April 29. As Osborne saw it:

Here are the highlights of the April 29 board meeting:

1. Januich claimed he had no knowledge of possible poorer financial data until April 21.
2. Januich observed that the death of the Osborne 1 had occurred faster than anyone could have predicted.
3. Dennis Bovin of Salomon Brothers, on behalf of the underwriters, stated that they would work with the company to raise money providing top

management remained and no evidence of fraud or misrepresentation was found. (Osborne and Dvorak, July 23, 1984, p. 47)

Another meeting was held on May 5, in which the board resolved that management should try to raise $30 million in new equity. At that time the equity base was $13 million. Existing venture capital investors added a new $12 million.

On April 17, the new model, Executive, was formally announced and shipped during the first week of May. Its price was set at $2495, and the price of the Osborne 1 was raised to $1995. The prices were too high for the immediate inflow of cash that was then needed: "Executives were not selling at $2495 and Osbornes were barely trickling out the door at $1995" (Osborne and Dvorak, July 23, 1984, p. 50). Competition from Kaypro continued to hold Osborne's sales down. For a company with small capitalization and large losses, an immediate upturn in sales was desperately needed. It didn't come. In September 1983, pattern D became history for the Osborne Computer Co. It filed for bankruptcy.

DYNAMIC SYSTEMS AND ACCOUNTING

Organizations are dynamic systems—systems in the sense of interacting and relating parts, and dynamic in the sense of activities unfolding in time. In the corporation, the quarterly and annual earnings are accountings which summarize the performance of the organization over the most recent period. These accounts do not, however, depict the dynamics of the activities that underlie these performance summaries. The power of systems dynamics techniques lies in the ability to analyze and clarify the dynamics of activities which result in the accounted performance.

SUMMARY

All business firms are dynamic systems. In new firms, particularly, problems and bad timing in balancing any of the factors of the system create crises which, if not overcome in time, may cripple or terminate the firm. A corporate system is an open system, consisting of inputs, outputs, and the transformation function of the system. A systems dynamics model of corporate growth describes the flows of materials and information of the corporate activity.

The general patterns of growth for initially successful new business firms are either continued growth or troubles, with several outcomes. One such trouble is a delivery delay, which tends to lose sales increasingly as the delay lengthens. The first crisis for a growing new firm can be a delivery delay either in current product or in the introduction of an improved product. Corporate growth for a new firm requires a careful balancing of the several factors in the dynamics of the corporate system.

REFLECTION

1. Identify several new firms that went public in the last five years. Find their prospectuses and trace their stock prices since going public. Have any encountered problems? What were they, and why did they occur?

FOR FURTHER READING

FORRESTER, JAY W., *Industrial Dynamics.* Cambridge, Mass.: MIT Press, 1961.

CHAPTER FIVE
INNOVATION PROCESS

CENTRAL IDEAS

1. Macro and micro levels of innovation
2. The science base of innovation
3. Stages of the innovation process in a firm
4. Culture, structure, and roles in innovative organizations

Example: National Level of Innovation—The 1981 Memory Chip War

Viewed as an overarching concept of business change by technology, innovation is an organizational process—creating and introducing into the market new products, processes, and services. At a micro level, innovation is a process in which individual firms develop new products, processes, and services for commercial introduction. At a macro level, innovation is a national process. An example of national innovation occurred in the early 1980s when the Japanese made a successful entry into the memory chip market—against one of America's strongest and most innovative industries at that time—the semiconductor industry of "Silicon Valley."

The time was January 1981. During the previous decade of the 1970s the industrial world had reeled from the escalation of energy costs. Manufacturing industries had been hit by inflationary price increases, losing asset value during the decade. But not the semiconductor industry—it had boomed right along, on a continuing wave of innovation. In 1981 the time was ripe for another innovation in the memory chip—a new generation of computer memory chips—the 64,000-bit chip. Both the Japanese and American firms were rushing to introduce that 64K chip—because it was the next obvious technological advance in computer memory chips, an incremental innovation over the 16K chip. Both the American semiconductor firms and the Japanese electronics firms had the vision. The difference was that the Americans had created and dominated the semiconductor chip market. How could the Japanese crack that market?

They had formulated a strategy. In the 1970s, the Japanese government had planned with Japanese firms to invade the semiconductor market. In preparation for the invasion, the Japanese government agency, the Ministry of International Trade and Industry (MITI), had funded a major R&D project in Japanese electronics firms to jump to the cutting-edge semiconductor technology of the 1970s—the large-scale integrated chip (LSI chip technology). LSI technology was seen as the next incremental innovation in the semiconductor industry production technology. LSI technology was necessary for building a 64K chip (Bylinsky, 1981a).

Memory chips contain many memory cells, composed of pairs of transitors that stay either "on" or "off"—when at any time turned on or off. By "on" or "off" is meant electrically conducting or electrically nonconducting. Computer designers think of the "on" state as storing the number 1 and the "off" state as storing the number 0. Mathematically, one can express any number as a sucession of 1's and 0's in what is called the "binary number system." In computer jargon, each 1 or 0 is called a "bit." Memory chips are thus devices for storing numbers expressed as a series of 1's and 0's in adjacent pairs of transistors turned on and off. A memory chip with 1000 (1K) transistor pairs can store 1000 1's and 0's or 1000 bits. A memory chip with 16,000 transistor pairs can store 16,000 1's and 0's, or 16K bits. The 64K chip would store 64,000 bits.

In the beginning of 1981, American confidence was high. Silicon Valley was the envy of the industrial world. The high-tech managers of Silicon Valley considered themselves superior to the managers of the motorcycle, television, and automobile industries, which had been stampeded by Japanese. The semiconductor industry had been preparing for future competition by spending large sums in research and development. Pit one group of innovative managers against another and you have a high-tech war.

December 1981—the race for the 64K-bit chip was over. The battle for market dominance in the new 64K chip market had been won by the Japanese with 70% of the market. American pride and pocketbook were hurt: "The American semiconductor industry, that bastion of innovation and enterprise, is reeling under its first major defeat by the Japanese—a defeat that came upon it with blinding speed" (Bylinsky, 1981b, p. 52). L. J. Sevin, the founder of Mostek Corporation (one of the hot semiconductor firms of the 1970s) was quoted: "The Japanese have finally done it. They have won the memory market. It's the thing we were all dreading. Here it has happened. Bang!" (Bylinsky, 1981b, p. 52).

How did it happen? It happened because of Japanese strategy in innovation, timing, and quality of production. Its consequence was to position the Japanese as the major competitors of the United States in the semiconductor industry for the rest of the 1980s. Let us next see an overview of the innovation process. From that view, we can see how the battle was won.

THE SCIENCE BASE OF
THE INNOVATION
PROCESS

An overview of the innovation process is sketched in Figure 5.1. Like most important processes, innovation is complex. It is full of interactions, some of which may be planned and some serendipitous. However, one can sketch a simplified logic to the process. It begins in research, then moves into development, and then into production and marketing of new products. Even though the logic is oversimplified, one can see in it the kinds of decisions that occur in any innovation (Haeffner, 1980).

Technological invention is the first step in technological innovation. At any point in time, technological invention draws on the current scientific knowledge base. Discoveries in science provide opportunities for technological invention. Accordingly, modern inventors must be versed in the latest scientific knowledge and techniques. For this reason, the corporate research laboratory is staffed with scientists as well as with engineers. The scientists perform (1) scientific work as complementary to their primary emphasis on (2) technological invention, (3) on research and development, and (4) on product and process design. This is lumped together under the term "research and development" (R&D).

The scientific research system of a nation is part of the nation's R&D system. Scientific progress is cumulative—research questions begin in some current state of scientific knowledge. These questions stimulate research projects from which scientific results are published in scientific literatures.

FIGURE 5.1 Overview of the innovation process.

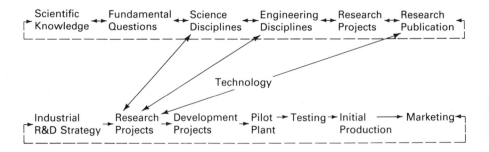

From the accumulation of scientific knowledge, scientists and technologists invent and develop new technologies.

Example: The MITI LSI Project

From 1976 to 1979, the Japanese government, through its Ministry of International Trade and Industry (MITI), sponsored a large-scale-integration project designed to bring Japanese electronics industry to the technological level of the United States in semiconductor technology (Ypsilanti, 1985). Together, the Japanese government and the Japanese electronics industry had understood the need for a common scientific and technological knowledge base for industrial competitiveness.

By the 1970s, the Japanese electronics industry had already emerged as the world's leader in consumer electronics. The opportunity for that emergence had occurred in the 1950s with the invention of the transistor. Although invented and developed in the United States, U.S. industry had emphasized the military applications of transistorized electronics, ignoring consumer applications. The Japanese electronics firms thus found a technological hole in the world's market, the transistor for consumer electronics. In the early 1960s they aggressively pushed the application of transistorized electronics into consumer products, and by the middle of the 1970s they had captured most of the consumer electronics industry. Many American firms (Philco, Admiral, and Emerson Radio, for example) had dropped out or became importers and distributors of Japanese products (Ypsilanti, 1985).

Yet in 1970, the Japanese government and electronics firms realized that they had an inherent commercial weakness—for they were importing from the United States the heart of the new electronics, the integrated semiconductor chips. The reason for this was that while the Japanese had learned how to make transistors, the innovative Americans had integrated many transistors on a single semiconductor chip. The Japanese decided that they would no longer play technological catch-up. Although they had market share and a manufacturing capability, they needed the technological edge.

In electronics technology, the Americans were making integrated circuits and researching the next technological generation of large-scale integrated circuits (LSI). MITI and the Japanese government and the Japanese firms decided to work together on LSI technology. The innovation capability of individual firms in a nation depends on the innovativeness of the whole industrial sector. If Japan was to have competitive Japanese electronics firms, they must have an innovative Japanese electronics industry. MITI then provided the equivalent of $10 million worth of research grants to Japanese electronics firms from 1970 to 1975. Some portion of the budget purchased advanced semiconductor manufacturing and testing equipment from U.S. manufacturers. Japanese firms subsequently registered about 1000 patents resulting from that project (Ypsilanti, 1985).

Thus by the late 1970s, Japanese firms had become technological equals of American firms in semiconductor production techniques. The MITI LSI project had created the innovative context for Japanese electronics manufacturers. Yet it was still up to the individual Japanese firms to use that new knowledge for innovation. To understand the next step in the 1981 memory chip war, we must examine the corporate level of the innovation process.

MICRO LEVEL—THE CORPORATE INNOVATION PROCESS

Although scientific knowledge and generic technological knowledge are the sources of knowledge for invention, the innovation process for creating new products occurs specifically within individual firms. The macro level of innovation is a national and international process, involving a science and technology interaction and involving industrial, university, and governmental research interactions. The micro level of innovation occurs in particular companies, beginning with ideas for innovation that are researched and developed into new products and processes and then commercially introduced (after testing and pilot production and marketing).

In these firms, the innovation of new products requires business strategies in which the perception of economic conditions and strategies for profit provide the motivation and resource base for industrial R&D. The steps of the innovation process start in industrial research and development.

Technological invention—an idea for a new means of accomplishing a desired function—is the first step. Invention arises from combining (1) the ideas of new technical possibilities with (2) the idea of an application for a new product or service. After invention, applied research is needed to create a functional prototype (a working model) of a new product. This is a laboratory model which shows that the product will function. Next comes developmental research to design a product that works better and can be manufactured at a reasonable cost. Developmental research creates the new product design (and any new production processes required to produce the new product). Next the new product is tested and new production processes are tested in pilot plants. Finally, initial quantities of the new product are produced and trial sale of the new product begins. Successful products then begin production expansion and sales growth.

Therefore, within a firm:

1. Research and development is performed within the context of business strategy.
2. Research invents new products or processes.
3. Applied research creates functional prototypes.
4. Developmental research creates manufacturable designs.
5. Testing checks and leads to refinement of designs.
6. Pilot and initial production leads to new product introduction.

Example: The 64K Chip Design

The Japanese firms performed the R&D for the specific new product of the 64K chip. To do this, they had to scale up from the 16K design to the 64K design, to increase the density of transistors on a single chip. In developmental research, the managerial question is always—just how much innovation? Enough to create a new and superior product but not enough to delay product introduction. In the management judgment for the 64K chip, the Japanese hit it just right. They went for a less innovative design—straightforward scaling up of the American Mostek's standard design for the 16K chip, while the American firms chose to be a little more innovative, wishing to reduce the size of the chip.

In retrospect, its easy to call a judgment, but in the heat of battle it is hard to make the right decision. In this case, the Japanese won. They got there first. It took the American firms one more year to get the bugs out of their slightly superior designs. That was bad but not deadly. What really hurt was that Japanese production quality turned out to be superior. Japanese chips were less likely to be flawed from production. Japanese quality control was good, very good. The Japanese were not only innovative, but they were quality producers and aggressive pricers. A strong combination—innovation, quality, and aggressive pricing.

Of course, only in movies do people or firms live happily ever after. In real life, competition continues. Because the American semiconductor industry was innovative, the 64K memory chip battle was lost, but the competitive war in semiconductors continued. By the middle of the 1980s the next market battle focused on the 256K-bit chip (while research went on to the million-bit chip). In 1983, the first 256K prototypes were announced by AT&T and in 1984 by IBM.

It can be seen in this example that a coordinated partnership for technological innovation had occurred between the macro and micro innovation levels of Japan. This was partly due to Japanese governmental/industrial culture and to national policies. Their technology policy was postulated on the basis that the role of government was to encourage the advance of fundamental scientific and technological knowledge which Japanese firms could build on to improve international competitiveness. This is also an example of an R&D infrastructure relationship (a topic that we discuss in Part IV).

At the micro level, the trade-off in judgments between engineering design innovativeness and production manufacturability was better made by the Japanese—not in any absolute sense, but temporarily. Recall that timing is critical to the commercial success of innovation.

CULTURE, STRUCTURE, AND ROLES IN INNOVATIVE ORGANIZATIONS

Thus we should begin to see that the innovation process is complex, involving different levels and different stages, and requiring difficult managerial judgments to beat competitors to the market with just the right product, quality, and price. To focus on the context of these difficult decisions, we examine next what has been learned about the factors or organizational culture, structure, and roles in encouraging innovation.

Culture

A culture that encourages and supports innovative activity improves the chances of the commercial success of innovation. Alan Frohman summarized three aspects in the corporate culture that facilitate the utilization of technology:

1. Top management orientation.
2. Project selection criteria.
3. Systems and structure.
   (Frohman, 1982, p. 97)

The orientation of top management toward innovation is important, for they control the resources and reward structures of the organization. They take the risks of entering new markets and commit to the long-term investments.

In supporting R&D, the corporation must have a clear (but flexible) set of technological and business strategies and policies to provide the decision criteria for selecting R&D projects. Selectivity in choosing which projects to move forward from research into commercial introduction is another critical factor in successful innovation. The company must also have the management systems and structures to organize innovative activities, integrating business and technological decisions. This integration strengthens the business capabilities, financial stability, and the competitive position of the corporation.

James Brian Quinn also emphasized that top executives must provide the atmosphere and vision for innovation: "Visions, vigorously supported, are not 'management fluff,' but have many practical implications. They attract quality people to the company and give focus to their creative and entrepreneurial drives" (Quinn, 1985, p. 78). In addition, Quinn emphasized that innovative organizations must be oriented toward markets and support multiple approaches toward technological development. Innovation succeeds when market needs are satisfied. Yet dramatic advances in technology often come from a fascination with pushing technological advance just to see how far it can be pushed. Therefore, innovative organizations must have both technological strength and marketing strength.

Multiple approaches to technological development can reduce the uncertainty in technological success. Technological development is inherently risky from two standpoints. First, the technology must succeed in attaining a hoped-for performance. Second, that performance must be just right for the market need. Quinn suggested that many innovative companies support competing approaches to a new technology and set a "developmental shoot-out" between the projects in the final stages (to determine which is really best for market needs). With such competition, Quinn also suggested that it is important for the organization to be supportive of, and reintegrate into the corporation, the losers from such shoot-outs (Quinn, 1985, p. 79).

Structure

No particular structure is best for all innovative organizations, but two structural principles should be encouraged by all organizations seeking to foster innovation:

1. Structures should be relatively flat in hierarchical levels.
2. Structures should encourage learning and tolerate flexibility and experimentation in developing technology and products.

James Quinn summarized these principles, calling the best organizational approach to innovation a kind of "incrementalist approach": "Major innovations are best managed as incremental, goal-oriented, interactive learning processes" (Quinn, 1985, p. 82).

Technological progress occurs in fits and starts and by unexpected pathways. This does not mean that it is blind or entirely fortuitous, but it does mean that managerial processes that encourage and foster innovation should tolerate high degrees of uncertainty, experimentation, false starts, and serendipity. Thus a structure that provides goal-oriented guidelines and directions but minimizes overly detailed planning and control is more likely to foster innovation than a rigidly planned, controlled, and hierarchically oriented organization.

This principle was proposed in early studies by Tom Burns and G. M. Stalker, in which they argued that the "mechanistic" types of organizational structures were best suited to detailed control of known production processes, while "organistic" types of structures were best suited to creativity in developing or changing production processes (Burns and Stalker, 1961).

Flatter organizational structures, minimizing the layers of management, can provide more informal communication vertically than can hierarchical structures with many layers. Informal communication often facilitates interactive learning in an organization. Management styles of innovative organizations should also delegate a great deal of discretion to lower levels while providing overall strategic control:

> Effective managers of innovation channel and control its main directions. Like venture capitalists, they administer primarily by setting goals, selecting key people, and establishing a few critical limits and decision points for intervention rather than by implementing elaborate planning or control systems. As technology leads or market needs emerge, these managers set a few—most crucial—performance targets and limits. They allow their technical units to decide how to achieve these, subject to defined constraints and reviews at critical junctures (Quinn, 1985, p. 83).

Roles

Organizational culture and structures for innovation should thus encourage discretion, experimentation, learning, and creativity of personnel. This increases the importance of attending to roles in an innovative organization. The concept of roles in the innovation process was proposed in a study called SAPPHO, in which four kinds of roles were seen as essential in industrial innovation: the Technical Innovator, the Business Innovator, the Chief Executive, and the Product Champion (Sappho, 1972).

Later, J. Smith and others studied a sample of 10 innovations at a particular firm, Union Carbide. They added more roles to the innovation process:

1. The Scientific Gatekeeper,
2. The Process User Gatekeeper,
3. The Product User Gatekeeper,
4. The Idea Generator,
5. The Process/Product Champion,
6. The Problem Solver,
7. The R&D Sponsor,
8. The Project Manager,
9. The Quality Controller,
10. The R&D Strategist,
11. The Business Sponsor,
12. The Top Management.
    (Smith et al., 1984)

Since innovation must move across the spectrum from research into production and sales, the number of roles and people involved are many. The first four roles are involved in creating the innovative idea. The Process User Gatekeeper and the Product User Gatekeeper are familiar with the production processes and user markets for which the innovative idea is aimed. The Scientific Gatekeeper and Idea Generator provide the scientific knowledge base from which a new technological idea may be applied to the process or product need in order to create the idea of an invention.

Once an inventive idea is conceived, it must be researched, reduced to practice, and developed into a useful product or process. In this part of the innovation, the next four roles play central parts. There must be a project manager to organize and manage the R&D project. There must be a Problem Solver who solves the technical problems in the research in making practical the inventive idea. There must be a Process/Product Champion who pushes for the R&D project and an R&D Sponsor to provide resources for the project.

The next step of the innovation process in moving a successful R&D project into commercial application requires the last four roles to be involved. First there must be an R&D Strategist who recommends to the proper business division the usefulness of the R&D project. Then there must be a Business Sponsor who accepts the recommendation and will commercialize and implement the product or process resulting from the R&D project. There must also be a Quality Controller who judges whether the performance of the R&D project will meet the commercially attainable goals of the Business Sponsor. Finally, there must be approval from Top Management for the capital commitments for commercialization of the R&D project results.

These roles can be played by one or several people. In Smith's study, The Scientific Gatekeeper and Idea Generator roles were usually members of the scientific staff of the research laboratory. Research managers in the laboratory often played the role of Idea Generator and usually the role of R&D Sponsors and Project Managers. Scientists and engineers working in the laboratory usually played the role of Problem Solver. The roles of Quality Controller and R&D Strategist were usually played by R&D program directors or vice presidents of R&D. The roles of Process User Gatekeeper and Product User Gatekeeper were often members of the firm in production or sales with whom the research staff were in communication. The roles of Business Sponsor and Top Management were in positions outside the research laboratory.

The innovation process is complex and requires participation of many roles and many players. It is difficult and complicated to manage—yet essential to master—for innovative organizations have the best chance at long-term survival.

SUMMARY

Innovation is a process, creating and introducing into the market new products and processes. There are several levels: the firm, the industry, the national R&D infrastructure, and international competition. The technological sophistication of an industry facilitates the innovative capability of firms in the industry. The R&D infrastructure of a nation facilitates the technological sophistication of industries of the nation.

Within the firm, the innovation process begins in research and development, guided by the firm's business strategy. After invention, applied research creates functional prototypes. Further research and development must create engineering and production prototypes before pilot production can be begun. The testing and product refinement continues. Finally, production and marketing can begin.

The culture, structure, and roles of an organization are all important to improve the chances of success of innovation. Culture requires top-management commitment to innovation and decision processes that select R&D projects focused on both technical and business criteria of success. Structure requires relatively flat organizations, encouraging creativity and discretion within goal-oriented guidelines and reviews at critical junctures. Since innovation must move from research into production and sales, the number of roles and people involved are many, including gatekeepers of technical and marketing expertise and product champions.

REFLECTION

1. Find, either in the literature or in a nearby firm, an example of a new product or new process innovation. Write a brief case study of the innovation, identifying the steps. Also identify the key personnel in the project and describe their roles.

FOR FURTHER READING

BURNS, TOM, and G. M. STALKER,   *The Management of Innovation*. London: Social Science Paperbacks, 1961.

CHAPTER SIX
FORECASTING
TECHNOLOGY

CENTRAL IDEAS

1. Technology S-curve
2. Progress in technology S-curve jumping by systems innovations
3. Natural limits to technological progress

Example: A New Technology—The Germanium Point-Contact Transistor

To be innovative, the manager must create and anticipate the uses of technological change. For example, in the 1920s and 1930s, the electron tube was new and wonderful. The functions it made possible—radio and long-distance telephones—were also wonderful. You could hear Rudy Vallee (a popular singer) singing from Schenectedy, New York. People could call California from New York. But at that time, if one had plotted decreases in power and size for electron tubes (as performance parameters), one would have seen a limit to their improvement—which in fact was reached around World War II.

In fact, by 1935, Bell Labs' scientists were already thinking about replacing that wonderful electron tube. Earlier, in experiments in telegraph and in radio, it had been discovered that an odd material, germanium crystals, could detect radio signals. It had also been discovered that silicon crystals could convert light into electricity and could change alternating current to direct current. Therefore, even before World War II, scientists knew that these materials of germanium and silicon had curious electrical properties—those of semiconducting materials.

In the 1930s, Bell Laboratories, the corporate research laboratory of American Telephone and Telegraph, decided to set up a research program in semiconducting materials—they called it "solid-state physics." The reason for this management decision was a hope to search for a technological replacement for the wonderful electron tube.

It was a program of basic research (as universities perform in the innovation process) to try to understand the electronic nature of germanium and silicon. The managers of Bell Labs knew that understanding nature often meant discovering ways to use natural things for inventions: "Quantum theory had opened up the possibility of understanding the properties of solids from their atomic and electronic structure. It was hoped that through interdisciplinary research, sufficient understanding of solids could be obtained to design and fabricate new materials that, according to the Bell directive, could 'be used in the development of completely new and improved components and apparatus elements of communications systems' " (Bardeen, 1984, p. 143).

However, the research was interrupted by World War II. Bell Labs' scientists contributed to the war effort by designing electronics for radar, communications, and control. But after the war, the solid-state physics group was reconstituted. William Shockley was head of the group, which included John Bardeen and Walter Brattain. Germanium as a pure crystal does not conduct electricity. But Shockley's group had learned that by doping (adding) other atoms into the germanium crystal during its growth, electricity would be conducted by the extra electrons (negative carriers) that the dopant atoms contributed—or by the deficit of electrons, "holes"—other dopant atoms contributed in the crystal (positive carriers).

Then in the summer of 1945, Shockley proposed controlling the number of electricity carriers in doped germanium crystals by applying an external electric field perpendicular to the direction of the current. Using quantum mechanics theory, Shockley had calculated that the effect of the field should be large enough to provide amplification of the controlling field by the current in the semiconductor. Shockley had a sample made, but it didn't work.

Bardeen had just joined the group. Shockley asked him to check the calculation. Bardeen suggested that electrons might be being trapped at the surface of the crystal, which prevented seeing the calculated effect. Brattain conducted some experiments confirming his conjecture. They were, after all, on the right track. They tried other configurations and got a small amplification.

The amplification was too small. They tried other arrangements—one of which placed two closely spaced gold strips on the surface of a doped germanium crystal and an electrical connection on its base. Relative to that base, one gold strip had a positive voltage (called the emitter) and the other a negative voltage (called the collector). They applied a signal between emitter and base, and voilà! It was amplified, greatly, in the voltage between the collector and the base. What happened was that holes introduced into the germanium from the emitter went not to the base but to the collector—this added to the positive current flowing from the base to the collector. It was amplification! It meant that transistors could do what electron tubes did. But the new transistor was smaller than the electron tube and used much less electricity.

AT&T acquired the basic patents for the transistor. In 1956, Shockley, Brattain, and Bardeen were awarded the Nobel prize in physics. AT&T licensed the transistor, and the new age in electronics began. The invention of the transistor started a new technology.

FORM OF
TECHNOLOGICAL CHANGE

The germanium transistor is an example of a radical innovation, transistorized electronics. It set off a long period of further innovation. The pattern of this further innovation showed a very general feature of technological progress, which people have called the "technology S-curve." In this chapter we examine this important concept and its use in technology forecasting.

Anticipating technological change is an important management function. One must do so to plan new products and new businesses. One must also avoid being technologically blind-sided by competitors with technologically superior products. Yet this is not easy to do because often technological progress is surprising. But sometimes it is planned. Technological forecasting tries to put as much planning as is possible into technological change.

Radical and systems innovations are usually the type that have been surprising. They are hard to plan. However, incremental innovations have often been planned—or, at least, sought after. The seeking or anticipation of technological innovation has been called "technology forecasting."

Historically, most incremental technological innovations have shown similar patterns in the rate of technological change. Sometimes, one can use the knowledge of this pattern to anticipate the rate of change of a new technology. Figure 6.1 shows the general shape of the rates of technology change. In the beginning of a major new technology, the rate of technological progress is exponential, as a plethora of new ideas are generated to tackle the obvious limitations of the new technology. Later the rate of technological change slows to a linear growth. Finally, the rate turns off to little or no growth, as a natural limit to the technology is approached. For example, Figure 6.2 (see p. 67) shows the density of transistors in the period 1960–1980. One can see how density grew.

All new technologies are awkward, expensive, inefficient, and unsafe—but they are functional. Wright's airplane flew, Bell's telephone transmitted voices, Ashley's computer calculated tables. The early histories

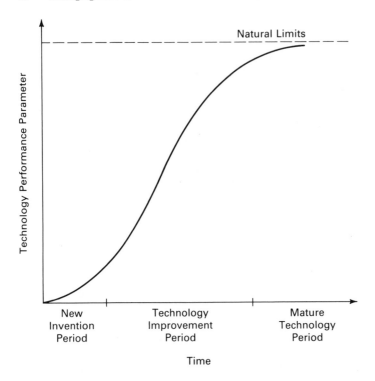

FIGURE 6.1 Technology S-curve.

of these and others all show similar characteristics of inefficiency, costliness, and danger. Accordingly, one popular reaction is always to laugh at the new technology—ha, ha—if God had meant people to fly, God would have given people wings (the Wright brother's first plane didn't fly very far). However, technologists have a different attitude toward new technology— hey, it works, and I have an idea how to make it work better!

Accordingly, the early history of all new technologies is a rash of additional new inventions, all aimed at improving the new technology— improvements in components and in peripheral devices and in materials and energy sources. The numbers of these new inventions begin quickly to improve the performance of the new technology at an exponential rate. Hence, the first part of the technology S-curve—exponential.

Example: Explosive Innovative Advance in New Technologies— The Silicon Transistor

That wonderful little transistor was still poor, fragile, and unreliable. It failed easily—it couldn't take hot temperatures. Not to worry! The S-curve would take care of these problems! Bell Labs and Western Electric proceeded to research and develop the transistor for communications purposes. Another innovative company, Texas Instruments, was looking for ways to improve their seismographic detection instruments (which they sold to oil companies for oil exploration). Since their instruments used electron vacuum tubes and were portable and subject to abuse in the field, they immediately saw an application of transistorized electronics to their instruments.

In 1952, Patrick Haggerty was president of Texas Instruments. He purchased a license from Bell Labs to make transistors, acquiring the right to pursue new technology. Haggerty assigned to Mark Shepard a research project to develop a reliable transistor that could be sold for $2.50. Shepard was a good engineer. He developed it. Then Haggerty told his engineers to develop a pocket radio made of germanium transistors. This became the first consumer electronics product with transistors, introduced in 1954.

But Haggerty was not yet through. He was still looking to improve the transistor. He knew of silicon, but it was brittle and difficult to purify for making into transistors. From Bell Labs Haggerty hired a physicist, Gordon Teal, who had been researching silicon. Haggerty told Teal and another researcher, Willis Adcock (a physical chemist), to develop a silicon transistor. They worked rapidly and secretly.

In May 1954, Teal took the new transistor to a professional conference. There he listened to several speakers tell of the difficult problems of trying to make a silicon transistor. When Teal's turn to speak came, he began: "Our company now has two types of silicon transistor in production. . . . I just happen to have some here in my coat pocket" (Reid, 1985, p. 37). Teal had an assistant come onto the stage, carrying a record player, which used a germanium transistor in its electrical circuit. The transistor was visibly connected, by long wires, to the record player. Teal put on a record and started playing music. Next the assistant brought onto the stage a pot of hot oil, setting it beside the record player. Teal dunked the wired germanium transistor into the hot oil— zonk! The music stopped as the germanium transistor failed in the hot temperature of the oil. Teal then produced one of the silicon transistors from his pocket. There was a pause, as Teal soldered the silicon transistor to the wires, replacing the failed germanium transistor. The music from the record player started playing again. Then Teal dunked the silicon transistor into the hot oil. The music continued. The meeting exploded in excitement! Texas Instruments had done it—silicon! The transistor revolution continued on its way, climbing exponentially up the S-curve of technological progress.

S-CURVE JUMPS FROM RADICAL TO SYSTEM INNOVATIONS

The rates of change in new technologies thus consist of a radical innovation and subsequent major improvements on the radical innovation. However, a second kind of innovation sometimes occurs which jumps the previous technology S-curve onto a new S-curve—these are systems innovations utilizing the previous radical innovation. Together these continue the explosive growth of technologies on new S-curves.

Example: A New S-Curve—The Semiconductor Chip

An example of a systems innovation build around the innovation of the silicon transistor was the innovation of the semiconductor chip. Engineers quickly began thinking up wonderful circuits to make from the new, wonderful silicon transistors. But now there was new trouble. Engineers are never satisfied. The many wonderful new circuits they could dream up to use the silicon transistor would often contain so many transistors that no one could wire that many transistors together. Was the technological S-curve of transistorized electronics to flatten off due to the natural limits of how many electronic components could be wired together by the human hand? Two inventors, an engineer and a scientist, independently invented the way out—the integrated-circuit (IC) semiconductor chip.

The engineer was Jack St. Clair Kilby. He had grown up in Kansas, a kid loving technical things. He built a ham radio set, using electron tubes, and improved it. He decided to be an electrical engineer. In 1941, he entered college at the University of Illinois. Four months later, the Japanese bombed Pearl Harbor. Kilby entered the Army and ended the war as a sergeant, assigned to an Army radio repair shop on a tea plantation in India. Afterward, he went back to the University of Illinois and studied electrical engineering. He graduated in 1947, trained in electron vacuum tubes. He went to work at a firm named Centralab, located in Milwaukee (Reid, 1985).

One evening, he attended a lecture at Marquette University given by John Bardeen, who described the new transistor. Kilby began reading everything he could find on the new solid-state device. In 1951, Bell Labs announced their licenses, and Centralab purchased one for the $25,000 fee. They sent Kilby to Bell Labs for a five-day course in semiconductors. From 1951 through 1958, Kilby helped design transistorized electronic circuits at Centralab. He became aware of the new problem that further dramatic progress in circuits would require more transistors than could be hand-wired together. But to solve this problem would require a research capability greater than existed where Kilby worked.

In 1958, Kilby sent his résumé to several larger firms, one of which went to Willis Adcock of Texas Instruments. Adcock hired him. TI was also worried about the integration problem of wiring together so many transistors. In 1958, Adcock was in charge of a "micro-module" project at TI, which was one approach to integration. Kilby was put on the project but immediately didn't like it. It was not the best approach, he thought. Kilby would have to think of something fast. That summer in 1958 many people were off on vacation. Since Kilby was new he had no vacation time yet, but he had the semiconductor lab to himself. He learned quickly what TI knew about transistors. One obvious fact stood out: TI led in silicon technology. Whatever good idea Kilby came up with had better be in silicon technology.

He came up with a good idea. Transistors were made of silicon, but the other elements of an electronic circuit were not made of silicon. Why couldn't they all be made of silicon? Why not make the whole circuit on a silicon chip? Then no component need be hand-wired! Kilby could solve the component-wiring problem by doing away with individual components. Henceforth, only whole circuits need be wired together. No one had thought of it before—because silicon was a ridiculous material of which to make components other than transistors. Examples of other components were resistors (best made from carbon) and capacitors (best made from plastics or ceramics and metal foil).

On July 24, 1958, Kilby took up his lab notebook (lab notebooks are essential to establish patent priority for inventions). He wrote down what he called his "monolithic idea": "The following circuit elements could be made on a single slice [of silicon]: resistors, capacitors, distributed capacitor, transistor." He then made rough sketches of how to make each component by properly arranging the silicon material (Reid, 1985, p. 38).

Kilby showed his notebook to Willis Adcock. Adcock said that if Kilby could demonstrate they worked, he would authorize an R&D project to construct an integrated circuit on a chip. Kilby carved out a resistor on a silicon chip and then made a capacitor from another chip. He wired the two into a test circuit, and they worked. Adcock gave his approval to build a circuit.

On September 12, 1958, Kilby was ready. A group of TI executives assembled in the lab for a demonstration. The circuit made on a chip was hooked to an oscilloscope, which (like a TV screen) would display the output voltage of the circuit on the scope. At first the scope showed a flat straight line. Then Kilby switched on the integrated circuit, designed as an oscillator circuit, and—it worked—a wiggling line appeared on the screen, the sine-wave form of an oscillator circuit: "Then everybody broke into broad smiles. A new era in electronics had been born" (Reid, 1985, p. 39).

At the same time, independently, another inventor had come up with a similar idea—Robert Noyce, a physicist and, in 1958, president of Fairchild Semiconductor. Fairchild was a new company begun by Shockley, one of the inventors of the transistor. Noyce had been worrying about the same problem Kilby was concerned with about the same time. On January 23, 1959, Noyce conceived a solution. He took his lab notebook and wrote down his monolithic idea: "It would be desirable to make multiple devices on a single piece of silicon, in order to be able to make interconnections between devices as part of the manufacturing process . . ." (Reid, 1985, p. 41).

Simultaneous invention or discovery has often occurred in the history of technology and science, the reason being that technological problems are apparent to many people in a technical community, having similar scientific and technical backgrounds. Thus both Texas Instruments and Fairchild Semiconductors filed for the patent on inventing the semiconducting chip. There followed years of legal argument about the patent. In 1966, several semiconductor manufacturing firms met together; TI and Fairchild agreed to grant licenses to each other and to share priority in inventing the semiconducting chip. Kilby and Noyce (in addition to many other prizes and tokens of recognition) both received the National Medal of Science for inventing the semiconductor chip.

THE LINEAR PORTION OF THE TECHNOLOGY S-CURVE

After the first radical invention, several other major inventions build on the first to create a rate of technological progress which (in terms of technical performance) advances exponentially. After that a linear rate of rapid advance continues the technical progress. Further progress requires improvement of the scientific understanding of the phenomena and materials underlying the technology.

Understanding the scientific base of phenomena and materials behind a new technology is a lengthy, detailed, and laborious process, requiring an enormous effort in universities and industrial research laboratories. The high rates of R&D investment in high-tech industries occurs during this phase. For example, in the electronics and computer industry, firms have been investing in R&D at rates of 4 to 14% of their annual sales.

Example: Natural Limits to Chip Density

Finally, some inherent physical limit is approached in the physical phenomena underlying the technology, and the rate of technology change levels off. From 1948 to 1958, in 10 years, the rate of technological change in electronics progressed exponentially from the inventions of (1) the transistor, (2) the development of the cheap germanium transistor, (3) the invention and development of the cheap silicon transistor, and (4) the invention of the integrated circuit of silicon semiconducing chips (ICs). From 1960 through 1980, progress in semiconductor chips continued linearly by increasing the density of the numbers of transistors on a chip.

By the 1980s, the chip went through two major advances in increasing the number of transistors on a chip—large-scale integration (LSI) of the 1970s and very large scale integration (VLSI) of the 1980s. The original integrated circuit had hundreds of transistors on a chip. In LSI, thousands of transistors were put on a chip; and in VLSI, hundreds of thousands of transistors were put on a chip. From 1960 through 1975, increases of transistor density on a chip were exponential; then linear from 1975 on (Robinson, 1984, p. 268).

Where would this stop? Figure 6.2 shows a projection made in the early 1980s of where scientists then thought the limits to performance might occur and when they might occur—with performance measured as chip density or numbers of transistors per chip. Then it was projected that a natural limit will be reached in the 1990s as lithographic limits become near the resolution of light or x-ray diffraction limits: "It could happen by the turn of the century, according to James Meindl, director of Stanford University's Center for Integrated Systems. Meindl's forecast came in the opening session of the three-day International Electron Devices Meeting" (Robinson, 1984, p. 267).

In the 1980s, at annual meetings, semiconductor chip engineers had reviewed progress in semiconductor chip technology, forecasting its future. In the meeting of 1983, they anticipated that the limits of semiconducting material technology might be found in a density of a billion transistors per

FIGURE 6.2 Technology S-curve for semiconductor chip density progress. (From A. L. Robinson, "One Billion Transistors on a Chip?", *Science*, Vol. 223, January 20, 1984, p. 268. Photo courtesy of J. D. Meindl, Stanford University, Stanford, CA 94305. Copyright 1984 by the AAAS.)

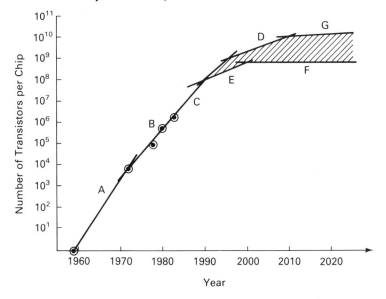

chip: "Meindl's message, then, is that moderation of the growth curve is in store. Depending on certain assumptions pertaining to the fabrication technology, the number of transistors per chip may climb to a number ranging from 'only' several hundred million to about 1 billion in the next 16 years. . . . Meindl calls this future era ULSI, for ultralarge-scale integration . . ." (Robinson, 1984, p. 267). After the IC came the LSI IC, then the VLSI IC, and finally the ULSI IC.

NATURAL LIMITS TO TECHNOLOGICAL PROGRESS

All technologies, based on natural physical phenomena, thus have limits to progress which is approached as the scale of the natural phenomenon is approached. For example, the physical limits which then were expected to be approached in the fourth generation, ULSI, would be due to thermodynamic limitations, materials limitations, and circuit limitations. After this, if further technical progress were to be attained, a new physical basis for the technology must be discovered. And that could come only from science.

In an earlier example, the change from the electron vacuum tube to the transistor had escaped the physical limitations of the tube size and the power consumption of the heated filament. To invent the transistor, the Bell Lab scientists had had to turn from the physical phenomenon of electron conduction in a vacuum (which underlay the electron vacuum tube) to electron-conduction in a solid material, semiconduction (which underlay the transistor and integrated circuits). Therefore, the physical basis of inventions ultimately limits the possible technical improvement of the inventions.

There will thus be a performance S-curve for every different physically based technology. For example, there was an S-curve for electron vacuum-tube performance and another for transistor performance. Then there was one for semiconductor chip performance. Changing from one physical basis for a technology to a new physical basis is like jumping from one performance S-curve to a new performance S-curve.

Because of the underlying scientific base of all technologies, it is important to corporate management to have a window on science and to encourage the scientific exploration of the phenomena utilized by corporate technologies. This is the reason that corporate research laboratories are important to corporate futures (a topic we examine in Part III).

SUMMARY

Anticipating technological change is an important management function. The general shape of technological change follows an S-curve. The technology S-curve is a plot of performance parameters of the technology over time. At first, innovations are exponential in rate, then linear, and finally, level off. The leveling off occurs when some limit to the technology is reached due to the natural phenomena underlying the technology.

Systems innovations that use a prior radical innovation also create new technology S-curves for subsequent technological progress. Further, technological progress requires the invention of a new technology, using different phenomena. If this occurs, technological progress jumps from one technology S-curve to a new one.

REFLECTION

1.   Think of a technology (device, system, or service) with which you are familiar. What are the primary measures of performance of the technology? Plot the change in performance over time. Did it take the shape of an S-curve? Did it jump from one curve to another? What are the natural limits to the technology, and on what are these based?

FOR FURTHER READING

JANTSCH, ERICH,   *Technological Forecasting in Perspective.* Paris: Organization for Economic Cooperation and Development, 1967.

CHAPTER SEVEN
TECHNOLOGY LIFE CYCLE

CENTRAL IDEAS

1. Impact of technological change on industrial volume
2. Phases in the longitivity of industrial technology
3. Product life cycle
4. Rates of innovation and industrial competition
5. Technologically obsolete industries
6. Relation of innovation to market saturation

Example: Technological Change in the Auto Industry

The S-curves of change in the technologies underpining an industry have important implications for the market growth of the industry. We can illustrate this by reviewing some of the history of the auto industry. Autos were once a high-tech industry, then became a mature technology industry.

In the 1880s, bicycles were invented and temporarily became a kind of high-tech boom. Some bicycle makers began experimenting with the addition of small motors to carriages, made of lightweight, high-strength materials (used in bicycle construction). They constructed a strong, light vehicle with low-friction bearings. This lightweight construction was technically important because it made possible the use of low-powered engines for locomotion. The early gasoline engine was certainly low powered—5 to 10 horsepower.

In the 1890s, the existing train industry built heavy vehicles with large, high-powered steam engines. Thus it was bicycle makers (not the train industry) who innovated the automobile (and, incidentally, the airplane). This is frequent pattern in innovation—a new industry springs up to create an innovative variation of an existing industry.

The year 1896 marks the beginning of the automobile industry. In that year, J. Frank Duryea made and sold 13 cars in Springfield, Massachusetts. This was the first time in America that more than one auto was constructed from the same plan, specifically for sale. From 1896 to 1902, many new firms were founded and a variety of configurations and motors marketed. In 1900, a gasoline-powered car defeated electric and steam cars at a racetrack in Chicago, establishing the dominance of the gasoline engine. That dominance was also assisted by the Olds Motor Works (predecessor of Oldsmobile). In 1902, Olds Motor Works constructed and sold 2500 small two-cylinder cars, priced at $650. This was a small beginning for a gasoline auto industry that was 50 years later to see $8 to $10 million sales a year (Abernathy, 1978).

There next came a time of growth when different manufacturers experimented with different configurations of the automobile. However, in 1908, there occurred a significant advance in standardizing the automobile configuration when Henry Ford built the classic Model T. This was the basic car for the people, particularly rural Americans (since in 1908 over half the people still lived on the farm). And it was the car you could buy in any color, as Ford said, as long as it was black.

Henry Ford's genius in organizing mass-production assembly lines to produce the Model T is well known. It is also important that the Model T created what is called "design standardization" for the auto industry. Standards are essential for market expansion in any industry.

The story was that Henry Ford long had in mind the idea of creating a cheap, dependable form of transportation. The key technological feature to doing that turned out to be again in materials—vanadium steel for the chassis. In 1905, Ford saw a French automobile crashed in a road race. After the race, he walked over to the wreck, examining it. He picked up one of the valve stems from the engine, noting that it was curiously light. Ford took it back to his factory to learn its composition. It was made of vanadium steel (steel with the element vanadium added as an alloy). Ford was excited, for the strength of the French vanadium steel was over twice that of American steel. With that strength, Ford could build the automobile for America. Ford envisioned that vanadium could reduce the weight while strengthening the car. In those days all roads in America were dirt, rutted, and potholed. An early car bounced and bumped and its chassis cracked, wrecking the automobile. The steel chassis was the framework of the car. Motors were then bolted directly to the chassis, and sometimes they were literally twisted in half in the violence of a pothole torquing the chassis. Ford was quoted as saying to Charles Sorensen (who helped design the Model T): "Charlie, this means entirely new design requirements, and we can get a better, lighter, and cheaper car as a result of it" (Abernathy, 1978, p. 31).

But how was vanadium steel made? Ford took the valve stem around to several steel companies, but none could duplicate it. Finally, he made a deal with a small steel company in Canton, Ohio, to research it, with Ford financing the trials. The first try failed, but the second try succeeded—vanadium steel, twice as strong!

Ford started on the Model T design; its chassis was to be built of vanadium steel. Its engine was to be in front and, rather than bolted to the chassis, suspended at three points on rubber mounts. The Model T would take the bumps and jolts of the farmers' roads. To this Ford added all the best ideas of the time—magneto ignition (no batteries), drive-shaft powering of the rear wheels (no bicycle chains), and so on. Ford designed the form of the automobile much as we know it today. The Model T became the design standard of the young auto industry.

And the Model T was, in fact, black. The reason was not because it was Ford's favorite color. The reason was technical. In 1908, colored finishes could not be cheaply produced on both the wooden and metal parts that made up the body of the Model T. It was not until 1923 that DuPont chemists created pyroxylin paint, which could reduce the painting time of a car from 12 days to 3 days (thereby making colors economically possible for what had by then become all-steel-bodied cars). Ford's Model T was the right product at the right time for the right market at the right price—performance, timing, market, and price—the four factors of successful technology management. Ford captured the auto market from 1908 through 1923.

PHASES IN THE INDUSTRIAL GROWTH DUE TO TECHNOLOGICAL CHANGE

The link between technological change and market growth has been sketched in a concept called the "technology life cycle." Generally, an industry is innovative in its beginning and middle phases of its technological history but uninnovative in the last phases. David Ford and Chris Ryan suggested that by plotting the market volume over time for any industry, one can identify the periods of changing innovativeness of the industry—that is, the technological aging of the industry (Ford and Ryan, 1981).

The typical form of volume against time appears as in Figure 7.1. When a new industry (based on new technology) is begun, there will come a point in time that one can mark as the inception point of the technology. In the case of the automobile, that was 1896, when Duryea made and sold those first 13 cars from the same design.

Then the first technological phase of the industry will be one of rapid development of the new technology—technology development. For the automobile this lasted from 1896 to 1902, as experiments in steam-, electric-, and gasoline-engine-powered vehicles were tried.

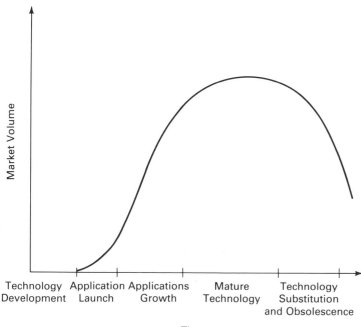

Time

FIGURE 7.1 Technology life cycle.

Then another phase occurs in which the new application has been worked out to a standard design and rapid growth of the market can begin. In any new technology, the early new products are created in a wild variety of configurations and with differing features. This is a creative period of product experimentation, lasting through the technology application and application launch phases. However, the variety of products are confusing to the customer, requiring much technical skill and knowledge simply to understand and use any of the variety. Moreover, each product may be strong in some aspects and weak in other aspects. Finally, when enough experimentation has occurred to map the general boundaries of possibilities of the product line, some managerial genius usually puts all the best features together in one design and creates the model which then becomes the standard design for the industry. Thereafter all product models follow generally the standard design. This makes possible large market volume growth. For the automobile, this occurred with Ford's Model T design.

After the applications launch, there occurs a rapid growth in the penetration of technology into markets (or in creating new markets). After some time, however, the innovation rate slows and market creation will peak. This is the phase of technology maturity. Finally, then, after more time passes (and until competing or substitute technologies emerge), the mature technology market continues at the same level. However, when competing or substituting technologies emerge, the mature technology begins to degrade in competition with the competing technologies.

PRODUCT LIFE CYCLE

A related concept to the technology life cycle is the product life cycle. Products have life cycles in moving from first innovation and developing with incremental innovations. If an industry is based on a single product line, the product life cycle and technology life cycles coincide. If an industry has several product lines, the technology life cycle will be the envelope of the several product life cycles.

The dominant design of a product denotes the best product design, including the features and configuration that have generally been found to be most desirable. This standardization of product design is essential for market growth in any new industry. William Abernathy and James Utterback pointed out that in a product life cycle, innovation initially focuses on product change and then later shifts predominantly to process change (Abernathy, 1978; Utterback, 1978).

If one charts the rate of innovations for a product life cycle as either product or process innovations, one will obtain a graph in the form in Figure 7.2. After product standardization, innovation continues, but principally as process innovation. Because the product design has been standardized, the rate of innovation in product design slows while the rate of innovation in process increases (Hill and Utterback, 1979).

As examples of the different product and process innovations in the auto industry, Abernathy listed some major innovations to engines from 1900 to 1964:

> From 1900 to 1908, a simple and reliable engine (the Model T) was developed, while multiple simultaneous machining processes were also developed to produce the engine.
> From 1910 to 1920, the V-8 engine (eight cylinders in a V shape) was first developed, while at the same time continuous pouring of molten iron was developed to produce engines.
> From 1920 to 1929, the light-weight piston of aluminum-alloy was developed, crankcase ventilation was introduced into engine design, and special materials for exhaust-valves were developed to stand the exhaust heat. At the same time, process innovations included cemented carbide tools to cut iron and dynamic crankshaft balancing to produce balanced crankshafts which could turn smoothly at high speeds.
> From 1930 to 1939, the down-draft carburetor was introduced, along with the automatic choke, and the design of a low-cost V-8 engine. In process innovation, cast crankshaft and camshafts were introduced, along with improved precision boring techniques, and surface tunnel broaching techniques. (Abernathy, 1978, p. 52)

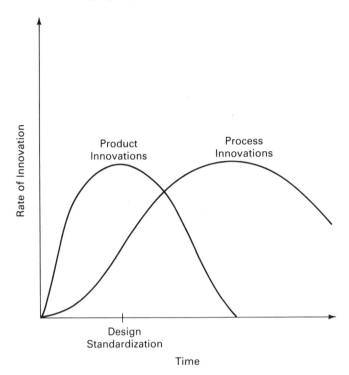

FIGURE 7.2 Shift in the rate of innovations from product to process in the life cycle of a technology.

INDUSTRIAL COMPETITION AND THE TECHNOLOGY LIFE CYCLE

The early phase in an industry is an exciting time, because product improvements continue and improved processes for producing cheaper, better products are innovated. However, during this same time, it is important in competition to balance innovation strategies with marketing strategies, because it also becomes a time of eliminating weak competitors.

In the early phases of an automobile industry, new companies spring up like weeds, started in garages (or in bike shops). Organizations are small at these times; life is entrepreneurial. Success is dramatic and swift. Failure is also swift. For example, in 1909 there were 69 auto manufacturing firms, but only half these firms survived the seven years to 1916. This is the general pattern in any new industry.

In the phase of market growth, the failure rate of firms for the industry continues to be high. Successful firms grow large. Organized (focused and continuous) corporate R&D becomes important to maintain incremental model improvement, to establish market segmentation, and to improve production processes, lowering production costs. For example, by 1923 in the automobile industry, only eight major American firms had remained, capturing 99% of the market—General Motors, Ford, Chrysler, American Motors, Studebaker, Hudson, Packard, and Nash.

In the phase of technology maturity, process innovations dominate. The firms that survive are very large, dividing the market among a few producers. Competition is primarily on price and in segmented market lines. Organizational life is bureaucratic, production is specialized and efficient. Products are treated like commodity items. During this phase of technological maturity, economies of scale and marketing dominance continue to whittle down competitors, to the final few. For example, by 1965, only General Motors, Ford, Chrysler, and American Motors had survived in the American automobile industry.

MATURE AND OBSOLETE INDUSTRIES

When an industry runs out of significant innovation (product and process), market size is determined principally by:

1. Demographics and replacement life, or
2. Foreign markets

Within the constraints of demographics and replacement product life, a mature industry can still continue indefinitely as long as there is a demand for the product line (and as long as the technology embedded in the product is competitive with any other technology). However, technology diffusion will probably occur internationally, and international competition for any market will become important. Dissemination of knowledge through education and product and process copying allows foreign competitors to compete in industries with mature technologies. Competitors with more abundant resources, cheaper labor, or subsidized capital can obtain a competitive advantage.

In addition to foreign competition, a mature technology may also face competing technologies. Competing technologies may also shrink market sizes. Products from competing technologies may substitute due to lower cost or superior performance for specific applications. For example, through the twentieth century, the market generally for materials had grown in the world. Yet in the United States, the market for steel has declined as aluminum and then plastics created materials substitution for steel. In the 1980s, an example of a declining U.S. industry hit by both foreign competition and competing technologies was the steel industry. In addition to the materials substitution competition, foreign steel producers had lower labor costs and sometimes subsidized capital.

There is, finally, a last phase in some industries—a dead industry. A technology becomes obsolete when it is replaced by a new technology with superior performance for the same function. For example, horses were replaced by tractors and autos, sailing ships by steamships and steamships by diesel. In an obsolete technology, the large industry dies, with survivors filling market niches, such as hobby and recreational markets.

Example: Technology Life Cycles and Corning Glass

The Corning Glass Company is an example of a corporation that has faced technology life cycles. In 1983, it was a 132-year-old company, integrated around products based on silicon chemistry, the basic element of glass. Over the course of its history various glass or silicon products served large markets and some aged. Due to aging markets, Corning's pretax income had declined 8% in 1980 and 15% in 1981, with return on stockholders' equity eroded by one-third from the value in the 1970s. The problem was not poor management or low productivity but old technology—Corning's traditional businesses in light bulbs and television tubes had been vanishing.

Corning's long corporate history descended from the glassblowers who made Thomas Edison's first bulb in 1889. Until 1945, providing bulbs to electric light manufacturers had brought Corning a third of its sales. Even in the early 1970s, light bulbs still provided 10% of sales and 9% of profits. Yet in the 1970s, an industry shakeout began. The lamp industry consolidated into three integrated producers: General Electric, General Telephone & Electronics, and North American Philips. Therefore, for Corning to have stayed in the light-bulb market would have required Corning to integrate vertically in light-bulb manufacture, a strategy they did not choose (Magnet, 1982).

In the 1960s, another of Corning's large businesses began to fall to foreign competitors. In 1967, two-thirds of Corning's earnings had come from TV picture tubes. By 1980, Japanese firms had totally driven the American manufacturers out of black-and-white picture tube production and had invaded the color-tube market. In 1982, only five U.S. makers of color television had survived to buy Corning's TV tubes. The officers of Corning in 1982 commented: " 'I'm very reluctant to say, even as difficult as the domestic TV business is, that we should pack it in,' declares MacAvoy (president of Corning). It's a luxuriant generator of cash, and it represents an investment of hundreds of millions of dollars. . . .' But given price and market pressures, cautions chief executive Amory Houghton, Jr., 'something dramatically different has got to happen for us not to be out of the business in the U.S.' " (Magnet, 1982, p. 92).

Corning had faced problems that all corporations eventually face—loss of major markets in mature technologies to international competition. Corning's solution? Innovation and new businesses. Corning was a corporation with a tradition of technical excellence. The tradition resulted from deliberate strategy in research and development. And from that excellence, new businesses did emerge in the 1980s—fiber optics, immobilized enzymes, and medical diagnostic equipment.

After the invention of the laser and the transmission of laser light through glass fibers, the possibility of light-transmission systems became evident. Yet, technically, the glass required for such fibers was so pure and complicated to construct that traditional techniques of making glass by melting sand would not work. Corning researchers invented a new technique. They heated extremely pure liquid chemicals in a revolving tube, letting the resulting vapors separate into the pure glassy layers required for fiber-optic transmission—an important process innovation. Corning then joined Western Electric in a cross-licensing agreement to make a market for the new fibers. In the early 1980s, AT&T and other communications companies had begun to lay thousands of miles of glass cable. It was the beginning of the rewiring of the world with glass.

Another new business in immobilized enzymes emerged from other research by Corning. In 1965, a Corning biochemist poured a mixture of proteins down a column filled with glass beads. He discovered that the proteins had stuck to the glass and preserved their enzyme activity while on the glass. A new technique had been created to hold an enzyme for biotechnology production. Using the technique, Corning formed a joint venture with Kroger Co. to convert the by-product of cheese making, whey, into a protein-rich sweetener. Still another of Corning's new enterprises in the 1980s arose from Corning research. Starting from Pyrex glassware for chemical laboratories, Corning had moved into medical diagnostic equipment, which by 1982 had grown into a $400 million-a-year business. The long-term R&D research of an innovative company, Corning, had continued to provide new business opportunities even as old businesses in technologically mature industries were being lost.

INNOVATION AND
MARKET SATURATION

Markets saturate, of course, when demand is satisfied. The importance of continuing technological innovation in an industrial life cycle is that it can delay market saturation by:

1. Creating succeeding generations products with significantly improved performance
2. Creating multiple applications
3. Lowering the price to facilitate ownership of multiple copies of products for convenience

Product or process innovations that dramatically improve the performance of a product and lower the price of the product delay market saturation by creating a performance–price advantage replacement market. For example, through the decades of the 1960s, 1970s, and 1980s, the mainframe computer market grew by successive product generations, which created replacement markets, delaying market saturation.

A second form of extending markets for innovative products is by creating different models lines for different applications. For example, in computers, the first line created came to be called "mainframe" computers. Then with advances in semiconductor chip technology in the 1960s, a second line of computers were introduced called "minicomputers." Minis expanded the market from organization-based computers to single-user computers in scientific and technical organizations. Organizational customers bought both mainframes and minicomputers. Then, again due to semiconductor advances in the 1970s, the "micro" or "personal" computer line was innovated, again expanding the market. Business customers bought mainframes, minis, and personal computers.

Process innovations can also delay market saturation. Product costs may eventually be lowered to the point where customers can own multiple copies of a product. For example, the continuing automobile expansion after World War II was based on family multiple ownership of cars. Prior to the war, most families owned only one car—the family car. Shortly after the war, the family cars were replaced by the beginnings of the 1950s. Then families began to own more than one car. This and a replacement period of an average of three years' ownership provided the expansion of the U.S. auto industry until the early 1970s, when the energy crisis changed the market.

MANAGING TECHNOLOGY LIFE CYCLES

We can now compare the concept of the "technology life cycle" to the concept of the "technology S-curve":

1. The "life cycle" depicts the impact on an industry from underlying technological change.
2. The "S-curve" depicts the rate of change of that underlying technology.

The basis of the technology life-cycle curve is the underlying technology S-curves. The exponential beginning of the rate of change of new technology in the beginning of the S-curve underlies the first three phases of the technology life cycle: technology development, technology application, and application launch. The linear period of the rate of technology change in the S-curve underlies the fourth phase of the application growth and the early part of the fifth phase of technology maturity of the life cycle. Finally, when the rate of technology change slows in the leveling off of the technology S-curve (after natural limits are approached), the life cycle enters the peak of the technology maturity phase of the cycle.

When a new technology begins, management should expect that over the next decade very rapid progress will occur. This will create rapid product obsolesence, with product lifetimes of only a couple of years. After a decade, progress will continue to be dramatic, but at a slower, linear pace. Product lifetimes will perhaps stretch to 5 to 10 years. Finally, after two or three decades, a natural limit will probably be approached. Accordingly, the industry will enter a mature technology unless a new physical basis for a substitute technology is discovered.

The fact that the rates of technological innovation affect the competitive conditions of an industry means that management should plan different strategies for different phases of the technology life cycle. For example, Richard Foster suggested that in times of changing technology, management:

1. Should decide which technology to develop,
2. Should manage the transition from one technology to another, and
3. Should prepare the corporation for technological change
    (Foster, 1982, p. 24).

SUMMARY

The technology life cycle is the pattern of the effects on product volume of an industry, due to the rate of change of its underlying technology. In any new industry, many firms are started, entrepreneural, and aggressive.

The next phase begins when a dominant product design emerges and applications growth begins. Then the market grows rapidly. Product innovation continues but slowly and incrementally, while process innovation becomes dominant. Organized corporate R&D becomes essential to keep competitive. During this phase, market segmentation begins and price competition increases. Big firms from other fields enter. An industrial shakeout occurs. Some of the new firms become big; many are acquired by other firms; some fail.

In the technological maturity phase, marketing and pricing become the dominant competitive factors. Only a few major producers remain. Mature markets may still be enlarged by innovation. When an industry runs out of significant innovation in a product, market size is determined principally by (1) demographics and replacement life, or (2) foreign markets. Innovation can delay the saturation of markets.

In aging-technology industries, international competition becomes very important, due to the diffusion of technological knowledge. Competing technologies also shrink markets for mature-technology industries. When a new technology with better performance and equal or lower cost emerges, the industry dies as the technology becomes obsolete.

Technological innovation can delay market saturation.

REFLECTION

1. **Identify an industry that was historically obsoleted. When and where did it begin? When was the technology most innovative? How did it end? Do remnants of the industry survive today?**

FOR FURTHER READING

ABERNATHY, WILLIAM J., KIM B. CLARK, and ALAN M. KANTROW, *Industrial Renaissance.* New York: Basic Books, 1983.

SLOAN, ALFRED P.,   *My Years with General Motors.* New York: Macfadden-Bartell Corp., 1963.

CHAPTER EIGHT
ECONOMIC LONG CYCLES AND TECHNOLOGY

CENTRAL IDEAS

1. Kondratieff waves
2. Economically pervasive, basic innovations
3. Excess capacity in mature-technology industries
4. Premium management for the long term

Example: Hard Times in the Steel Industry

Technology life cycles, in addition to affecting markets and industrial competition, can also have long-term economic impacts. Research into the nature of economic cycles has clarified the role of technological change in long economic cycles—long waves.

Signs of hard economic times: Youngstown, Ohio, region in the 1980s—shutdown steel factories; 50,000 unemployed; an empty union hall, Local 1307 of the United Steelworkers of America; billboard at the entrance of one of the former factories of U.S. Steel Corporation—"USS Industrial Park . . . Now Leasing."

Since the nineteenth century, steel had been the backbone of the industrial revolution. In America, in the twentieth century, giant steel mills disgorged metal for a century—railroads, automobiles, bridges, skyscrapers, ships, appliances—steel, the skeleton of industry. As late as 1974, steel production in the United Stated had grown annually, but that year it peaked, at 151 million tons. At that time 500,000 people had worked in steel. The industry provided a 4.5% return on $40 billion sales. Imported steel had only 12% of the U.S. market.

In 1984, ten years later, U.S. steel production had shrunk to half. In 1983, the industry lost 7.4% on sales. Steel imports climbed to 21% of the U.S. market. In 10 years, from 1974 to 1984, 500 steel factories had closed.

On September 19, 1977, at Youngstown, Ohio, the Youngstown Sheet & Tube Company closed its factory, putting 5500 people out of work. On November 19, 1979, also at Youngstown, the U.S. Steel Company closed down its McDonald Works, putting 3500 people out of work. Both days had occurred on a Monday; in Youngstown, people called each "Black Monday" (Waters, 1984).

What had happened? Could anyone have been blamed? It was a long wave of economy rolling through history.

KONDRATIEFF WAVES

In the 1930s, a Soviet economist named Kondratieff saw an interesting pattern in the industrial revolution. He had identified three major capital expansions in the Western economies, occurring in periods lasting about three decades and interrupted by major depressions. When he presented his analysis to Soviet authorities, Kondratieff was banished to a Siberian salt mine, perishing there—since his long-wave concept implied periodic capitalist resurgence rather than the Marxist doctrine of the inevitable capitalistic collapse.

The long cycles which Kondratieff proposed continued to be controversial, but research in the 1970s and 1980s produced evidence that, historically, technological innovation has contributed to major periods of economic expansion. In 1975, Gerhard Mensch proposed what he called a "metamorphosis model" to account for the dynamics of the long wave (which had been identified by Kondratieff and studied by Kuznets). Mensch's model superimposed on the Kondratieff cycles, curves of market growth due to basic innovations. He argued that basic new technology began the economic expansion in each long wave (Mensch, 1979).

Following up on Mensch's approach, Jay Forrester, Alan Graham, and Peter Senge argued that basic inventions and innovations underlaid the beginnings of economic long cycles (Graham and Senge, 1980). Forrester and his colleagues also modeled the U.S. economy using the technique of systems dynamics, a technique that specifically described the timely interaction between aspects of the economy. It captured the timing of the kinds of economic interactions, including lead times and delays, and the interaction between technical innovation and economic change. These types of models provide temporally dynamic patterns which can be compared to actual economic history.

In running his model, Forrester found Kondratieff waves: "The National Model generates . . . the same patterns of change that have been observed in real life. The Model exhibits business cycles of three to seven years' duration. It shows Kuznets or construction cycles of fifteen to twenty-five years in length. It manifests stagflation and reveals the causes of simultaneous unemployment and inflation. The National Model produces an economic long wave, or Kondratieff cycle, of 45 to 60 years between peaks . . ." (Forrester, 1983, pp. 10–11).

Example: The Auto Industry in Trouble

An illustration was provided by the economic troubles of the U.S. automobile industry in the 1970s. Economic turmoil, triggered by the fuel-price increases of the 1970s, also marked the beginning of intense international competition in automobiles, then a mature-technology industry—and the declining side of a Kondratieff cycle—excess production capacity in an industry of aging technology.

Kondratieff had pointed out that the technological advances of the automobile at the turn of the nineteenth century (together with the innovations of the electrical industry) had provided the foundation for the major economic expansion of 1896–1930 (interrupted by World War I). In those early days of the automobile, technical advances were many, and the market expanded.

After World War II technological advance in the auto industry became meager, with most management attention paid to marketing and cost control. Still these were expansive years of the auto industry, due to the pent-up demand from the Great Depression and war. American manufacturers created large cars with poor fuel efficiency. While the American auto industry stood still technologically, the European and Japanese industries rebuilt from the war devastation. In particular the Japanese learned how to sell small cars in the United States—a market niche that the U.S. industry had ignored.

In the early 1970s, an oil cartel of less developed countries, OPEC, created a demand for higher technical performance of autos by raising the price of oil. Suddenly, gas milage was the key performance criterion. The American auto industry, long committed to large, fuel-inefficient cars plunged off the crest of an economic expansion. It surfed down a Kondratieff-sized wave. In 1982, a study by the National Academy of Engineering and the National Research Council summarized the turmoil in the industry: "The U.S. auto industry is in crisis. Vigorous import competition, drastic shifts in consumer preferences, and anemic final sales combined to make 1980 and 1981 one of the most difficult years in the industry's history" (National Academy of Engineering and National Research Council, 1983, p. 10).

The U.S. auto industry had to change, and it did. The key to survival was innovative technology in materials (plastics and ceramics), control (electronics), and in production processes (CAD/CAM and robots): "If the industry is to survive, the next five years (1982–1987) will see wrenching changes in its productive and financial base as new product technologies are introduced, manufacturing plants are retooled, and new relations are established among management, labor and government" (NAE/NRC, 1983, p. 10).

And return to innovation—process innovation—is just what the auto industry did in the 1980s. For example, General Motors (under Roger Smith) made four large moves from 1982 to 1985: reorganization of the North American car division, formation of a new car division (Saturn Corporation), acquisition of a large data processing company (Electronic Data Systems), and acquisition of a large high-tech aerospace/defense company (Hughes Aircraft). These moves followed on a grand strategy to make GM more entrepreneurial and the world leader in computer-integrated manufacturing techniques (*The Economist,* 1985b).

Other leading auto manufacturers also turned to the new process technology integrated by computers: "An example of what can now be done is in the new VW production system for the Golf II model at its Wolfsburg assembly plant. . . . In addition to a fully automated and flexible body-welding line and robotised paint-shop—features common to many factories—the VW facility also takes the first steps to automated final assembly with robots installing the engine, brakelines, battery, and wheels" (*The Economist,* 1985a).

THE LONG-WAVE PROCESS

How does a long-wave process occur? The process behind a long wave is an interaction between (1) new technology, (2) business opportunities the new technology creates, and (3) an eventual overbuilding of capital after the technology ages. The stages are:

1. Discoveries in science create a phenomenal base for technological innovation.
2. Radical and basic technological innovations create new products.
3. These products create new markets and new industries.
4. The new industries continue to innovate in products and processes, expanding markets.
5. As the technology matures, many competitors enter internationally, eventually creating excess production capacity.
6. Excess capacity decreases profitability, and increases business failures and unemployment.
7. Subsequent economic turmoil in financial markets may lead to depressions.
8. New science and new technology may provide the basis for a new economic expansion.

The first Kondratieff cycle began in 1787, expanding through 1813, upon the innovations (1) of applying steam engine power to textile spinning and weaving, and (2) in the invention of the Bessemer process for producing iron, using coal as an energy source. A depression followed in England from 1814 to 1827, after which the textile and iron industry revived from 1828 through 1842.

The second cyclic expansion in England occurred due to the new railroad technology (in applying the steam engine to steel-wheeled vehicles rolling on steel track). This provided an expansion of prosperity in England from 1843 through 1869, followed by a depression from 1870 to 1885.

A third cyclic expansion (particularly in the United States) began in 1898, and lasted until 1929, based on the new technologies of electricity and automobiles. With electricity came the telegraph, the electric light, the electric motor, and the telephone.

A fourth expansion in the United States began after World War II, based primarily on chemicals and computers (and renewed expansion of the automobile market, which had been depressed in the 1930s and deferred in the first part of the 1940s).

This picture of technological innovation and industrial expansion is of course, oversimplified. But basic innovations (such as the electric light bulb and electric motor, and dynamo, turbine, alternating-current, and polyphase systems, etc.) have been major factors in the business opportunities of major business expansions.

By the 1980s, economists had not reached a consensus about the validity of economic waves or about the role of technology in generating economic expansion. George Ray, an economist with the National Institute of Economic and Social Research in Sweden in 1980, summarized Schumpeter's and Kuznets' contributions: "Most important was the work of Schumpeter who put emphasis on innovation and on the subsequent burst of entrepreneurial investment activity as the engine in the upswing of the long cycle, à la Kondratieff. This was hesitantly supported by Kuznets, who added that if that was so, the investment burst must stem from innovations with very far-reaching impact across the whole economic system . . . " (Ray, 1980, pp. 79–80).

Kuznets' point—that the investment burst must stem from innovations with very far-reaching impact—is very important. Some technological innovations have had such far-reaching impacts. Historical examples were the steam engine and the train, the gasoline engine and the automobile and airplane. Other examples were the electronic vacuum tube, the transistor, and the semiconductor chip.

For example, in 1982, the uses of the semiconductor chips in the European market were divided as follows:

32% of the chips found end-use in computers,
18% in communications,
17% in office automation and other industrial products,
22% in consumer products, and
11% in military products.
(Ypsilanti, 1985)

The first part of an economic long wave is expansion based on new business opportunities that new innovations create. The second part of the long wave follows after technological innovation has slowed and competition overbuilds for a no-longer-expanding market: "[The long-wave process results in an] overbuilding of capital-producing sectors, during which they grow beyond the capital-output rate needed for long-term equilibrium" (Forrester, 1983, p. 10).

RECENT LONG WAVES

In the 1980s, where was America in long waves? Forrester, for example, argued that the long-term interaction between technology and business opportunity was the major factor in the economic turmoil of the time:

> To understand today's economic difficulties, we should avoid several common attitudes that prevent a clear view of economic conditions. . . .
> First, the focus of attention regarding economic change should be shifted away from the business cycle. . . .
> Second, political changes should receive less attention as an explanation of economic difficulties. . . .
> Third, economic ideology should receive less attention. . . .
> Instead, present economic conditions can be better understood by considering the growing forces that, on a worldwide basis, are causing unemployment, high real interest rates, excess capital plant, and burdensome debts. Such symptoms of economic deterioration come from long-term changes that have been gathering momentum for more than two decades. (Forrester, 1983, pp. 1–2)

Other observers agreed with Forrester's assessment. For example, Bruce Merrifield, the assistant director for technology and productivity in the U.S. Department of Commerce in the Reagan administration: "Actually, this new cycle has already started. Fixed asset intensive companies in the U.S. have been liquidating themselves in "real terms" for seven of the last nine years. And the key factor in their liquidation is their inability to further increase productivity in obsolescent facilities" (Merrifield, 1981, p. 14). Merrifield thought that autos, chemicals, and steel were troughing in a Kondratieff cycle but that at the same time, a new wave was beginning in bioengineering, advanced electronics, materials, and other areas (Merrifield, 1981, p. 14).

THE LONG-WAVE HYPOTHESIS

New and superior performance-to-cost options for many and new applications—that is the cutting edge of technological competition and the driving force behind long waves of economic activity. High-technology products displace old technology products when the ratio of performance to cost of the new product exceeds that of the old product. For this reason, the technology life cycles of major industries affect long cycles in national economies.

It is important to note that history is not deterministic. One should not read any kind of historical inevitability into the long-wave hypothesis. New technology creates business opportunities which may lead to economic expansion. The following economic expansion may lead to overcapacity and subsequent economic trouble after significant innovation in the technology has ceased. It is not inevitable that new technology will be created and begin a new wave. New technology comes from the science, and science from discoveries of nature. The long-wave hypothesis merely describes past connections among (1) pervasive basic innovations; (2) long-term economic expansions; and (3) excess capital formation in technology-mature industries. It does not determine anything in the future.

Example: Entrepreneurship at the Bottom of the Wave

Back in that bleak Youngstown of the 1980s, there was one ex-manager of U.S. Steel with entrepreneurial commitment. He was David Houck, and he had witnessed the closing of the McDonald Works of U.S. Steel on the second Black Monday. Houck had been a steel man for 29 years with U.S. Steel. He had been a superintendent at the McDonald Works. In 1979, upper-level management had asked him to draft a plan for the reprieve of the McDonald plant. Houck studied the problems and potentials of the plant. He recommended changes to improve the competitiveness of the plant, a $208 million investment. He sent the report to corporate headquarters in the middle of November 1979. One week later, on Monday, U.S. Steel announced the shutdown of the plant (Waters, 1984).

Hard. Bleak. Dark. But Houck had an idea. He took part of his study and drafted a business plan for reopening part of the plant. In particular, the plant had one outstanding facility, a mill that worked 14–inch thicknesses of steel. It was unique and had been supplying 30 customers with a variety of shaped steel products, from simple rods (used in construction) to filigreed forms (used in truck-wheel rims). Its 30 customers would not be able to find an alternative supplier in this country. Houck took his plan to two venture capitalists in Youngstown, David Tod and Daniel Roth.

Initially, Houck received a cool reception. After all, had not an industrial giant just closed the place down? Then as Tod and Roth studied the plan, they warmed. Houck appeared to know what he was proposing. The numbers looked solid. There was a technically outstanding tool in the 14–inch mill. There were real customers with a known demand. And there were profitable financial projections. Finally, there was Houck's experience and determination. Todd and Roth decided to back Houck—it was venture capital and entrepreneurship in Youngstown, Ohio.

The McDonald Steel Corporation was created in 1981. In 1984, after three years, it did about $28 million in sales and was operating in the black. Its production capacity had been increased from one mill to two, and it had put 100 people back to work. So okay; it wasn't a big deal. Yet it showed that management committed to productivity and markets and technology and to the future could find business opportunities, even in the bleakest of times.

PREMIUM MANAGERS

Management is a complex activity, and there are many styles of management. Whatever the style, however, there must always be some willingness in management style to adapt to changing business conditions. In the 1980s much business concern went to renewing attention to the venturesome aspect of management, entrepreneurial management, as illustrated by Houck's initiative in Youngstown.

Richard Rosenbloom and William Abernathy critized some management practices that became common in the inflationary period of the 1970s, which had tended to ignore this balance in understanding the business: "American managers, guided by what they took to be the newest and best techniques for management, have increasingly directed their attention to matters other than innovation. . . . In consequence . . . American managers may have made themselves vulnerable to competitors whose strategic thrust leads them to technological superiority and market leadership" (Rosenbloom and Abernathy, 1982, p. 218).

An important ingredient of good management, including entrepreneurial management, is having a thorough understanding of the business, from finances to production to sales to technology. It was for example, this kind of balanced business understanding that enabled Houck to restructure some business out of the closed plant. Rosenbloom and Abernathy have also argued that American management should renew attention (1) to integrating technical with financial perspectives, and (2) to balancing short-term against long-term perspectives in corporate strategy (Rosenbloom and Abernathy, 1982).

Abernathy argued further that one of the reasons that this kind of integration and balance had been neglected was due to the changing origins of American managers. After World War II, American managers with purely financial and legal backgrounds were increasingly recruited. From 1953 to 1977, the proportion of corporation presidents in the 100 top U.S. companies with finance and legal backgrounds increased by 33%, while those with technical backgrounds decreased by 33% and those with marketing backgrounds decreased by 20% (Hayes and Abernathy, 1980.)

Managers with either technical and financial backgrounds should gain experience with all functions of the corporation: "During the past 25 years the American manager's road to the top has changed significantly. No longer does the typical career, threading sinuously up and through a corporation with stops in several functional areas, provide future top executives with intimate hands-on knowledge of the company's technologies, customers, and suppliers" (Hayes and Abernathy, 1980).

Hands-on knowledge particularly means to understand the technologies and markets of the corporation. Hayes and Abernathy's prescription for good management was a bit old-fashioned:

1. To invest and innovate,
2. To lead, and
3. To add value.
   (Hayes and Abernathy, 1980)

Good management never goes out of fashion, in the best of economic times and in the worst.

SUMMARY

Economic long cycles depict major periods of expansion due to new technologies. There are several stages, which begin with basic, pervasive innovations, then continue with rapid industrial growth. After significant innovation ends, markets eventually saturate. If capital investment continues to build production capacity, exceeding market need, a recession in the industry follows. When the industries play major economic roles in society, such recessions may occur as major depressions.

New science may provide knowledge bases for new basic technologies. When new basic innovations are economically pervasive, they may stimulate major economic expansions, due to the business opportunities created. Premium management requires management for the long term, a commitment to innovation, improving productivity, and creating new products and new businesses.

REFLECTION

1. **The chemical and electrical industries began in the nineteenth century. Identify as many basic innovations as you can which laid the basis for these industries. Who innovated them? Why were these innovations economically pervasive?**

FOR FURTHER READING

MENSCH, GERHARD,   *Stalemate in Technology.* (Cambridge, Mass.: Ballinger, 1979).
SCHMOOKLER, JACOB,   *Invention and Economic Growth.* (Cambridge, Mass.: Harvard University Press, 1966).

CHAPTER NINE
SOURCES OF INNOVATION

CENTRAL IDEAS

1. Forms of high technology
2. Market pull and technology push
3. Technology maps

HIGH TECHNOLOGIES

High technology has been a buzzword—high-tech startups, high-tech investments, improved productivity, growth markets. Precisely what is high technology? High technology is a business area of rapidly changing technology. The technological change can be in new products, production processes, knowledge-based services, or in new applications for new markets. In the forms of high technology, there are high-tech components, high-tech devices, high-tech processes, high-tech systems, high-tech materials and resources, and high-tech services. Examples include:

High-tech component: semiconductor chip
High-tech device: laser
High-tech process: computer-integrated manufacturing
High-tech system: fiber-optic communications systems
High-tech material: conducting plastics
High-tech service: medical practice

Semiconductors

We recall that the transistor was invented by industrial scientists at Bell Labs in 1947, and that the integrated semiconductor chip was invented independently at Texas Instruments and Fairchild Semiconductor. Transistorized electronics were the high-tech component driving force in the second half of the twentieth century.

Lasers

The laser was invented by Charles Townes, who first invented a means of amplifying microwaves—the maser. Next he conceived of the idea of generating coherent light—the laser. Coherent light is light of the same frequency. Although such light existed in nature at submicroscopic levels of existence (quantum levels), it had not before occurred at our macroscopic level of existence.

It was spring morning in 1951. Sitting on a park bench in Washington, D.C., Townes was admiring the azaleas when the bright idea came, an idea for which he had been searching for some time—new ways to produce radio waves at very high frequencies. The idea was to fill a container with atoms of a substance that could be stimulated to its higher quantum states by the passage of electrical fields through the atoms. Then light of the right frequency would be pulsed through these atoms, triggering a cascade of light photons of the same frequency when electrons of these atoms fell back to their lower state. Townes called it light-amplification-stimulated-emission radiation—laser (Townes, 1984, p. 153).

Townes was a Columbia University professor of physics and also worked as a consultant to Bell Labs. A colleague at Bell Labs, Arthur Schawlow, suggested that the laser light could be collected by putting mirrors at each end of the laser chamber. In December 1958, Townes and Schawlow published the first paper on lasers. In 1960, Theodore Maiman, a physicist at Hughes Aircraft Company, built the first operating laser.

Computer-Integrated Manufacturing

Several component, device, and process advances came together in the early 1980s to have begun another major step in the industrial revolution. Computer-aided design (CAD) was linked with computer-aided manufacturing (CAM) in CAD/CAM. This, in turn, was linked with robots in flexible manufacturing. This, in turn, was linked with computer networking in computer-integrated manufacturing (CIM). Together it was another industrial revolution.

Fiber-Optic Communications Systems

In fiber-optic cables, lasers provide an enormous bandwidth for information compared to electrical circuits. To utilize the bandwidth capabilities, all-optical circuits were needed for switching from one cable to another to connect different callers. The key to that was the invention of an optical analog of the electronic transistor, called a "bistable optical device."

In 1975, the phenomenon of optical bistability was invented by a Bell Labs scientist. Yet it worked only at very low temperatures. Hyatt Gibbs at Bell Labs decided to work on improving the device. He went to the University of Arizona and applied to the National Science Foundation for a grant. Gibbs, then a university professor, worked with two of his old colleagues, Sam McCall and Art Gossard at Bell. Gibbs invented the first fast-switching, room-temperature optical equivalent of a transistor. Laser transmission, fiber-optic cables, and optical logic switching began a new electronics revolution in communication systems in the 1970s and 1980s.

Conducting Plastics

In the 1970s, Alan McDermiad at the University of Pennsylvania invented plastics that could conduct electricity. New battery designs using the conducting plastics were invented next. These promised batteries lighter in weight and superior in performance to metal-based batteries such as the lead auto battery.

Medical Practice

Medical practice has been a high-tech service since the nineteenth century, when medical practice was increasingly based on biological science. In the 1970s and 1980s, molecular biology advanced the level of understanding of genetics so that new drugs and treatments for old diseases, such as cancer, might be attained in the twenty-first century.

MARKET PULL AND
TECHNOLOGY PUSH

Where do ideas, such as these, for high technology come from? What are the sources of innovation? They come from two kinds of considerations:

1. New ideas in markets services and goods that seek new technology
2. New ideas in technology that seek applications.

These have been called "market pull" and "technology push." Market pull is the advancement of technology, oriented, however, primarily toward a specific market need and only secondarily toward increased technical performance. Market pull is particularly effective when markets are well established. Technology push is the advancement of technology, oriented primarily toward increased technical performance and only secondarily toward specific market need. Technology push is particularly effective when it creates wholly new markets.

There have been many arguments as to which creates more

innovation—push or pull. Each side has had adherents. For example, Eric von Hippel has emphasized the importance of market orientation in innovation. In the 1970s he studied samples of innovations in the scientific instrumentation industry. He examined four types of instruments: gas chromatography, nuclear magnetic resonance spectrometry, ultraviolet absorption spectrophotometry, and transmissions electron microscopy. Von Hippel classified these innovations as invented by "users" or "manufacturers," with users being scientists. He found that the user-scientists made 80% of the innovations and manufacturers 20% (von Hippel, 1976).

Two important facts about scientific instruments are that (1) they are essential to scientific discovery, and (2) scientists invent most of the scientific instrumentation. Von Hippel's study illustrated that innovation comes from coupling market pull with technology push. The "users" here are technically more advanced than the manufacturers. Scientists are able to invent new scientific instrumentation because (1) they advance the technical frontiers of knowledge, and (2) they know the use to which the instrumentation can be put. Conjoining technical expertise with user needs is really the source of innovation.

Many other studies on the source of innovation have been done, and similiar lessons can be seen. Eric von Hippel conveniently summarized several of the studies (von Hippel, 1982). For example, von Hippel also studied innovations in semiconductor and electronic subassembly manufacturing equipment. There he found 21% of the ideas for the innovation came from users of the equipment (market pull) and 46% came from frequent customer–manufacturer interactions. Again the important point was that most of the innovations came from interaction between technologically sophisticated users and manufactures—matching market needs to technological opportunities (von Hippel, 1977).

Some of the other innovation studies produced results similar to von Hippel's, in that users were more often the source of innovations rather than manufacturers: J. Enos studied process innovations in the petroleum industry (Enos, 1962), C. Freeman studied process innovation in the chemical industry (Freeman, 1967), and W. G. Lionetta studied process innovation in the pultrusion industry (Lionetta, 1977). In all these samples, the users were technologically sophisticated customers, having both the technical knowledge to suggest innovations and the user need to motivate innovation.

However, other studies found that manufacturers created more of the innovations. For example, K. D. Knight studied innovations in the evolution of computers and found that manufacturers (rather than users) dominated innovation in computers 1944 to 1962. The important point was that for that industry at that time, the industry was more technologically advanced than computer users (Knight, 1963). A. Berger studied innovation in scientific instruments and in plastics and also found many more innovations by manufacturers than users (Berger, 1975). J. Boyden studied innovation in the plastics additives industry, again finding manufacturers much more innovative than users (Boyden, 1976). P. Wiseman studied a time series of patents in chemical processes for producing synthetic fibers, finding these affected both by market demand and by technological opportunity (Wiseman, 1983).

The conclusion is that both manufacturers and users can be sources of innovation. The critical requirement is to match technological opportunity to market need. Technologically sophisticated customers are excellent sources of ideas for innovation. Technologically unsophisticated customers are poor sources of ideas for innovation (since their lack of technical sophistication provides little imagination for how things could be done otherwise). On the other side, technology pushers (scientists, engineers, and inventors) must have direct experience with users in order to have the functional focus to create new uses for technology. Therefore, the management problem in innovation is to ensure that technical imagination is focused on user needs. Christopher Freeman summarized this view: "Perhaps the highest level generalization that it is safe to make about technological innovation is that it must involve synthesis of some kind of [market] need with some kind of technical possibility" (Freeman, 1974, p. 193). Market pull innovations most often are incremental innovations since an established market inspires the need. Technological push is often the source of the radical innovations.

TECHNOLOGY MAPS

The concepts of technology push and market pull are useful to map the areas and directions of rapid technology change—high technology. First classify areas of rapidly changing technology into (1) components, (2) devices, (3) processes, (4) systems, (5) materials and resources, and (6) services. Next, for each of these areas, identify changes being pushed by advances in technological opportunity and changes being pulled by market needs. Such a map shows the dominant areas of rapid technological change during a decade. As an illustration, Table 9.1 summarizes a technology map of the 1980s. As components, rapid technological change continued in semiconducting chips which had far-reaching impacts, due to new functions made possible by technological advance and by new market applications.

In the device category, computers, robots, lasers, and various scientific instruments had rapidly changing technologies, both pushed by new components, architectures, and systems and pulled by new applications. In the process category, optical circuitry, genetic engineering and biotechnology, and chemical processes were areas of very rapidly changing technologies. In the systems category, communication system, computer-integrated manufacturing systems, and military systems were areas of rapidly changing technologies of great economic and national importance. In the resources area, materials advances, particularly in composite materials, advanced rapidly in the 1980s.

TABLE 9.1   Technology Map of the 1980s: Areas of Rapidly Changing Technology

Components

1. Semiconductors

   Technology push:
   1. Integrated chips: VLSI design and fabrication, VHSIC

   Market pull:
   1. Custom chip design applications in electronics, computers, consumer appliances industrial control, communications, aircraft and missiles, automobiles and transportation

Devices

2. Computers

   Technology push:
   1. Supercomputer architecutre: parallel processing
   2. Computer peripherals: printing, memory, display
   3. Computer graphics and three-dimensional display
   4. Expert systems, software, and user friendliness

   Market pull:
   1. Segmented computer markets: mainframes, minicomputers, microcomputers
   2. Applications markets: business and office systems, manufacturing systems, scientific systems, personal computers, home entertainment and information

3. Robots

   Technology push:
   1. Manipulation and control
   2. Sensing: vision, tactile
   3. Flexible manufacturing: tools, materials, scheduling, handling
   4. Production and sales system integration

   Market pull:
   1. Automobile
   2. Aerospace and defense
   3. Electronics

4. Lasers

   Technology push:
   1. Lasing techniques and materials: frequency and power
   2. Laser tools

   Market pull:
   1. Laser communications: transmission, fiber optics
   2. Optical logic devices and circuitry
   3. Holographic imaging and measurement
   4. Laser tools
   5. Laser weapons

5. Scientific instrumentation

   Technology push:
   1. Nuclear magnetic radiation (NMR) measurement and imaging
   2. Synchrontron radiation

TABLE 9.1   (cont.)

  3. Millimeter, infrared, and ultraviolet radiation sensing and measurement
  4. Automated instrumentation
  5. Remote sensing
  6. Computerized databanks and shared models
  7. Automated testing

Market pull:
  1. University research
  2. Aerospace and defense research
  3. Chemical and petroleum industries
  4. Medical and pharmaceutical industries
  5. Electronic and computer industries

Processes

6. Optical circuitry

Technology push:
  1. Fiber-optic transmission
  2. Laser equivalents of tranistors: bistable devices, photronics

Market pull:
  1. Communications
  2. Defense

7. Genetic engineering and Biotechnology

Technology push:
  1. Recombinant DNA techniques
  2. Tissue culture and monoclonal antibodies
  3. Genetics
  4. Fermentation and separation

Market pull:
  1. Scientific instrumentation and products
  2. Medical products: analysis and treatment
  3. Agricultural products and processes: plant stocks, pesticides, animal breeding, vaccines
  4. Specialty chemicals

8. Chemical processes

Technology Push:
  1. Instrumentation and chemical analysis
  2. Molecular design of compounds and reactions.
  3. Laser-induced chemical reactions
  4. Catalysis, separations, multiphase processes
  5. Coal-and-biomass-feedstock chemical processes

Market pull:
  1. American chemical industry
  2. Japanese and European chemical industries
  3. Third-world chemical industries
  4. OPEC

TABLE 9.1   (cont.)

Systems

9. Communications

   Technology push:
   1. Distributed processing: local and global computer networks
   2. Computer security
   3. Integrated communications: voice, video, data

   Market pull:
   1. Business: automated office
   2. Telephone and data transmission
   3. Media: television and movies
   4. Publications: technical and general and video text
   5. Databases: scientific and consumer

10. Computer-integrated manufacturing

    Technology push:
    1. Color computer graphics
    2. CAD design principles and algorithms
    3. CAM and flexible manufacturing tools
    4. CAD/CAM peripheral equipment

    Market pull:
    1. Aerospace and defense
    2. Electronics
    3. Automobiles
    5. General manufacturing

11. Military systems

    Technology push:
    1. VLSI an VHSIC electronics
    2. Laser weapons
    2. Composite materials

    Market pull:
    1. Smart weapons
    2. Electronic warefare
    3. Star Wars
    4. High-performance materials

Resources

Materials

   Technology push:
   1. Organic and metallic composites
   2. Ceramics: electronics, high-temperature
   3. Polymers: materials, fibers, adhesives
   4. Conducting plastics
   5. Semiconducting materials and processes
   6. Low-temperature materials and processes

TABLE 9.1 (cont.)

Market pull:
1. Textiles, fabrication, construction
2. Aerospace and defense
3. Automobiles
4. Electronics, computers, and communications
5. Scientific instruments

A technology map is useful for strategic planning. Unless a company knows all the areas of rapidly changing technology, the company cannot correctly foresee the potential impact of technology on the company's businesses or see new business opportunities. Successful innovation requires the company to understand wherein opportunities lie for innovating new technology for market needs: "In short, innovative success appears to be a function of good communication, purposeful allocation of resources, top-level support with the organization, and careful matching of technology with market" (Kantrow, 1980, p. 8).

SUMMARY

High technology is a business area of rapidly changing technology. The technological change can be in new products, production processes, knowledge-based services, or in new applications in new markets. In the forms of high technology, there are high-tech components, high-tech devices, high-tech processes, high-tech systems, high-tech materials and resources, and high-tech services.

The sources of ideas for innovation are either from market needs (market pull) or technological opportunities (technology push). Technologically sophisticated customers are excellent sources for ideas for innovation. Technologically unsophisticated customers are poor sources for ideas for innovation. Technology pushers (scientists, engineers, and inventors) must have direct experience with users in order to have the functional focus to create new uses for technology. Technology maps are useful to management strategy in providing an overview of the most rapidly changing areas at a given time.

REFLECTION

1. **Identify two high-technology areas. Find the major changes in the technologies for the last 10 years. Were these innovated by users of technology or manufacturers of technological products?**

FOR FURTHER READING

LAYTON, CHRISTOPHER, *Ten Innovations*. New York: Crane, Russak, 1972.
VON HIPPEL, ERIC, The User's Role in Industrial Innovation, in *Management of Research and Innovation*, B. V. Dean and J. L. Goldhar, eds., New York: North-Holland, 1980.

CHAPTER TEN
TECHNOLOGICAL SYSTEMS AND COMPETITION

CENTRAL IDEAS

1. Business opportunities in a technological system
2. Major devices in technological systems
3. Technology effects on the structural relationships within an industry
4. Development of technological systems

Example: Business Opportunities in Technological Systems—Personal Computers

As businesses are types of systems, technologies can also be kinds of systems. In particular, a radical new innovation may create many business opportunities when it is a technological system—a system of products and services. In a technological system, there are many places for innovating new products and services. We recall that the concept of any system is an operating whole—composed of parts, relationships between parts, and an environment in which the system operates. We can examine how new business opportunities occur within a technological system by reviewing the early history of the personal computer market.

In the late 1970s, the personal computer was a new computer product line, coming in at the low end of computer systems. It arose from the technical advances in semiconductor chip technology at the stage of large-scale integration (LSI). However, the personal computer was innovated not by existing computer companies but by individual entrepreneurs, who started new firms to exploit the new technological opportunities.

Origin of the personal computer industry Around 1970, computers were being produced in two product lines, mainframes and mini's. Semiconductor chip technology had progressed to the point where all the circuits for the central processing circuits of a computer (CPU)—the circuits for mathematical and logic operations—could be put on a single chip. When this occurred, the personal computer industry began.

Because of the existence of big computers, many people with technical backgrounds wished that they had their own computer. But computers were expensive and were only purchased by large organizations. One of the first hobbyist groups, the Amateur Computer Society, was started around 1966 by Stephen B. Gray. The ACS published a bimonthly newsletter containing problems, answers, and information about where to get parts, schematics, and cheap integrated circuits. Still, trying to put together a computer was a massive job, beyond the range of individuals (Gray, 1984).

The situation for amateur computer makers remained this way until 1973. Then Frederick Faggin, at Intel, designed a microprocessor on a chip, produced as the Intel 8008 chip. Nat Wadsworth, a design engineer at General DataComm in Danbury, Connecticut, attended a seminar given by Intel about its new 8008 chip. The chip used an 8-bit word length and could perform all the mathematical and logical functions of a big computer. Wadsworth suggested to his management that they use the chip to simplify their products, but they were not interested. Then Wadsworth talked to his friends: "Why don't we design a nice little computer and each build our own to use at home?" (Gray, 1984, p. 12).

Two friends joined Wadsworth. They designed a small computer. They laid out printed-circuit boards and ordered several constructed by a company. Then Wadsworth decided to manufacture a small computer, and in the summer of 1973, Wadsworth quit his job, incorporating the Scelbi (Scientific, Electronic, Biological) Company. In March 1974, the first advertisement for a personal computer based on a microprocessor appeared in QST, an amateur radio magazine. Unfortunately, Wadsworth had a heart attack in November 1973 at the age of 30. Then he had a second attack in May 1974. He sold about 200 computers—half assembled and half in kits. While in the hospital, he began writing a book, *Machine Language Programming for the 8008,* which sold well.

Meanwhile, another entrepreneur was also building a personal computer. H. Edward Roberts, working at the Air Force Weapons Laboratory at Kirtland Air Force Base in Albuquerque, New Mexico, had tried manufacturing several electronics products, forming, with Forrest Mims, a company called MITS. In 1971, when he decided to manufacture electronic calculators, Roberts bought out his partners in MITS. At first the calculators made a profit, but by 1974, big firms had moved into the business, and MITS was $200,000 in debt. Roberts then decided to jump the industry by developing a more powerful product, a computer. He, too, used the Intel 8008 chip (Mims, 1984).

Luckily for Roberts, about the time he was ready with his computer, the editorial director at *Popular Electronics,* Arthur Salsberg, was looking for an advanced computer project using the new Intel chip. He learned of Roberts' project. Salsberg called Roberts and told him that if he could deliver an article in time for the January issue, he would publish it. Roberts said that he would deliver a computer. He shipped the completed prototype to the magazine and flew to New York. The machine did not arrive (it was lost or stolen at Kennedy Airport). But Roberts had the circuit diagrams with him and explained the operation of the machine. The new machine was called Altair and was featured on the front cover of the January 1975 issue of *Popular Electronics:* "Project Breakthrough! World's First Minicomputer Kit to Rival Commercial Models." Art Salsberg titled his editorial: "The Home Computer Is Here!" (Mims, 1984, p. 27).

The publicity worked. Orders came pouring into the company. The product was awkward and difficult to use. That first Altair in 1975 cost $429 in kit form and came without memory or interfaces. It had no keyboard and had to be programmed directly in binary by setting switches. But it was a computer. Moreover, Roberts had used a standard bus, the so-called S-100 bus. This was to become the first standard for the new personal computer industry. In 1977, Roberts sold MITS.

Major Devices in Technological Systems

Specifically, a technological system is a system providing a functional capability. For example, automobiles provide a transportation function, as do airplanes. These are major devices in air and land transportation systems.

The parts of a technological system are (1) the major device; (2) components, materials, and resources; and (3) peripheral devices. The relationships within the technological system are the controls, standards, and applications of the technology. The environment of a technological system is the infrastructure of sales, service, supplies, and education required to use the system.

In the example, the infrastructure of the computer industry had created a latent market for personal computers—engineering and technical hobbyists. Amateur groups had formed and hobbyist magazines were looking for the right product. The components part of the computer industry, semiconductor chips, had advanced the integrated circuit, the microprocessor on a chip, to the point where a personal computer was technically feasible. With this component advance, the major device because feasible— the personal computer.

The first products were created by entrepreneurial engineers, who left employment in large companies and government labs to start their own companies. Publicity of new products in hobbyist journals was essential to the commercial success of a new consumer technical product. Although illustrated by the personal computer origin, these lessons are perfectly general—technical entrepreneurs selling first products for a hobbyist and scientific market, with education and communications and publicity playing important roles in early commercial success. Thus both the major device and the infrastructure of a technological system are necessary to begin an industry based on a new technologial system.

Example: Growth of the Personal Computer Industry—Parts and Relationships

Growth of the new industry can also depend on additions and improvements in parts or relationships in the technological system. The first products in any new technical area are never really easy to use and are limited in performance and costly. Accordingly, the room for improvement is large and competition begins immediately. But don't be too hard on first products. They show the general shape of things to come and demonstrate the market—very, very important to innovation. Improvements in parts and relationships can create major technological advance in the system as a whole—and subsequent market growth.

For example, one important relationship in a computer system is the programming language. One of the first questions in personal computers was what high-level language should be offered for programming. A Dartmouth professor had developed an easy-to-learn language which he called Basic. The use of Basic made programming in an interactive mode easily self-teachable. In 1975, Bill Gates and Paul Allen wrote a Basic language interpreter for the Altair (Gates, 1984).

Further infrastructure developments occurred. In 1975 in Los Angeles, Dick Heiser started the first retail computer store. At the same time, another entrepreneur, Paul Terrell, opened a retail store in Mountain View, California, the Byte Shop. Thus after the major device of the new personal computer system had been innovated as a new product, the infrastructure of the system continued to grow (Ahl, 1984).

Advances continued in the major device. Other microprocessing chips were being used. Frederick Faggin, the designer of the 8008 chip, left Intel to start a new company, Zilog, producing the Z80 chip. Chuck Peddle, at MOS Technology, created a new 8–bit microprocessor chip with an extended instruction set, the 6502. These two chips, the Zilog Z80 and the MOS 6502, were to become the basis of the first expansion of personal computers.

The Apple Computer   The personal computer that finally ignited the mass market was the Apple. In January 1976, at a west coast electronics trade show (Wescon), Chuck Peddle decided to sell the new MOS 6502 chips at $20 each. (The first Intel 8008 chip had cost Roberts $100 a chip.) One of the first cutomers for Peddle's 6052 chip was Steve Wozniak, who was then a technician at Hewlett-Packard. Wozniak took the chip home and wrote a Basic language interpreter for it. Then he made a computer—Apple I, he called it. He showed it in the spring of 1976 to the Homebrew Computer Club in Palo Alto, California. Again, it was only partly complete—no keyboard, no case, no power supply. Yet two friends, Steve Jobs and Paul Terrell, were impressed. Jobs formed a company to sell the computer. Terrell ordered 50 units for his Byte Shop, but as assembled machines. He did not want to sell kits (Ahl, 1984).

With orders in hand and needing cash for production, Jobs sold his Volkswagen and Wozniak sold his two HP calculators. Wozniak stayed on his job at HP, while Jobs hired his sister and a student to assemble the units. In 29 days, they delivered their first 50 units. Then the garage-based company sold another 150 computer for $666 each. By the end of the summer, Wozniak was designing the successor product, which was to have a keyboard, power supply, and plug-in slots for the S-100 bus. The entrepreneurs understood that they had to improve their first design for better marketability.

So Jobs and Wozniak almost had it together—an engineer, manager, first products sold, improved model—what was missing yet was solid business experience and capital. The next member of the Apple team to be added was A. C. "Mike" Markkula. Markkula was trained as an engineer and had worked for Intel and Fairchild during their meteoric growth in the days of the first integrated circuits. Intel stock options had made him a millionaire, and he had retired at age 34. He visited the garage of Jobs and Woz and was impressed. He invested $91,000 of his own money and began an active role in planning and management. He hired Mike Scott as president. The four of them, Wozniak, Jobs, Markkula, and Scott, set out to make Apple a Fortune 500 company. And they did.

Apple became one of the four major competitors for the major device product in the initial stage of industrial growth of the personal computer. The other early competitors were Tandy's Radio Shack, Jack Tamiel's Commodore, Texas Instrument, and Warner's Atari. The major device product competition by 1980 was thus lined up.

Further system parts and relationships in the personal computer system   The next steps in innovation were in peripheral devices and in generic applications. The tape cassette had early been used to store programs, but it was slow. In the middle of 1978, two companies, Apple and Radio Shack, introduced floppy disk drives for their computers. This facilitated software applications.

Earlier in 1975, Michael Shrayer had purchased an MITS Altair, and he had written a "text editor" routine for it. A text editor is a software tool to make it easier to write programs and to alter programs. On completing the routine, he wrote a second piece of software to document (i.e., write instructions) the first, which he called the Electric Pencil. It was the first word-processing software for the personal computer, which he began selling in 1976. Word processing became one of the major applications of personal computers (Shrayer, 1984).

Later, a second major application was the spreadsheet. In 1978, Dan Bricklin was a student in the Harvard Business School. He and his friend Bob Frankston had been working on a spreadsheet program for the Apple. Spreadsheets were just what business students needed. Bricklin had an assignment in his consumer marketing class to analyze a Pepsi Challenge campaign. Bricklin used his new spreadsheet routine, projecting the financial results of the Pepsi campaign five years out (instead of the two years projected by all his other classmates). His professor liked it. Bricklin and Frankston knew that they had a useful business tool—VisiCalc. They introduced the new product at the National Computer Conference in New York in 1979 (Bricklin and Frankston, 1984). With the spreadsheet application, Apple sales really took off. The personal computer had become a useful personal business tool for the business manager.

By 1980, the major device, parts, relationships, and infrastructure of the personal computer system had developed, and the industry began extraordinary growth. IBM watched its growth and decided to enter. In 1981, they introduced the IBM PC. IBM sanctioned the serious status of the personal computer.

COMPETITION, INDUSTRIAL STRUCTURE, AND TECHNOLOGICAL SYSTEMS

Industrial structures are altered by product differentiation and by product pricing. Since technological change can create product differentiation and can lower product costs, industrial structure can be altered by technology. As we saw in the personal computer industry, technical advances in semiconductor chips created the microprocessor-on-a-chip. Adding other circuits and devices created the personal computer, thus differentiating a lower end of the computer product line. This new product line was not innovated by the established computer manufactures, allowing entrepreneurs to create the new market. Thus the computer industrial structure was altered by the technological change.

Michael Porter emphasized that to understand the competitive conditions in an industry one must analyze the elements of the industrial structure:

1. The competitors within the industry,
2. The potential for new entry by competitors and for product substitution from other industries, and
3. The relationships between suppliers and buyers to the industry. (Porter, 1985, p. 5)

The competitors within an industry can gain competitive advantages either through differentiation of their products or through cost advantages. Differentiation can be either on quality or on market focus. Cost advantages may be through lower prices or higher profit margins (allowing greater expenditures for marketing, research, etc.). Thus the relationships between competitors and buyers can be changed by technology which either differentiates products or lowers prices.

Technology may also affect the barriers for entry of new competitors. For example, the microprocessor on a chip dramatically simplified the technical problems of making a computer and lowered the costs of producing a computer. This allowed a rash of new competitors to enter the microcomputer market, challenging established computer makers. Thus Apple went from a trio of entrepreneurs to a major competitor to IBM in personal computers.

New technology can also affect an industrial structure through product substitution into a industry's market by products from another industry. For example, the lowering of prices by microcomputers and the improvement of technology created product substitution along computer product lines. Microprocessors began to take the lower part of the market for minicomputers in the small business market. In addition, personal computers invaded the market of "dumb" terminals on time-sharing mainframe computers. Thus new technology can affect the relationships in an industrial structure; and these alterations can be complex and surprising because the technology itself may not be a simple entity but also a system.

Example: The Computer as a Technological System

To understand better the complexities of creating a technological system, let us look in more detail at the origin of the computer (of which the personal computer is only one product line). The computer is both a major device of a computing system and a system in itself. We recall that essential components for a computer as a system include the semiconductor chips, in which are embedded the electronics for the architecture of the computer. These chips and their relationships form the architecture of a computer. They include a central processing unit (CPU), a memory, input–output circuits, and a data bus. There are also essential peripheral devices to the computer, including (1) the terminal for input (video screen and keyboard or other data sources), (2) the tape or disk drives (floppy, hard, or optical) for data storage,

(3) the printer for hard copy, and (4) the modem for communications. All these and the computer are usually called the hardware.

Two important control relationships for the computer system are (1) software to program the computer, the assembly language code, and higher-level-language codes; and (2) software to run the computer, the operating system. A third important relationship in the computing system is the applications software for the computer, such as accounting packages, word processing, spreadsheets, data management bases, games, and scientific data analysis packages. A fourth important set of relationships are the standards for common operating systems, disk formats, data buses, graphics, and so on.

Finally, as part of the computer system, its environment is the infrastructure for sales, service, education, and communications to other organizational systems. Thus business opportunities in the computer industry have occurred in all these aspects of the computing system, particularly when a change in the technology of any one part of the system affected the market for computing systems.

Origin of the modern computer   We will now look at the original innovation of the major device of a system, seeing that it often requires many ideas and much time to be created when the device is a complex system. The history of the origin of the modern computer (which preceded the personal computer) illustrates this well. The ideas for a machine that can calculate came from antiquity, as counting aids such as the abacus. Yet the modern ideas are usually traced from Blaise Pascal (a sixteenth-century French mathematician and philosopher) and Charles Babbage (a nineteenth-century English inventor). Both their calculating machines used mechanical gears (Ceruzzi, 1983).

The first modern type of mechanical calculating machine with key-boards and printing) was innovated by Dorr Felt in 1886 and by William Seward Burroughs in 1892. The company that Burroughs founded was still a major company a hundred years later. In 1896, Herman Hollerith added a way to encode information into a machine. Hollerith used the idea of punched paper cards to encode data from the U.S. Census (his idea was derived from the use of Jacquard cards to control patterns in weaving cloth). With such cards, data could be analyzed mechanically. The machine read the holes in the cards and added the counts to counting dials. Hollerith formed the Tabulating Machine Company, which later expanded into the International Business Machine Company, IBM.

In the 1920s an important extension of Babbage's ideas was created by Vannevar Bush, a professor at MIT. He designed a mechanical machine that could perform mathematical operations at the level of calculus. He called it a differential analyzer.

Other ideas (besides calculation) were important to the modern concept of the computer—Boolean logic and binary number systems. The idea of expressing logic in a formalized, computational form traces from the seventeenth-century German mathematician and philosopher Gottfried Leibniz. But such a logic was formally created by the nineteenth-century English logician and mathematician George Boole, In the 1930s, Claude Shannon (inspired by Bush's machine) designed electrical circuits that could perform both mathematical operations and logical operations.

Thus a long history of ideas, techniques, and technologies lead up to the first real computers. The ideas were for machines to compute and perform higher mathematical and logical functions. The techniques were binary arithmetic, Boolean logic, and machine architectures for logic and mathematical operations circuits. The technologies were encoding of data into machines, gears, and electronic circuits for performing calculations. Also, the world had to wait for computers until practical electrical components were developed—first electronic vacuum tubes, then transistors.

It was not until the 1930s and 1940s that the first electrical computers were made, independently by Konrad Zuse in Germany and Howard Aiken in America. Because of the war situation, they did not know of each other's efforts. Howard Aiken was a professor at Harvard University, interested in creating a computer to compile useful calculations such as navigational tables. With the backing of Tom Watson at IBM, he constructed a massive calculator using electromechanical relays. It was called the Harvard Mark I, first turned on in 1943.

Computer research was also occurring in Great Britain during the war. The British constructed electromechanical computers and used them in cracking German codes at the secret Bletchly Park in England. These were called the Colossus series and involved several people, including Max Newman, T. H. Flowers, A. W. M. Coombs, I. J. Good, D. Michie, and Alan Turing.

Also in 1942, the electronic computer, using vacuum tubes only, was created at the University of Pennsylvania. John Mauchly and J. Presper Eckert proposed to the U.S. Army that they build a computer made completely with tubes. With $400,000 of government funds, they built the first electronic computer, the ENIAC (Electronic Numerical Integrator and Calculator), switched on in February 1946.

John Von Neumann, a mathematician, while working on the Manhattan atomic bomb project, learned of the ENIAC project and began consulting with Mauchly. Von Neumann then conceived of storing the programs as well as the data in the machine—and thus the whole idea of the system of the modern computer was finally born.

After the war, commericial interest in the computer began at IBM, Bell Telephone, and Sperry-Rand. The first commercially successful computer system, the UNIVAC I, was designed by Mauchly and Eckert. Delivery of the first commercial machine was to the U.S. Bureau of Census in March 1951.

DEVELOPMENT OF TECHNOLOGICAL SYSTEMS

What we have seen in the computer illustration is that a new technological system begins with the innovation of the major device within the system. The device itself is a smaller kind of system, requiring the creation of ideas, the invention of techniques and of parts, and the development of technology before the ideas can be realized in a practical system.

A long time may elapse between early conceptions and practical realization because of the requirement for the techniques and technology to be ready for the invention. Moreover, the commercial innovation may be further delayed until the technical feasibility has been demonstrated, often in a military application.

Thus the major device in a new technological system is a radical innovation, beginning a new technology S-curve, whose progress depends upon innovations: in parts, relationships, peripherals, applications, standards, and infrastructure. This radical innovation also forms the basic innovation for the growth of a new industry. Further technological development may provide the basis for dividing the industry into several markets.

SUMMARY

In radical innovation, many business opportunities occur when the innovation is a technological system. A technological system is composed of a major device, components, peripherals, applications, standards, and infrastructure.

Entrepreneurs can compete not only in the major device part of the system, but also in the components, periperals, applications, standards, and infrastructure. Technological change in parts of the system can not only create business opportunities in existing product lines but also open up whole new products lines. Individuals can start new companies with these new product lines when existing firms ignore the potential new markets.

A new technological system begins with the innovation of the major device within the system. The device itself is a smaller kind of system, requiring the creation of ideas, the invention of techniques and of parts, and the development of other technologies before the ideas can be realized in a practical system.

REFLECTION

1. Choose a major system innovation (such as the automobile, airplane, train, radio, television, movies, etc.). Trace out its early

industrial history. How many and what kinds of firms were started? What infrastructure firms were also started? How were the industries that supplied parts for the system affected?

FOR FURTHER READING

EVANS, CHRISTOPER, *The Making of the Micro,* New York: Van Nostrand Reinhold, 1981.
LEVERING, ROBERT, *Michael Katz, and Milton Moskowitz, The Computer Entrepreneurs.* New York: New American Library, 1984.

CHAPTER ELEVEN
TECHNOLOGY AND
MARKETING

CENTRAL IDEAS

1. Impact of marketing leadership and technology leadership on long-term competitive advantage
2. Marketing flexibility
3. Emphasis on market positioning
4. Use of marketing experimentation

Example: Problems of Technology Leadership—Xerox, Apple, and IBM

Technology leadership is exerted through "function," in producing products with advanced performance or features. Marketing leadership is exerted through "application," in service, distribution, and pricing. Both technology leadership and marketing leadership are important to ensure that the commercial benefits of innovation will be captured by the innovating corporation. An example of the advantages and perils of technology leadership can be seen in the early 1980s in the experience of three competitors in the personal computer and office automation market: Xerox, Apple, and IBM.

We have seen that personal computers emerged as a mass market by 1980. Then, in 1984, the second generation of personal computers was introduced, focused on office systems and user-friendly technology. "Office systems" consisted of networks in which personal computers served as distributed workstations. "User friendliness" consisted of the integration of applications software and improved human/computer interfaces (such as higher-resolution screens, iconic menus, and multiwindows). Continuing incremental innovation created the second generation of personal computers. The user-friendliness innovations gained public attention in 1983 when Apple Computer introduced a new personal business computer called Lisa and in 1984, a less-expensive version called the Macintosh. Yet the technology story behind this second generation (for example, Lisa and Macintosh) began not in Apple but in Xerox.

Up until the early 1970s, Xerox had been only in the reprographic business, grown from the small Haloid company, on the basis of Carlson's xerography patents. However, in 1970, anticipating competitive pressure in the copier market in the long term, Xerox had a new vision. Xerox formulated a long-range plan of office automation as a coming technological revolution. Xerox planned to expand their products to encompass the totality of office systems. Copiers would be a key component, but the whole of the system of office practice would be the product domain. To research and develop products for this new business strategy, Xerox built a new corporate research laboratory (in addition to the older research laboratory in Rochester, New York, which was to continue being devoted to reprographic research) (Uttal, 1981).

George Pake, a physicist, was hired to head research and development for Xerox and to build the new laboratory. He chose to locate it in "Silicon Valley" next to Stanford University. Stanford had become the major center of the semiconductor electronics industry in the 1970s. Stanford University's research and educational capability in computers and electronics would provide a stimulating intellectual environment for Xerox's new research laboratories efforts. The new laboratory was named PARC—Palo Alto Research Center: "On a golden hillside in sight of Stanford University nestles Xerox's Palo Alto Research Center, a mecca for talented researchers—and an embarrassment. For the $150 million it has lavished on PARC in 14 years, Xerox has reaped far less than it expected. Yet upstart companies have turned the ideas born there into a crop of promising products. Confides George Pake, Xerox's scholarly research vice president: 'My friends tease me by calling PARC a national resource' " (Uttal, 1983b, p. 97).

PARC technologically pioneered the new concepts of office systems, of user friendliness, and of distributed computer networks. In the late 1960s, an MIT professor, J. Licklider, had envisioned an easy-to-use computer. PARC researchers, influenced by Licklider's vision, determined to make it practical. PARC's Alan Kay even projected Licklider's ideas further as a machine which was to be portable, about the size of a book, and easy to use (Bartimo, 1984).

The PARC scientists developed a system called Alto, installing it in PARC. Alto had several unique features. First, it used a new programming language called Smalltalk, facilitating programing with windows, ikon, and "mouse" controllers. Alto was easy to use with an ikonic menu pointed to be a movable desktop "mouse"(for example, to file a report or program, the mouse was used to move an arrow on the screen to point to a tiny image of a file drawer). Alto also had multiple window displays (so one could look at several applications at once), called "desktop" organization of display. Al-

tos were also hooked up in a network (Ethernet) of communicating workstations. Each researcher had an Alto on his or her desk, sending mail on the
computer to one another and printing on a common Xerox laser printer.
Alto was the first experiment in the concept of the paperless, automated
office.

All this had occurred in the late 1970s at PARC, even before the world
realized that a personal computer revolution was brewing in the hobbyist
world of computer kits. Xerox's office products division, however, focused on
competition in the dedicated word-processing market (in which Wang had
leapfrogged both IBM and Xerox). Xerox Office Products Division chose
then to follow Wang's distributed workstation concept in implementing
PARC's vision of office automation rather than the personal computer form.
In 1981, they announced a series of products—a smart typewriter, a personal
computer, the Star workstation, and a local-area network, the Ethernet. Yet
only the workstation and Ethernet incorporated PARC's far-seeing vision:
"By the mid-1970's the center [PARC] was hard at work on the Alto. . . .
Alto and its software became . . . popular inside Xerox. Product development, however, was the turf of another Xerox group, which was championing
a rival machine called the Star . . ." (Uttal, 1983b, p. 98).

The Alto could have been sold as a personal computer, but the Star
could not, since it only worked hooked to other Xerox equipment. Xerox's
office product systems management appeared not to appreciate the complete set of ideas in Alto and Smalltalk. However, another, rival group did:
"Lisa is the unkindest cut of all. In December 1979, Steve Jobs . . . visited
PARC with some colleagues to poke around. They saw Smalltalk. . . .
'Their eyes bugged out,' recalls Lawrence Tesler, who helped develop
Smalltalk. . . . Seven months later Jobs hired Tesler, having decided to use
many Smalltalk features in the Lisa" (Uttal, 1983b, p. 100).

Xerox's Office Product Division launched a too-expensive and too-
closed workstation instead of an advanced personal computer. The personal
computer it marketed was a mundane, look-alike personal computer, which
did poorly even in the booming market of personal computers. It turned out
to be a case of a technology leader without marketing flexibility. The Xerox
Star workstation was revolutionary enough to show PARC's vision—to the
competition. Apple followed two years later first with its Lisa and then with
its Macintosh personal computers. Software for the IBM, the Lotus 1-2-3,
followed quickly after Lisa. They all had the user-friendly visions of PARC.
In sequence, then, MIT inspired Xerox, Xerox inspired Apple, and Apple
inspired software companies for IBM.

Apple's president, Steve Jobs, understood the market. It was personal
computers that were to lead the way into office systems. He had seen the
technical significance of PARC's advances and targeted them toward the
right market, the personal computer market. Xerox's Office Products Division had failed to envision the impact of the personal computer on the office

system. Technology management requires correct strategy on two sides—technology and market. In reporting on the Xerox–Apple innovations, Bro Uttal commented: "From this Xerox might appear to have muffed the chance to make it big in personal computers with PARC's creations. . . . To mourn the Alto, though, is to blame unfairly those who killed it. Xerox was out to produce office equipment, and no office equipment supplier, including IBM, forsaw that personal computers would compete with their wares" (Uttal, 1983b, p. 100).

Flexibility in marketing strategy for new-technology products is very important. When the personnal compuer emerged, Xerox might have made use of it as a workstation, which is eventually how it was used. The PARC scientists had correctly anticipated the decentralized network of computers. This approach might have been used as an alternative at Xerox. Committing too many eggs into one market basket early in a new technology is costly if later it turns out to have been the wrong basket.

MARKETING FLEXIBILITY AND MARKET POSITIONING

The reason that anticipating markets for new technologies is difficult is that technologies and their applications are developed interactively. As new technology develops, new applications are often discovered as well as new relationships to existing technologies and applications. Successful product innovation of the new-generation technology requires that corporate management recognize its significance and correctly focus the marketing of the new product lines. However, this is the hardest thing to do, since the new technologies will probably affect new markets in unenvisioned ways. Therefore, it is important that technological development in a corporation be accomplished in a manner that strongly encourages a shared vision of the directions and rates of technological advance between the research laboratories and the production divisions. The research personnel will be most creative about technological opportunity, while the production and sales divisions while be most sensitive to market needs.

Technology leadership must thus be aimed for the right market at the right time and at the right price, or else the technology leader may end up showing the way to competitors without capturing a dominating lead. Since this may not happen in the first pass, it is important for the innovating corporation to be flexible and quick at adapting the new product to evolving market situations.

To emphasize this learning aspect for new technology products, Shanklin called the making of new markets by new technology a kind of "supply-side marketing," by which he meant "any instance when a product can create a market." Traditional market analysis for new products approaches the task by market segmentation, identifying the customer group (industry or consumer) upon which to focus the new product or service. This can be done because earlier or similar products have defined the function and applications of the product. Incrementally innovative new products can target a segmentable market. In radically new products, however, the largest market has often turned out to be different from the initially envisioned market. For example, Kodak's plastic photographic film was intended for a professional photographer's market, which at that time used glass plates, but it quickly found a larger market in the amateur photography market, which the film created (Shanklin, 1983).

Trying to anticipate the market for radically new technologies is therefore difficult since new applications are invented as the technology improves and declines in price. For this reason, technology strategy should emphasize product flexibility, improvement in performance, and lowering of cost—in order to seek new applications and create new markets. The more radically new the innovative product, the more flexible should be the view of the potential market. Critical points of market acceptance are when the application, performance, safety, ease of use, and price match a new market group of customers.

Ryans and Shanklin called this kind of marketing for innovative products "postioning" the product: "Stated simply, market segmentation is a too narrowly defined term to describe the target marketing activities that need to be employed by the high-tech company. Rather, positioning seems to best describe the steps that the high-tech marketer needs to follow if it is to identify correctly the firms's target markets and to place them in priorities" (Ryans and Shanklin, 1984, p. 29).

By positioning, Ryan and Shanklin suggested that the marketer first identify a broad range of potential users, listing applications, performance, ease of use, and price required for each group. Next, the marketer should prioritize these groups in terms of preferred market for the product. In the product design, flexibility which covers a wider range of groups, or is easily adapted from group to group, will increase the likelihood of commercial success.

E. Peter Ward has reviewed the steps in market positioning:

1. Focus upon the range of applications possible with the new technology;
2. Project the size and structure of corresponding markets for the applications;
3. Judge the optimal balance of performance, features and costs to position for the markets;
4. Consider alternate ways to satisify these markets;
5. Analyze the nature of the competition;
6. Consider the modes of distribution and marketing approaches.
   (Ward, 1981)

MARKETS FOR RADICAL INNOVATION

Market positioning for radically new innovations usually begins with the niche markets which are receptive to new technologies. These markets are the military, scientific, hobbyist, and technically oriented industrial markets. The military market is highly organized to fund new technology and new applications. The scientific market is trained to create and improve new instruments. The hobbyist market enjoys learning and views technical tools as a pleasurable avocation. Technically oriented sections of industrial markets (such as engineering design) have technically trained personnel to adopt and improve technical applications. These markets are the first to adopt new high-technology products. They are the traditional markets for small high-tech companies.

To move high technology products into the mass markets of consumers or of general business, a company must be both a technology leader and a marketing leader. The reason is that mass markets are sensitive to both education and price. They require substantial training and service to accept an innovative product. They also require a relatively low price, high level of safety, and ease of use.

In a mass market, a technology leader runs the risk of demonstrating a new market, which can later be captured by a technology follower with stronger marketing and lower-cost production capability—the "me-too" competitor. The advantage to the "me-too" company is that the potential market factors for success has been explored by the technology leader and thereby delineated. The competitor can then improve its product, more carefully target and price the market, and provide features and service, which together may cancel the lead-time advantage of the technology leader.

Example: IBM PC

In computers, marketing leadership has gone to the company which had hardware performance almost as good as anyone else's but had provided superior software for applications. With this principle, IBM dominated the mainframe computer market from the 1960s through the 1980s. In the new personal computer market in the beginning of the 1980s, IBM had watched Apple and the growing personnel computer market, then attacked with the IBM PC. Introduced in 1981, it claimed 7% of the market that year. In 1982, it matched Apple's share at 27%. In 1983, IBM emerged as the clear and dominant leader with 36% and Apple had slipped even further, to 24%.

IBM played a "close-follower" technology strategy in 1981 in entering the personal computer market. It used just a right balance of technology leadership and marketing leadership—a little technology leadership and a lot of marketing leadership. The IBM PC had a 16-bit central processing chip, superior to the 8-bit chip of the Apple and competitors in the personal computer market in 1981 (superior in the sense that it allowed a larger memory address). Yet since the IBM PC used an 8-bit bus, the combination made it easy for software applications to be written for the IBM PC (using the larger memory which the larger addressing capacity of the 16-bit processor made possible). Therefore, the principle of IBM's entry into the personal computer market in 1981 was just a little technology leadership, but not too much.

One marketing aspect of IBM's successful entry into the personal computer market in 1981 was that IBM focused on the business market, pricing it right for that range and marketing it through its own sales personnel, opening new retail outlets, and distributing it through the new personal computer dealer networks. The important marketing edge was the IBM name, the installed base of IBM business customers, and IBM's reputation for service. This combination of the right balance of marketing and technology leadership worked for IBM. There was an IBM for small businesses and for sharp business executives who knew that IBM mainframes served their businesses. Another factor for success was the choice of an open architecture and operating system (imitating Apple), which facilitated the rapid transfer and development of software applications for the new IBM personal computer.

It was to survive IBM's attack that Apple determined to seize technology leadership in 1981. Apple rushed through the Lisa project to grab technology leadership from IBM (and Apple had found the ideas for technology leadership at Xerox). In 1983, Apple introduced the Lisa to compete with IBM—but met with disappointment. While recognized as a technology leader, Lisa had been priced too high at $10,000, almost twice the cost of the IBM PC XT (Morrison, 1984).

Moreover, some of the software advantages, the integrated programs, had not been strong enough to knock IBM out immediately—for me-too software products for the IBM PC quickly began to appear. One such program became the best-selling software in the middle 1980s, "Lotus 1-2-3." This program had copied one of Lisa's program integration features (database and spreadsheet), yet ran on IBM PCs, which by then dominated the market.

Apple responded in 1984 by introducing the Macintosh, a smaller version of the Lisa and priced in the IBM PC range $2000 to $3000 (*Business Week,* 1984a). This model sold well initially (in contrast to the Lisa model) and kept Apple as a major competitor to IBM in the personal computer market in the middle 1980s. Apple had made the strategic choice of playing technology leader against IBM's market leadership. Without IBM's prestige, mainframe business, and extensive business installations, Apple could not then match IBM's marketing strength. Wars in business competition are fought battle by battle, in products pitted against each other in technology, marketing, and pricing.

MARKETING EXPERIMENTATION IN NEW TECHNOLOGY

Roland W. Schmitt emphasized the importance for marketing personnel to work closely with research personnel, in order to facilitate the linking of technological opportunity with market need: "These [marketing] experts should not, however, give blind allegiance to the latest analytical techniques or the dogma of marketing supremacy. Rather, they should have the temperment of a research experimentalist, putting forth hypotheses about the market and devising economical and efficient market experiments" (Schmitt, 1985, p. 126).

Marketing experimentation is the key to improving the understanding of the eventual market implications of new technologies. The more radical the innovation, the more an experimental marketing attitude is required.

SUMMARY

The competitive advantage goes to the company that balances technology and marketing leadership. Technology leadership is exerted through "function," in producing products with advanced performance or features. Marketing leadership is exerted through "application," in service, distribution, and pricing. Radically new technology creates markets—supply-side marketing. In radically new products, the eventually largest market is often quite different from the initially envisioned market.

Radically new technology sells first to the technically sophisticated customer who needs little training and who can develop applications. In positioning for new markets with high-technology products, the marketer should first identify a broad range of potential users, listing applications, performance, ease of use, and price required for each group. Next, the marketer should prioritize these groups in terms of preferred market for the product. The more radical the innovative product, the more flexible the product should be designed for potential markets, and the more experimental should be the marketing approach.

REFLECTION

1. **Identify a major product innovation and trace its subsequent product lines and markets. What were its first markets? What**

were eventually its largest markets? How did it affect previously existing markets? Were the firms that eventually dominated the markets, technology or market leaders or both?

FOR FURTHER READING

KARGER, D. W. and ROBERT G. MURDICK,   *New Product Venture Management.* New York: Gordon and Breach, 1972.

CHAPTER TWELVE
CORPORATE DIVERSIFICATION AND TECHNOLOGY

CENTRAL IDEAS

1. R&D, corporate culture, and diversification
2. Corporate technological competence
3. Conglomerates—reasons for diversification
4. Profitability of conglomerate acquisitions
6. Diversified portfolio strategy and R&D

Example: The 3M Corporation

Corporate diversification should pay attention to the relationships between the company's distinctive technological competences, organizational structure, and strategic orientation. When a corporation diversifies with some underlying strength, the corporation has a distinctive competence on which to draw in both good times and bad times. The 3M Company is an example of a corporation which had grown wholly by diversifying through new product innovation.

In 1980, 3M had made about 45,000 products (including product variations in size and shape). They were diverse products from sandpaper and photocopiers to tape, skin lotions, and electrical connectors. The source of this product diversity was 3M's innovations, with 95% of the company's sales ($5.4 million in 1979) having come from products related to coating and bonding technology. This was 3M's secret for diversification success—they knew their businesses, for they had invented most of them (Smith, 1980).

3M prized innovation, even giving, for example, annual prizes to its best innovators—the Carlton Award. The award was named after Richard Carlton, who was president of 3M from 1949 to 1953. It was given annually to a few scientists who have made major contributions to 3M's technology. For example, Paul Hansen developed a self-adhesive elastic bandage sold by 3M under the Coban label. Dennis Enright developed telephone-cable splicing connectors. Arthur Kotz developed an electronic system for microfilming directly from computers. W. H. Pearlson's research in fluorine chemistry led to the development of agrichemical products for 3M and to their Scotchgard fabric-protection spray (Smith, 1980).

In 1980, there were 40 business divisions created from these kinds of products developed from 3M's research. Earnings for 3M had risen each year from 1951 through 1980 (except in the 1972 oil-crunch year). Growth through innovation had been 3M's strategy since its early days. Minnesota Mining & Manufacturing Co. began in 1902 at Two Harbors, Minnesota, when local investors purchased a mine. The mine was supposed to have contained high-grade corundum, a hard mineral used in abrasives. Instead, the corundum was low grade, useful only for ordinary sandpaper. Sandpaper even then was a commidity business with low profit margins. The disppointed investors decided to look for products with higher value.

The new company sent its sales personnel searching for innovative ideas. They went onto the shop floor of their customers to look for needs for which no one was providing a product. In automobile factories, they saw workers choking on dust from the dry sandpaper. They reported this to 3M, and researchers created a sandpaper that could be used when wet. This was the first step in starting 3M's technological capability—adhesives and coatings. It was also the first step in 3M's success formula—communication between sales people and researchers for innovation.

The next product also came from observations by the salespeople. They also noticed in automobile plants that workers had a difficult time keeping paint from running on two-tone-painted cars. Richard Drew, a young technician in 3M's lab, invented masking tape. Another famous 3M product also came from Drew's inventiveness. In 1930, Drew conceived of how to put adhesive on cellophane. Cellophane itself had been invented at DuPont in 1924. Then a sales manager at 3M, John Borden, created a tape dispenser with a blade on it—and the "Scotch Tape" product was born.

About half of 3M's innovative products have come from 3M salespeople looking for needs in their customers shops and offices—market pull. The other half have come from bright research ideas looking for applications—technology push. For example, 3M's research lab came up with a synthetic fabic from pressing rayon or nylon fibers together; it was unique in that it had no weave (sort of like felt material). They thought first of using it for disposable diapers, but it was too expensive. Then they thought of using it for seamless cups for brassieres but again it was too expensive. The health care division came up with the right application—surgical masks, which would be more comfortable to doctors and nurses than woven masks because they could be pressed into the right shape—and hospitals could afford it.

R&D, CORPORATE
CULTURE, AND
DIVERSIFICATION

Large American companies have generally moved toward organizations which are diversified in businesses and structured in multidivisional forms. At one extreme, the principles of order that connect diversified corporations may be purely financial, as in pure conglomerates. At the other extreme, diversified corporations may have underlying competences in shared technological or marketing strengths. Jon Didrichsen, for example, distinguished between corporations that have a broad technological competence in a scientific area, such as DuPont in chemistry, and corporations that have a strong kind of technological branching competence, such as 3M in adhesives (Didrichsen, 1972).

In 1980, Edward Roberts summarized some of the lessons applicable to creating corporate growth through new ventures. He emphasized (1) proper organization, (2) top management commitment to innovation, (3) funding for innovation, (4) product teams, (5) reward systems for entrepreneural activity, and (6) performance measures for innovation (Roberts, 1980).

In 3M, for example, the organization structure was organized around product lines that had been created from 3M's innovations. The fact that 3M's divisions were created from innovations contributed to an organizational culture in which innovation was seen to be of high priority to the corporation. Furthermore, each product-line division had an associated product-development department, to maintain and improve the technology and applications of product lines.

Above the divisions, the 3M board and chief operating officer ran the corporation with a vice president of R&D. Reporting to the VP-R&D were two central corporate units, a corporate research laboratory and a new business development unit. Thus 3M was organizationally structured for business diversification by innovation—divisions created from innovations and a central corporate research laboratory creating new innovations, which were nurtured into businesses by a new business development unit.

Roberts pointed out that in 3M's culture, the top management commitment to innovation was clearly articulated policy: "From top to bottom 3M's management provides active, spirited encouragement for new venture generation. Many at the company even speak of a special eleventh commandment: 'Thou shalt not kill a new product idea' " (Roberts, 1980, p. 139).

The company also provides multiple sources of funding support within the company for new ventures. Any of the different groups can provide funding. If an idea is taken to one group and turned down, the proposer is free to try his idea with any other 3M group.

The 3M company uses product teams, which they call "business development units" (which we have called venture teams). Early in the development of a new product, a complete product team is recruited—from research, marketing, finance, and manufacturing. These teams are voluntary, in order to build in commitment and initiative. The incentives to join a new venture for 3M employees are the opportunities for advancement and promotion which the sales growth of a new venture will provide. The 3M company also emphasizes direct financial measures of performance for each new venture: return on investment, profit margin, and sales growth rate.

The value added to an innovative product is knowledge. If the knowledge is not being generated within the firm, it cannot be added. Invention may come from corporate research or from outside licenses. However, the expertise to develop the invention into a useful product must be within the firm.

CONGLOMERATES—
REASONS FOR
DIVERSIFICATION

Most modern large corporations have some degree of diversification, but only a few are true conglomerates. One commonly used definition of a conglomerate is a firm having at least four unrelated businesses, with no one business contributing more than 50% of sales. There are several reasons for diversification: safety in recession, escape from low-growth markets, and financial flexibility.

A major reason for diversification is to counter common business cycles. Different businesses are affected differently in a recession. One example of a merger put together specifically to counter the effect of business cycles was the formation of the Martin-Marietta Company in the 1950s. Martin was then an aircraft firm and Marietta a construction materials firm, selling cement and crushed concrete. The merger followed a belief that defense and domestic economies are often on opposite cycles.

A second reason is to escape from the confines of a low-growth or low-return industry. The first conglomerate, Textron, was created by Royal Little for this reason. In 1923, Little founded a company called Special Yarns Corp. in Boston, Massachusetts. The 1930s depression was hard, and the company strugged to stay alive. After the war, the textile business turned out to be highly cyclic, with a low return on capital. One of the reasons for this was that the industry expanded production capacity by reinvesting profits, reluctant to pay out high dividends or taxes (Little, 1984).

On June 30, 1952, Roy Little held a special stockholders' meeting to change the articles of association to buy businesses outside of textiles. His first acquisition was the Burkart Manufacturing Co. (which had begun by making horse blankets in St. Louis and then turned to making auto seat stuffing). Little then bought two more companies in 1954, Dalmo Victor and MB Manufacturing. In 1955, Little bought Homelite Corp., and the first conglomerate was under way.

A third reason for diversification is to take advantage of financial flexibility, using profitable businesses to acquire or to enter other businesses. The 1960s were the go-go years of conglomeration. The stock market in the late 1950s and 1960s expanded enormously, and companies with increasing sales and profits had their shares sold at very high price-to-earnings ratios. Buying growth was one way to raise that ratio, which in turn provided a way to buy companies with a lower price/earnings ratio through exchange of the higher-priced stock.

For example, in 1954, Litton Industries began from a company called Electro-Dynamics Corp (which was taken over by Roy Ash and Tex Thornton). Ash and Thornton changed the name to Litton Industries and acquired at least 20 different businesses, using high price/earnings ratios (as high as 47 at one time). Then in the early 1960s, they acquired two companies with problems, Ingalls Shipbuilding and Royal McBee. In 1968, Litton's quarterly earnings declined for the first time. For a long time thereafter, the shares were down, and finally the company returned to being a strong performer (Little, 1984).

PROFITABILITY OF CONGLOMERATE ACQUISITIONS

Not all conglomerate acquisitions have proved valuable. Some acquisitions redefined the core businesses of a company. Others could not be integrated into the company or perceived as valuable enough for management attention or resources. In the 1970s and early 1980s a large number of corporate divestitures occurred by sales of divisions to other companies or by leveraged buyouts.

For example, Royal Little, the founder of Textron, commented:

> The spinoff trend started in 1972. The conglomerates had bought too many small companies, and they begain selling the ones with the least growth potential to put more capital into the most promising divisions. . . . By 1972, of course, I was out of Textron, but I was running Narragansett Capital Corp. . . . and we were able to pick up dozens of divested cash cows that weren't growing. We used leveraged buyouts, which enabled us to give the managers a piece of the action. So in a way I had the best of both congolomerate cycles—when they were diversifying in the 1950's and 1960's and when they were selling off in the 1970's. (Little, 1984, p. 60)

Are conglomerates good or bad? Neither, simply another form of business organization, relying primarily on financial mechanisms and controls for performance. Like all companies, when well managed they do well. But they, too, have their problem times. Underlying technological competences can strengthen conglomerates.

Example: Problems with Portfolio Strategy in Conglomerates— RCA in the 1970s and 1980s.

In 1981, Thorton Bradshaw became chairman and chief executive of RCA Corp. He had become the fourth chief executive for RCA in the six years from 1975 to 1981, a rapid turnover for a major company. Edgar Griffiths, Robert Sarnoff, and Anthony Conrad had preceded him (Nulty, 1981).

RCA had been a leading and major company in the electronics revolution which began with radio and continued through television. In the 1960s, RCA became a conglomerate in which the National Broadcasting Corporation (NBC) and Hertz, the leading car-rental company, were major businesses. In addition, many other businesses had been acquired.

When Bradshaw's predecessor, Edgar Griffiths, became the chief executive officer, RCA's financial position was poor. Griffith instituted stronger financial controls, increased factory automation, decreased the payroll, and began a process of divestiture. He sold Random House books, an Alaskan telephone system, two food companies, and manufacturers of x-ray equipment, aircraft radar, and mobile radios. He turned again toward the electronics busi.iess, increasing the research budget from $112 million to $197 million (Nulty, 1981).

Still Griffiths was strong on diversification and in 1980 purchased a financial firm, CIT Financial, for $1.4 billion in cash and stock. This doubled RCA's debt and left the company highly leaveraged. RCA's per share earnings had increased from a little over $2 to about $3.50 from 1976 to 1979. But from 1979 to 1981, the per share earnings dropped to minus 19 cents (Ehrbar, 1982).

Over the course of the 1970s, RCA had taken several heavy write-offs. In 1971, RCA wrote off $490 milion in withdrawing from the computer business. In 1981, RCA wrote off $230 million: $130 million in TV-picture-tube operations; $59 million in truck leasing, which Hertz had begun in 1978; and $34 million on TV shows in NBC's inventory. When Bradshaw began managing RCA in 1981, the company had the negative earnings and large debt from the most recent acquisition of CIT Financial. In 1984, Bradshaw sold off CIT Financial (for nearly what RCA had paid for it).

The Hertz company had initially prospered under Robert Stone, after being acquired by Robert Sarnoff. From 1971 to 1977, Hertz profits increased fivefold, to $131 million. Stone was replaced in 1977 and Hertz profits declined from 1979 through 1981. In 1985, RCA sold Hertz to United Airlines.

Some of the companies acquired by RCA and then sold off prospered after the sale. For example, Banquet Foods was acquired by RCA and later sold. It did well before and after RCA. Bradshaw commented: "We didn't know how to run it, and we should not have had it" (Ehrbar, 1982, p. 67).

This is the heart of the diversification strategy—don't acquire or get into a business that you don't know how to manage. Managing includes understanding the market and the technology. There are always two related questions to ask in corporate diversification, phrased nicely by George White and Margaret Graham:

Are we doing the right job?
Are we doing the job right? ·
(White and Graham, 1978)

Epilogue—in December 1985, the General Electric Corporation acquired RCA.

CONGLOMERATES AND BUSINESS PORTFOLIO STRATEGY

The problem with managing conglomerates is the temptation to manage the corporation by a kind of portfolio analysis. Portfolio strategy was popular in the late 1960s and early 1970s. Some advocated (1) comparing profit margin against market share, and (2) comparing sales growth against market share. George Day summarized some of these approaches toward strategy, comparing businesses along the dimensions of market dominance and market growth. Figure 12.1 illustrates that categorization of businesses as "stars," "problem children," "cash cows," and "dogs" (Day, 1975).

The strategic implications of this categorization appears at first obvious, simply in the naming of the categories. One funds the stars, milks the cash cows, decides what to do with the problem children, and gets rid of the dogs. However, that attitude toward strategy is too simple. James Brian Quinn, for example, has suggested: "Perhaps the most difficult task for top managers is to balance the needs of existing lines against the needs of potential lines. This problem requires a portfolio stategy much more complex than the popular four-box Boston Consulting Group matrix found in most strategy texts" (Quinn, 1985, p. 81).

One of the reasons that more complex strategy is required is that the simple characterization in terms of markets and margins only misses many of the other important factors in a business. For example, Kantrow emphasized several factors that should go into a company's diversification strategy: "It is of great importance to identify and assess the nature of the relationship

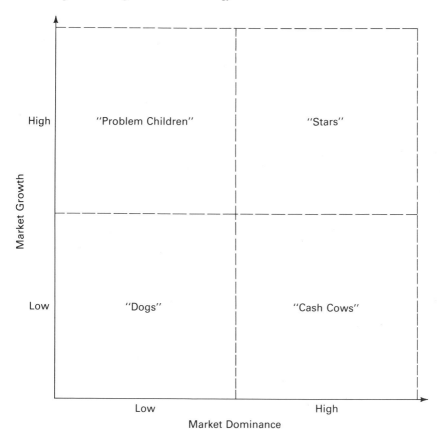

FIGURE 12.1 Business portfolio strategy.

among a company's distinctive technological competence, its organizational structure, and its overall strategic orientation" (Kantrow, 1980, p. 12).

Richard Hamermesh and Roderik White also agreed that a typical flaw in this kind of strategic portfolio analysis was to ignore completely any effects of the organizational relationships within the corporation. The aspects of interaction that are important are (1) autonomy of the business unit managers, (2) line responsibility for direct and complete control of key functions, and (3) incentive compensation of business unit managers linked to unit performance. They argued that "the nature of a business unit's relationship to headquarters can have as much effect on its performance as its competitive position and the industry's environment" (Hamermesh and White, 1984, p. 103).

In stable environments, a high degree of autonomy, line responsibility, and closely linked incentives improve the performance of business units. In dynamic environments, the relationship with corporate headquarters matters, because strong performance in business units can still result in high sales growth with low return on investment. The trade-offs among the many variables in a dynamic environment should involve decision-making at the central level as well as at the unit level.

In the business environment, one particular factor of stability or change which is important is the rate of technological change of the industry of the business unit—the technology life cycle. For example, if businesses were stars or problem children due to growth of a new technology, the strategy should be to strengthen both, if possible.

Even for cash cows and dogs in technologically mature areas, it is not necessarily sensible to merely milk the one and get rid of the other. Although highly competitive, markets in mature technology areas tend to be very large. If one merely milks the cash cow, without doing a sufficient amount of defensive R&D (that is, R&D that improves models and lowers production costs and targets applications), one may lose cash cows to aggressive competitors.

Even dogs in mature technology areas may be repositioned against competition by defensive R&D, and a small shift in market share in a large market may turn a dog into a cash cow. Technology-mature markets can last for long times (until obsoleting technologies occur). Moreover, management may be unprepared for problems when they occur in the cash cows and these suddenly are transformed into dogs. Then investors see a company that is partly valuable and partly valueless. Corporate raiders may think of breaking up such a company, for the parts are more valuable than the whole. In these situations, management becomes vulnerable to raids and takeovers.

For example, in the 1981–82 recession, Bendix tried to take over Martin-Marietta (when its stock was depressed by the construction business side while its defense business side boomed). Instead Bendix was acquired by United Technologies. Martin-Marietta survived independently but paid a stiff price in acquiring new debt. Subsequently, it sold off parts of its businesses.

Business strategy in handling a portfolio of diversified companies must not only optimize short-term gains but also provide for long-term growth and strengthen integrative competences which make the corporation more than a sum of its parts.

SUMMARY

Corporate diversification should pay close attention to the relationships between company's distinctive technological competences, its organizational structure, and its overall strategic orientation. The principles of order that connect diversified corporations may, at one extreme, be purely financial, as in pure conglomerates. At the other extreme, diversified corporations may have underlying competences in shared technological or marketing strengths.

New business ventures provide an important source for business diversification in firms that have learned to institutionalize innovative activity. Portfolio business strategies should not optimize short-term returns but prepare for long-term futures and strengthen underlying competences that integrate the corporation.

REFLECTION

1. Select a conglomerate and write a case history of its origin and performance. Has the conglomerate focused on any integrating competencies? What has been its stock-price history? Have any takeover attempts occurred?

FOR FURTHER READING

PORTER, MICHAEL E., *Competitive Advantage*. New York: Free Press, 1985.

CHAPTER THIRTEEN
LINKING BUSINESS AND TECHNOLOGY STRATEGY

CENTRAL IDEAS

1. Role of technology strategy in business planning
2. Formal planning processes
3. Technology strategy in formal planning
4. Impact of innovation on business strategy
5. Technological scenarios

Example: Technology Strategy and Long-Range Planning at Monsanto

We have seen the importance of technology to business; how is it to be included in business planning? The basic role of technology strategy in any business planning is to pose three fundamental questions:

1. In the future, in what businesses should the firm engage?
2. How should the firm be positioned in these businesses?
3. What research, production, and marketing will be necessary to attain those positions?

An example of a major change in business plans, arising from technological considerations, occurred in Monsanto in the early 1980s. From the late nineteenth century through the middle of the twentieth century, the chemical industry was a continuously innovative and growing high-tech industry. Chemicals are central to many industrial production processes, provide resources for many products, and provide materials and fabrics. The pace of technological change in the chemical industry followed the classic S-curve, exponentially exploding in the early twentieth century and growing rapidly but linearly into the later twentieth century. Then in the late 1970s there arose the possibility that the basic chemicals side of the industry would become a mature-technology industry. At the same time, worldwide industrial capacity to produce commodity chemicals outgrew demand. Technology transfer of chemical knowledge to less developed countries had shifted the competitive edge from knowledge advantages to resource advantages.

Petrochemicals were going through a technology life cycle:

> It happened in steel, it happened in copper, and now it is starting to happen to basic petrochemicals. . . .
>   A once-thriving domestic industry reaches maturity . . . . Then upstart producers in developing countries, which often have lower costs for raw materials and labor, build spanking new plants. This floods the world with excess capacity and forces many manufacturers in the developed countries to shutter their higher-cost operations.
>   This oft-repeated trend is under way in the petrochemical industry. It has sparked a shakeout among the nation's manufacturers of basic petrochemicals such as methane and ethylene, used as building blocks for more sophisticated chemicals. (*New York Times,* 1984).

In the later 1970s, the third-world oil-producing countries began to build petrochemical production facilities to compete in petrochemicals in the world markets. They were able to do this since production techniques for current bulk chemical processes were invented in the period from the 1880s through the 1950s and, by the 1970s, technical knowledge of these processes has been widely disseminated, through education and technical literature.

Thus in the 1980s, additional new petrochemical production capacity began in less developed countries: "The way chemicals are traded around the world will soon change. South Korea, Mexico and other developing countries are building petrochemical plants to supply their own needs; more important, some importers, particularly Middle Eastern countries, are about to become big exporters themselves. The traditional exporters in the United States, western Europe and Japan are now looking for ways to safeguard their home markets" (*The Economist,* 1983).

Shades of Kondratieff—technological maturity—excess production capacity—falling profit margins! The large American chemical firms had to plan new strategies. In the early 1980s, chief executives of Monsanto, John Hanely and Richard J. Mahoney (succeeding Hanely), redirected the company. On September 1, 1983, when Mahoney became president, Monsanto was a $6 billion company, headquartered in St. Louis. Mahoney led Monsanto in long-term strategy to (1) reduce costs in its traditional business areas while (2) positioning it in new technologies and new businesses (Labich, 1984).

At that time, a technical journal, *Chemical & Engineering News* (C&EN), published an interview with Mahoney:

C&EN: Where do you believe Monsanto is going in the next decade?

Mahoney: We've set out on a pretty clear course that will see us evolving over time into a company that will be, in some ways, like we are today, and, in other ways, quite different. (*Chemical & Engineering News,* 1983, p. 10)

The traditional business of Monsanto (basic chemicals) would become only one-third of Monsanto's future businesses. Monsanto sold a number of losing businesses in the United Stated and abroad, including some fiber operations, a petrochemical plant in Texas, nylon operations in Europe, and a subsidiary chemical and plastic firm in Spain. At the same time, Monsanto bought a number of small companies to fit into new electronics operations and invested heavily in biotechnology (Labich, 1984, p. 60).

This is one result of strategy based on integrating technology into business planning—parts of the company continue, parts are discontinued, and new parts acquired or begun. Long-term business planning looks toward the nature and balance of the company's future businesses.

Monsanto had turned its long-range strategy toward the hottest new, major technology then unfolding—biotechnology. Biotechnology was an example of a major technological change, a technological revolution pervasive enough to be a component of a new economic long wave: "Mahoney: Probably the one that gets most press at Monsanto is the biological component. Here I'm talking about our existing business in agriculture and a new business in nutrition chemicals, which we started up a few years ago to move into animal health and nutrition, and what we hope will be a substantial effort in the human health care area . . . " (*C&EN,* 1983, p. 10).

Accordingly, biotechnology was a major component in Monsanto's R&D spending: "Mahoney: We have perhaps $100 million of the $300 million per year in discovery—basic research. And $200 million in one form or another of applied research. Of the biotechnology area, virtually all of it is a component of the $100 million—say $30 million or thereabouts. So about one third of our basic science is going into biotechnology . . . " (*C&EN,* 1983, p. 13).

In October 1984, at a cost of $150 million, Monsanto opened a new research laboratory in the life sciences. It was located in a suburb of St. Louis and consisted of four building, containing 250 laboratories, 26 rooftop greenhouses, and 123 plant growth chambers (capable of duplicating most climate and soil conditions anywhere on earth). Initially, 600 researchers worked in the center, with staff planned to double in two years (Labich, 1984).

Faced with major changes of increased international competition in a technologically maturing industry, Monsanto had adopted new strategies for existing and new businesses, linking business direction with technology strategy:

C&EN: At the end of your tenure as chief executive officer, what do you wnat Monsanto to be?

Mahoney: I want Monsanto to be the envy of the chemical industry. I would like it to be the finest company in the fields that it's in . . ." (*C&EN,* 1983).

TECHNOLOGY STRATEGY

Technology strategy should be formulated wihtin the the larger context of business planning, since technology is only one component of the business system. Michael Porter suggested using the concept of the "value chain" of corporate production to clarify competitive strategy. The value chain of a firm is the set of strategically relevant activities in the production of goods and services of the firm. For example, the value chain includes the inbound logistics, operations, outbound logistics, marketing, and sales and service (Porter, 1985, p. 167).

The role of technology strategy in business planning should therefore identify the potential impact of technological change on any part of the value chain. This means that changes in the technologies of resource acquisition (or availability and prices) of resources and supplies would affect the value-adding activities of inbound logistics. Changes in the technologies of production processes would affect the value-adding activities of operations. Changes in the technologies of transportation and distribution would affect the value-adding activities of outbound logistics. Finally, changes in the technologies of products would affect the value-adding activities of marketing, and sales and service.

In the Monsanto example, management saw the changes in the availability of resources affecting their future basic-chemicals businesses, since Middle Eastern oil-producing companies with chemical plants would have a cost advantage in competing for world markets. In addition, they saw little technical change in either the processes or products of the basic chemical business. Their strategy was then to create new businesses (new products) based on the new processing technologies of biotechnology. Thus both technological change and the lack of technological change affected the value-chain of Monsanto's businesses; and Monsanto planned to use this understanding of technological change to restructure its businesses.

In planning technology strategy for competitive advantage, Porter also suggested a general approach to formulating a technology strategy:

1. Identify all the distinct technologies and subtechnologies in the value chain.
2. Identify potentially relevant technologies in other industries or under scientific development.
3. Determine the likely path of change of key technologies.
4. Determine which technologies and potential technological changes are most significant for competitive advantage and industry structure.
5. Assess a firm's relative capabilities in important technologies and the cost of making improvements.
6. Select a technology strategy, encompassing all important technologies, that reinforces the firm's overall competitive strategy.
7. Reinforce business unit technology strategies at the corporate level.
   (Porter, 1985, pp. 198–200)

Porter's prescription was first to be inclusive in identifying all the technologies in the firm's value chain (and in those of other relevant industries). Next, Porter suggested that one should determine the probable directions of technological change, focusing on the impact these changes may have for industrial competitiveness. Finally, Porter suggested that one should select a technology strategy and emphasize it at the appropriate business unit level of the firm.

FORMAL PLANNING PROCESSES

To accomplish a systematic approach to technology strategy (such as suggested by Porter), it is helpful to have in place some kind of formalized planning process—otherwise, the inclusiveness and focus of strategy tend to get lost in complexity or details. In formal planning, the key concepts are (1) objectives, (2) planning environment, (3) goals and strategies, and (4) tactics and budgets. Formal plans define the objectives the companies seek in the environments that the companies envision. The goals and strategies delineate broad sets of outcomes to be sought and actions to be taken. The tactics and budgets operationalize these actions in the next year. To some extent, all companies plan. But in the range and form of the planning process, some companies plan longer range and more formally, others short range and informally.

Firms should always have both some short- and long-range strategies, to avoid being blind-sided by competition, now or later. The short-range strategy is expressed in the budget plan for the next year. The long-range strategy is expressed in long-term financing, capital expansion, marketing plans, and new product and R&D strategies. Yet in form, the strategy of some firms sometimes consists only of budget preparation and projection. Others prepare detailed plans for five years, with extrapolated and alternative scenarios. The effective use of technology strategy requires a planning format of longer focus than mere budgeting and of greater substance than mere projection of sales. Formal planning processes have repeatedly been a subject of controversy in management theory—some praising, others damning formal planning processes.

To clarify planning situations, it is helpful to identify different levels of planning sophistication. In 1980, Frederick Gluck, Stephen Kaufman, and A. Steven Walleck published a study of the planning practices of 120 companies. They distinguished a spectrum of formalism and effectiveness in corporate planning practices:

1. Basic financial planning,
2. Forecast-based planning,

3. Externally oriented planning,
4. Strategic management.
   (Gluck, Kaufman, and Walleck, 1980, p. 154)

At the first level, basic financial planning provides the least range and scope of strategic planning. An annual budget is prepared each year and is only functional in focus (focused on organizational divisions). Budgets are, of course, essential for cost control.

At the second level, forecast-based planning is begun, usually when additional financial planning becomes necessary to estimate future capital needs and to compare alternative financing plans. The advantage of this level is that it requires managers to confront longer-range issues than presented in annual budgeting plans. Financial forecasts are an attempt to anticipate the financial future of the corporation.

At the third level, externally oriented planning is usually begun when the environment of the firm has started to change rapidly, so that the forecasts of the financial planning turn out to have been wrong. Externally oriented planning trys to understand the basic marketplace phenomenon that is creating the changes—changes in the structure of natural resources in availability and pricing, changes in the structure of the market (due to changes in life styles, demographics, socioeconomic statuses), and changes in the regulatory, financial, or international structures. Typically, formal planning may then be restructured as strategic business units or as profit centers. The value of externally oriented planning is the focusing of strategic thought on changes in markets and competition.

At the fourth level, strategic management is usually begun when the formality in the externally oriented planning begins to outweigh the benefits. Annual planning meetings begin to consume too much time, produce too many details, require too much review, fragment the view of the corporation into a bunch of unconnected profit centers, and confuse decision-making responsibility.

Strategic management focuses on major changes that affect more than one profit center and on themes cutting across the corporation. Strategic management should attend to changes in directions. Assuming that budgets, projections, and structural changes continue, what changes must be taken to achieve desired futures? Formalism in the strategic planning process should assist management to focus systematically on the important long-term problems and opportunities of the corporation. Too little formalism is of no help; and too much formalism obscures the issues.

Example: Formal Planning Process at Henkel KGaA

We will illustrate the concepts of planning in a formal process implemented in a German company, Henkel KGaA, in 1983.

Objectives   In 1983, Henkel was organized by product areas, geographical areas, and functional areas. Both organization and planning were market oriented: "Thinking and activity within the company is therefore strongly oriented to the careful observation of market activities and the input of corresponding measures. The planning must correspond to the conditions for handling the 'marketing-mix' " (Grunewald and Vellmann, 1981, p. 20).

The procedures in Henkel's planning process began with their management board setting overall targets and the corporate purpose. These targets used information from a forecast that extrapolated past performance into the future. The targets were decisions about desirable levels of investment, cash flow, and return on investment. The length of term over which forecasts and targets are formulated is called the "planning horizon" (the period of time over which planning should occur). The criterion for setting a planning horizon is the length of time for a future possibility to occur that requires a present decision to inauggerate. For example, such decisions are the lengths of time for plant construction, market expansion, and new product innovation.

The objectives of a company should focus on the markets the company intends to serve. Objectives should consist of two kinds of objectives, financial and market. Financial objectives are returns on investment and assets, cash flows and after-tax profits, and dividend policies. Market objectives are market areas and niches, market regions and shares, marketing strengths, and distribution capabilities.

Planning environment   The second step in Henkel's process was to translate these forecasts and targets into the level of externally oriented planning. At Henkel, a planning, controlling, and accounting unit translated the objectives into a "strategic plan" and also provided an "environmental analysis" to the divisional and functional units.

A business planning environment consists of a set of linked forecasts between economic, market, and technological changes. The planning environment depicts the competitive context that a firm expects to face into the planning horizon. The first component of a planning environment should be an economic forecast of the condition of the national economy (and relevant international economies) and other factors that may affect business conditions (such as governmental policies and capital or resource markets). The second component of a planning environment should be a baseline market forecast, estimating trends in the sales of product lines by application and customer class. The third component of a planning environment should be a baseline technology forecast, estimating trends in the performance/cost and features/cost ratios of current product lines.

The planning environment should link the three forecasts in a set of what-if future scenerios. Technological change can alter the baseline market forecast through (1) improved performance/cost products, (2) improved features at similar performance/cost ratios, and (3) new functional applications.

The most significant of these scenerios in terms of market impact should then be classified in terms of current judgments as to technologically impossible, possible, and probable. It is important to list the assumptions made in arriving at these judgments, for if any of these assumptions prove false, the judgments should be reviewed. Such a planning environment requires a close working relationship between the marketing and research personnel. In fact, the exercise of preparing linked marketing/technology forecasts for a planning environment is an important organizational mechanism for fostering working relationships between research and marketing.

In the Henkel illustration, its environmental analysis emphasized the underlying factors behind the company's businesses: "As the company is inevitably related to its environment, ideas and targets concerning nonoperating factors also affect the company-internal activities. It is the challenge of good planning, to take the probable effects of these external factors into consideration as far as possible" (Grunewald and Vellmann, 1981, p. 22).

Goals and objectives The next step was for the "profit centers" (that is, the divisional and functional units) to review the corporate targets and the planning environment. First they proposed any changes in structure or markets of which they were aware which would alter the planning environment forecasts. Then after any changes this produced in the overall plan, they formulated divisional-level strategies that would contribute to the corporate goals.

The planning environment and objectives provided the backdrop for the strategic plans. These strategic plans consisted of the goals and strategies the profit centers of the company proposed for each year of the planning horizon to contribute to the corporate objectives. At Henkel KGaA, corporate objectives were in narrative form and were also translated into operational targets:

> The corporate purpose as a planning element can be summarized in four interelated areas:
> Fields of activity for the company with overall statements on the kind of products, technologies to be used, consumer groups, geographic orientation.
> Orientation and limitation of the factor combination of fixed assets, financial assets, personnel and management structure with statements on financing methods, management structure, personnel development.
> Quantified figures as a measure for the financial success of the company and its sub-units; with the anticipated annual growth rate of gross profit and gross return on investment as well as net return on equity for the total company. . . . (Grunewald and Vellmann, 1981, p. 23)

The goals are qualitative and statistical statements of performance delineated in the appropriate year within the planning horizon: goods and services to be offered, market share, return on investments, debt retirement, and dividend policies. The strategies are the long-term means of achieving these objectives: product lines, market areas and regions, product innovation and technological innovation, and capital investment.

Tactics and budgets   The current and next-year planned budgets summarize the tactics and resources devoted to implementing the stategic plan in the current and coming year. The tactics are immediate steps in the strategic plan: production schedules, construction schedules, resource acquisition, projected sales, costs and profits, projected working capital, and short-term and long-term financing. The next-year budget and personnel plan detail the necessary financial resources to implement the tactics.

At Henkel, the individual plans were then assembled into a total corporate plan, approved by the management board, with appropriate adjustment of targets. In the process, the "corporate purpose, environmental analysis and guidelines" provided the common interpretive framework, while the "targets" provided the interaction between the top-down and bottom-up planning decisions.

Although formal planning processes at the levels of forecast-based planning and externally oriented planning (as described in the Henkel example) are laborious to set up initially, their maintenance, if computerized, is not laborious. The strategic process should then become a rolling process, preparing for the annual budget formulation. The annual planning process should be brief and concise, focusing only on changes in corporate direction. It should consist of (1) a historical view of where the corporation has been, (2) current status of where it is going, and (3) issues determining whether any of the current directions should be changed.

PLANNING GROUPS

Sometimes, to facilitate communication between line and staff groups, it may be useful in some firms to form special planning groups, as additional aides to the planning process. Special groups are useful in providing detailed reviews of special areas or existing product lines. For example, Domenic Bitondo and Alan Frohman advocated the use of "R&D strategic brainstorming" groups. They suggested that the makeup of such groups should include (1) marketing personnel, (2) engineering personnel, (3) manufacturing personnel, (4) research personnel, and (5) staff of relevant business units (Bitondo and Frohman, 1981).

IMPACT OF INNOVATION
ON BUSINESS STRATEGY

Anticipating the kinds and impact of technological change on the corporate future is essential to business planning. We recall that Abernathy and Clark suggested classifying the impacts of innovation upon competencies of the corporation, under the categories of (1) production/technology and (2) markets/customers (Abernathy and Clark, 1985).

Under production/technology, they inncluded product design, production systems, skills and knowledge base, and materials and capital equipment. Under markets/customers, they included customer bases, customer applications, channels of distribution and service, and customer knowledge and modes of communication. The range of impact of innovation on any of the factors might be from strengthening existing competencies to obsoleting existing competencies.

With these impacts in mind, Abernathy and Clark then proposed to scale any innovation along two dimensions:

1. Along a production/technology dimension, innovations could be classified as obsoleting existing competence or conserving existing competence.
2. Along a markets/customer dimension, innovations could also be classified as obsoleting existing competence or conserving existing competence.

This schema then provided categories for understanding the potential impact of an innovation on the corporation's activities:

1. Architectural Innovations
   —obsoleting both existing Technology/Production factors
   and existing Market/Customer Linkages.
2. Revolutionary Innovations
   —obsoleting Technology/Production factors
   but conserving existing Markets/Customer Linkages.
3. Niche Creation Innovations
   —conserving existing Technology/Production factors
   but disrupting existing Markets/Customer Linkages.
4. Regular Innovations
   —conserving existing Technology/Production factors
   and conserving existing Markets/Customer Linkages.
   (Abernathy and Clark, 1985, p. 8)

This classification is useful in indicating the areas of change that potential innovations may require in corporate strategy. Architectural innovations will make the most pervasive changes in the industry, obsoleting both existing technologies and market structures. Regular innovations will require the least change, conserving both existing technologies and existing market structures. Niche creation and revolutionary innovations require changes either in technologies or in market structures, while preserving the complementary factors.

Strategic planning which identifies the transilient nature of innovation can then focus on what corporate changes must be planned to exploit the business opportunities created by the innovation. For example, the genetic engineering innovation was an architectural type of innovation, requiring that Monsanto restructure some of its technology/production competencies and addressing new market/customer linkages.

TECHNOLOGICAL
SCENARIOS

Envisioning the impact of technological change on business opportunities and threats is the important role of technological scenarios in the planning process. Such scenarios can be relatively simple or complex and detailed. For example, Donald Pyke proposed a hierarchy of mapping categories to sketch systematically the impact of technological changes on markets. He proposed scenarios of three levels:

Level 1: environmental
Level 2: scientific and engineering capabilities
Level 3: product lines

The point is to trace over time the likely connections between changes in each of these levels (Pyke, 1973).

As an example, for automobiles in the 1960s, public concern about air quality of the environment resulted in pollution control laws. Automobile companies were caught technically unprepared for pollution control standards and had to spend a decade on defensive R&D to jury-rig existing engine designs with pollution control devices. This resulted in messy engineering and in products that saddled the public and auto companies with expensive and awkward solutions to auto emission control.

In summary, technology scenarios in strategic planning should help the corporation focus on (1) technological opportunities, (2) market needs, and (3) business opportunities. Alan Kantrow succinctly stated the technology–business connection: "In short, what makes technology go is exactly what makes business go: coherent strategy and managers closely committed to it. To be effective, then, technological decisions must be strategically sound, for technology strategy and business strategy are of a piece" (Kantrow, 1980, p. 20).

Another observer, Richard Rosenbloom, also nicely emphasized the importance of strategic thinking for linking of technology and business:

The strategy framework is particularly appealing because it integrates in two relevant dimensions.

First, the concept of strategy formulation calls for a perspective that cuts across the boundary of the organization, matching capability . . . with opportunity. . . .

Second . . . the concept of strategy implementation requires the translation of higher-level strategic abstractions into more concrete and implementable terms. (Rosenbloom, 1978, p. 226)

The role of technology strategy in business planning is to include the foresight of technological change in the business vision of the corporation.

SUMMARY

The basic role of technology strategy in business planning is to help ask the questions of in what businesses the corporation plans to be and how positioned. Effective planning then identifies the present decisions required to create desirable and competitive corporate futures. In particular, technology strategy must anticipate the transilient impact of technological innovation on the future competencies of a corporation.

An appropriate level of formal planning provides systematic and documented strategy. The inputs to the process occur through participation of staff and line management and of special planning groups. Technology scenarios shoud help management focus on the interaction of changes between technology and changes in markets, resources, regulation, and competition.

REFLECTION

1. Think of a major technology that has effected dramatic changes on markets, industry, and social and environmental patterns of living. Construct a historical scenario that describes the interactions among the environment, technology, and products. Was government regulation involved in that history? Were social infrastructures altered? Where do you think this scenario is likely to go in the next 50 years?

FOR FURTHER READING

JELINEK, MARIANN, *Institutionalizing Innovation: A Study of Organizational Learning Systems.* New York: Praeger, 1979.

QUINN, JAMES BRIAN, *Strategies for Change: Logical Incrementalism.* Homewood, Ill.: Dow Jones–Irwin, 1980.

CHAPTER FOURTEEN
MANUFACTURING
STRATEGY

CENTRAL IDEAS

1. Manufacturing as a strategic competence

2. Types of manufacturing choices

3. Levels of manufacturing competitiveness

4. Sources of manufacturing competitiveness: new technology and superior managerial integration

5. Stages of manufacturing revolutions

6. Computer-integrated manufacturing

7. Managerial strategy in flexible manufacturing systems

8. Simultaneous culture of factories of the future

Example: Flexible Manufacturing Strategy in the Deere Factory

Within the context of business and technology strategy and together with product and marketing strategies, manufacturing strategies should also be central to technology planning. In any successful innovation, competitors will eventually force product competition on quality–price factors. Quality and price are critically dependent on manufacturing strength. Such strength should be envisioned from the beginning and built up equally with other business functions in innovation of new businesses. Moreover, with the technological revolution in manufacturing techniques in the 1980s—flexible manufacturing—it became both feasible and desirable to utilize economies of scope in planning new business strategy.

An example in 1983 of flexible manufacturing innovation in the United States was a new Deere & Company factory: "When Deere & Company decided in 1974 to build a new tractor assembly plant in the rolling farm country of northeast Iowa, the mandate from top management was to build one at the leading edge of manufacturing technology. That leading edge turned out to be 'flexible manufacturing' . . . " (*New York Times, 1983,* p. 1).

The new concept was to organize production under computer control. Just as adding mechanical power to a machine was a revolution, adding computer control to a machine was another revolution. In flexible manufacturing, the same machine, that is, the same manufacturing line, can turn out many different products quickly and simply by reprogramming the computers that control the machines in the line. For example, at that Deere factory: "The centerpiece of the plant is a system that turns 1000-pound raw castings into fully machined transmissions cases, which are a major part of the structure of Deere's big tractors. A lone worker loads castings on carts that are pulled along by a chain in the floor, much like a cable car. For each one, the worker punches a code into a computer terminal. From there on, a computer is in charge" (*New York Times,* 1983, p. 30).

What the computer did was to direct the cart to a machine with the least backlog of work. At that machine, the computer then told the machine which of the different cases was to be made. It then directed the machines to find the piece (by putting out a probe to touch the material) and to load the right tool bit. Then the computer told the machine to bore, drill, and mill the part in the sequence necessary to create the desired case. When the machine was done, it had, under computer tutelage, transformed the raw casting into a precision component for Deere's tractors.

When the machine was finished, the computer told it to roll the part off to the side, where a cart picked it up to take it to the next machine for the next step of the manufacturing process. The labor involved had been reduced, since no highly paid machinist was needed. In addition to labor savings, flexible manufacturing had important implications for Deere's management strategies. In inventory, for example, it reduced in-process inventories from a three-month supply of finished parts to a three-day supply.

In product lines, it encouraged Deere to consider further product diversification: "Nor is Deere limited to its current model line-up. By simply reprogramming the machines and modifying them somewhat, it could process entirely different components. 'We can make aircraft parts or washing machine parts or almost anything within a certain size range,' Mr. Mattox said. Indeed, Deere has set up a group within the company to seek out defense, and other nontraditional business, to make use of its versatile facilities" (*New York Times,* 1983, p. 30).

The productivity increases of computerized manufacturing were enormous: "Deere's new factory, completed in 1981, stood it in good stead during the ensuing collapse in farm and construction equipment sales. It gave Deere the ability to make a profit while keeping production at 45% of capacity, a figure well below the national average. While its two major rivals, the International Harvester Company and Massey-Ferguson Ltd., lost hundreds of millions of dollars and skirted bankruptcy, Deere has remained profitable" (*New York Times,* 1983, p. 1).

MANUFACTURING DECISIONS

In general, manufacturing productivity depends on the efficiency and effectiveness of the technology of production—how cheaply and how well things are made. Sales depend on function, price, and quality.

Therefore, manufacturing ability directly affects corporate competitiveness through efficiency and quality. In the 1980s a renewed American respect for manufacturing competence was generated, partly due to Japanese competitiveness and competency in manufacturing and partly due to new manufacturing technology using computers and robots. For example, Steven Wheelwright and Robert Hayes noted: "The past several years have witnessed a growing awareness among American managers of the central importance to competitive success of first-rate competence in the work of production. At the top of many corporate agendas now rests the determination to boost productivity, product quality and new product innovation" (Wheelwright and Hayes, 1985, p. 99).

Wheelwright and Hayes also listed types of choices in manufacturing strategy. One must choose the facilities, equipment, and capacity for manufacturing, and the degree of integration of the production process. One must also choose how many parts and components to make internally and how much to purchase from vendors. One must also consider the organization of production, and the personnel.

Wheelwright and Hayes also pointed out that managerial strategies for manufacturing can be at various levels of sophistication, and they noted four levels. The first was simply "to minimize manufacturing's negative potential," the second "to achieve parity with competitors," the third "to provide credible support to the business strategy," and the fourth "to pursue a manufacturing base competitive advantage" (Wheelwright and Hayes, 1985, p. 100).

These levels reflect increasing determination to use manufacturing ability as a competitive advantage. At the lowest level, one simply plans to control production, but at the highest level one plans to beat competitors with a manufacturing advantage.

SOURCES OF MANUFACTURING COMPETITIVENESS

The competitive advantage from manufacturing ability comes from two sources: manufacturing technology and managerial integration. Manufacturing technology is the knowledge of the production processes. Managerial integration is the management system for planning and controlling manufacturing processes. In the 1980s, major technical progress was made in both areas. New technologies, centered around the computer, created a new stage of industrial revolution—which some called the "seventh" industrial revolution.

The original industrial revolution began in the eighteenth century when the new steam engines powered the spinning and weaving machinery in textile factories. Together with the earlier improvements in steel production (using coke), these began the age of steam and iron of the nineteenth century. Throughout that century and into the twentieth century, continuing revolutions occurred in industrial manufacturing techniques. For example, William Abernathy distinguished five more stages: (1) standardized products with interchangeable parts, (2) model variation in product lines, (3) updating of product lines through innovation, (4) use of parts suppliers, and (5) assembly-line manufacturing (*New York Times*, 1983, p. 1).

Around 1800, factories (such as Whitney's) made devices, including firearms, clocks, and watches, using interchangeable parts. Isaac M. Singer produced different sewing machines with the same mechanics but different cabinets. In the 1850s, Samuel Colt began to improve his revolvers as new technology made improved performance possible. Manufacturers, particularly in the bicycle and carriage industries, began to use suppliers for parts of their products. A fifth stage of manufacturing revolution was the mass production methods of Ford (introduced with the Model A in 1920): "Henry Ford, of course, is the symbol of the fifth stage of manufacturing, the uniting of man and machine on the assembly line, which transformed auto making from a craftsman's trade into something resembling a pipeline out of which flowed cars in great volume" (*New York Times*, 1983, p. 1).

In the late 1970s, a new stage began in revolutionizing manufacturing processes, centered on the computer. It was called computer-integrated manufacturing, or flexible manufacturing. In computer-integrated manufacturing (CIM), engineers could design new products on the computer. The computer could instruct the machining of parts of the product and the assembly of the product, while controlling the flow of materials to machining and assembly. Management could use computerized models of sales to control scheduling of production.

CIM was thus based on integrating several pieces of new technology:

1. Computer-aided design (CAD)
2. Computer-aided manufacturing (CAM)
3. Robotic assembly and automated materials handling
4. Manufacturing planning and scheduling

Computer-Aided Design

Computer-integrated manufacturing began with computer-aided design (CAD). Designing products on the computer is different, more efficient, and more effective than traditional engineering design (using the older tools of paper, pencil, and slide rule). There are many advantages, among which are (1) automatic three-dimensional perspective, (2) automatic simulation of operation, and (3) automatic instruction of machining and assembly.

What CAD looks like is a high-resolution video monitor, powerful computer, software programs for design and simulation, and communication of data. All the tools an engineer needs are in the software of the computer and displayed on the screen. The power of CAD is that it facilitates the creative design process, using pictures to communicate. (Since the right brain is spatial and synthetic, the CAD system augments the natural creative process of the engineer.) In addition, the CAD system provides a testing ability (within the computer using simulation software): "Donald D. Parker, a Fisher Body engineering executive says in praise of CAD: 'We do the design work on graphics and look at the results on graphics—all totally devoid of real parts to test. We can go through the whole process and have a good idea what the part is going to weigh, how strong it will be, how stiff, how well it will perform. We fix parts before the car is built' " (Bylinsky, 1981c, p. 106).

Computer-Aided Manufacturing

CAD is integrated into the manufacturing of parts through computer-aided manufacturing (CAM). CAM consists of the computer instructing machinery as to how to machine and assemble the parts to be manufactured. At first, CAM controlled lathes for turning metal from parts and drills for drilling holes and mills for milling metal from parts. Later, CAD was developed, and then efforts were made to link the software for design (CAD) with the software for manufacturing (CAM). Together, the combination (CAD/CAM) could design and control the machining of parts, all by the computer.

Robotics and Automated Materials Handling

Robots completed the computer-controlled automated factory. Materials were received and stored by computer control and robot handling. They were fetched and routed to manufacturing workstations, and moved between workstations, by robots under computer control. At workstations, parts were machined by robotic machinery and then assembled into products by robots.

By the early 1980s robots had been around for some time, but their intelligence was limited. Intelligence came from two sources: computer power to instruct the movement of robots, and sensors to allow the robot to perceive its environment. With the innovation of single-chip microprocessors in the 1970s, computer power for controlling robots began to arrive. Therefore, although the idea for industrial robots stems from the 1920s and 1930s (the term "robot" comes from a story of that period), robot technology had to await the innovation of microprocessors.

Sensing the environment was also a technical problem for the robot. This did not begin to be solved until the 1980s. First robot vision and then robot touch had to be developed. A robot that can think, see, and touch was called a "smart robot": "Widespread adoption of these [smart] capabilities could spark a population explosion in automatons. . . . There were 6,300 robots in the U.S. in 1982 out of a total 57,400 in the world—of which 31,900 call Japan their home. . . . Only 155 robots in U.S. factories are what could be considered intelligent robots having either tactile or vision capabilities. In contrast, Japan claims to have nearly 3000 robots with these capabilities" (Keller, 1983, p. 117).

Example: Productivity in the Factory of the Future

In the 1980s, early examples of flexible manufacturing showed the kind and scale of productivity gains made by the new technologies of flexible manufacturing systems (FMSs). In West Germany in 1983, the firm Messerschmitt-Bolkow-Blohm used FMS to build the wing structure for a fighter plane. The system reduced the lead time for the production of the plane parts from 30 months to 18 months. Required personnel were cut by 44%, floor space by 30%, parts-flow time by 25%, and capital investment costs by 9% (Jurgen, 1983, p. 36).

In another example, in Japan in 1983, Toshiba Tungaloy Co. used FMS units. Each unit handled 4000 different types of parts. This factory reduced the number of machine tools required by 88%, reduced personnel by 77%, reduced floor space by 76%, and reduced average processing time by 77% (Jurgen, 1983, p. 38).

One of the most dramatic examples of the new factory (factory of the future) in the 1980s was Fujitsu Fanuc's plant to produce robots—robots making robots. These were the sights of the new factory: "Yamazaki Machinery Works Ltd. operates a flexible automation plant near Nagoya that makes parts of computerized numerically controlled lathes and machining centers; the latter combine several metalworking machines and incorporate automatic tool changers. In the daytime 12 workers man the $20-million plant. At night only a lone watchman with a flashlight is on duty while the machines keep on working" (Bylinsky, 1981c, p. 112).

The productivity increases in that factory were enormous. Yamazaki estimated that in the old way, they would have required 215 workers and four times the machines and three months longer to turn out the same number of parts that the new factory made in three days. Moreover, they calculated that in the first five years of operation, the new factory will provide profits of $12 million, compared to the profits of $0.8 million that an old plant would have provided (Bylinsky, 1981c, p. 112).

Compare these figures in terms of productivity, capacity, and profits:

1. The workers are 12 instead of 215, a labor productivity increase of 1800%.
2. The plant produces as much in three days as a conventional plant would produce in three months, an increase in manufacturing capacity of 3000%.
3. The return on investment of $20 million averages $2.4 million annually (instead of $0.16 million annually), an increase of 1500%.

MANAGERIAL INTEGRATION OF FLEXIBLE MANUFACTURING SYSTEMS

The quickness of time and reduction of changeover costs through computer-integrated manufacturing provided the "flexible-manufacturing" capability. The strategic business impact of flexibility was important. A company with a flexible manufacturing system had more options as to which businesses it could pursue. Bela Gold emphasized the integrative importance of CIM: "Managers must understand that [CIM] is different because it is a 'contagious' technology—that is, it offers progressively greater benefits as it integrates more sectors of a plant's operations. . . ." (Gold, 1982, p. 92).

Managerial integration required the linking of technological innovation more closely with marketing opportunities. To utilize CIM and flexible manufacturing capabilities, management focused on identifying market opportunities. New products, quickly innovated, could be focused on market needs and niches and produced economically at many levels of lot sizes (from small to large).

Market modeling and sales forecasting were also required to be in the computer, since in the factory of the future, computers communicate with computers. A computerized manufacturing planing and scheduling (MPS) model began with a demographic and regional model of customers, needs, and applications. It included an analysis of competition in sales and products. It then assisted managers to plan market opportunities and to generate sales forecasts. Past sales forecasts were compared with actual sales to establish the reliability and accuracy of the model.

The sales forecast model generated a production schedule, which determined how many products of which kind were to be produced by what date. An optimization routine then planned and instructed the factory system on materials, production, inventory, and shipping.

Computerization of production also required computerization of marketing and sales strategies. This capability to enter and leave markets became an even more important factor in competition in the factory of the future: "The strategic implications for the manufacturer are truly staggering. Under hard automation the greatest economies were realized only at the most massive scales. But flexible automation makes similar economies available at a wide range of scales. A flexible automation system can turn out a small batch or even a single copy of a product as efficiently as a production line designed to turn out a million identical items. Enthusiasts of flexible automation refer to this capability as 'economy of scope' " (Bylinsky, 1981c, p. 114).

Manufacturers began to be able to cover more market niches: "As the new tools come increasingly into use, 'some companies will find themselves blind-sided by competitors they never imagined existed,' says Joseph D. Romano, a vice president at A.T. Kearney Inc., management consultants" (Bylinsky, 1981c, p. 114).

FLEXIBLE MANUFACTURING AND ORGANIZATIONAL CULTURE

Management and personnel emphasis in the factory of the future turned toward research and development, marketing responsiveness, market niches, product innovation, and service. New business ventures became increasingly important as the pace of business change increased. This implied a major change in corporate culture—toward a more closely interacting and integrated culture. Arnold Putnam summarized the changes in American manufacturing traditions in the 1980s:

> Since World War II, the United States has become a nation of manufacturing specialists. We have established a system to funnel every product through a fixed sequence of specialized tasks. A product moves from engineering development . . . to engineering detailing. Production engineering gets the product next. . . . Industrial engineering steps in to funish detailed routings and order necessary materials. Only then come production, assembly, inspection, and testing. In short, the venerable American tradition is to design first and do manufacturing engineering and quality control later. (Putnam, 1985, p. 139)

Computer-integrated manufacturing provided a means of integrating these functions into a simultaneously interacting system: "How can U.S. companies reduce the risk of design failure and the stiff cost of revamping programs, set realistic product launch dates, reduce engineering changes, and increase certainty about product quality? Managers may try to tackle these questions separately, but the notion of integrated manufacturing is an answer these all have in common" (Putnam, 1985, p. 139).

The development engineer and production engineer began to work together more earlier in product design, communicating through CAD computers. Engineers also began to work more closely with other types of personnel, such as marketing people. The organizational culture of the factory of the future moved from a sequential interaction of functions toward a simultaneous interaction of functions—the simultaneous organization.

SUMMARY

In any successful new venture, competitors will eventually force product competition on quality–price factors. Manufacturing strength should be envisioned from the begining of a new business venture and built up equally with other business functions as the venture grows. New manufacturing technologies, using computers, created a new stage of industrial revolution in the 1980s, reasserting the importance of manufacturing strategy and new product innovation.

Computer-integrated manufacturing was based on integrating several pieces of new technology: CAD, CAM and robots. The quickness of time and reduction of changeover costs in computer-integrated manufacturing gave rise to the "flexible-manufacturing" concept, with its "economy of scope." To utilize flexible manufacturing capabilities, management focused on identifying market opportunities and accurately forecasting sales. A company with a flexible manufacturing system had more options as to which businesses it could pursue. Management and personnel emphasis in the factory of the future turned toward research and development, marketing responsiveness, market niches, innovation, and service. Organizational culture emphasized simultaneous interaction of business functions.

REFLECTION

1. Consider a product with which you are familiar. How many product lines currently exist for the product, and what markets do they serve? Could markets be expanded for the product if it could be economically tailored to smaller niches? Could the industry currently producing these product lines attack complementary markets with flexible manufacturing capabilities?

FOR FURTHER READING

WHEELWRIGHT, STEVEN C., and ROBERT H. HAYES, *Restoring Our Competitive Edge: Competing through Manufacturing.* New York: Wiley, 1984.

CHAPTER FIFTEEN
CORPORATE RESEARCH

CENTRAL IDEAS

1. The corporate research laboratory and scientific technology
2. Organization of the central corporate laboratory
3. Objectives of corporate R&D
4. Corporate research function and product lifetimes
5. Relationships between research units

Example: The General Electric Research Laboratory

We have understood how technology is integrated into the corporation; we must next understand how technology is created through research. Early American managers believed in technological futures. In the beginning of the twentieth century, they created the world's first corporate research laboratories. These creations were of historic importance, because prior to 1900, the world had never experienced continuing technological change in the form that has become the hallmark of the twentieth century—steady and systematic.

An example of one of the first corporate research laboratories is the Research and Development Center of the General Electric Corporation, created in 1900. It still exists, located at a site overlooking the Mohawk River, on the outskirts of Schenectady, New York. There in 1982 the GE Center employed about 2100 people. GE's total research and development budget for that year was $1.5 billion, of which about 48% was funded from company sources and 52% sponsored by external contract. About $150 million of this was spent by the GE R&D center.

The General Electric Company traced its origin to the Edison Electric Light Company, which was established in 1878 to support the incandescent-light experiments of Thomas Edison. In 1900, GE had hired a young professor, Willis R. Whitney, to devote two days a week to research at GE's largest manufacturing works. At that time, Whitney was an assistant professor of chemistry at the Massachusetts Institute of Technology. GE's management had been considering strengthening the technological position of the company by starting a research laboratory. They offered its directorship to Whitney, and he accepted.

Whitney resigned from MIT, becoming director of one of the world's first industrial research laboratories. This turned out to be a typical pattern. Academically trained scientists, either fresh from a Ph.D. or early into their academic career, entered industrial research from the university. They created a pattern of industrial research using a scientific approach to technological development. This has been called "scientific technology."

The reason GE had created the center was the necessity for the young company to remain competitive in advanced products. In 1900, General Electric's principal business was electrical lighting, based on the inventions of Edison. The electric bulb then was made of a high-resistance carbon filament. However, newer inventions had made it technically obsolete.

One of these new inventions was the "glower" lamp, invented by Walther Nernst, a German chemist. This used a ceramic filament, heated to incandescence at a higher temperature. Another was the mercury vapor lamp, then being developed by Peter Cooper Hewitt, an American inventor. At that time, General Electric had not been exploring for alternative lamps. Yet its major competitor had—George Westinghouse had been supporting Cooper Hewitt's work and had obtained the American rights to Nernst's lamp.

Therefore, to remain competitive, General Electric established the Research and Development Center to develop new products. This stimulus was and is the basis for all corporate research—to maintain technological competitiveness in products and processes. The idea to create the laboratory came from both industrial leaders and scientific leaders.

Charles Steinmetz was employed by GE in electrical research. Steinmetz made major contributions to science and to electrical engineering in the theory of alternating currents. Steinmetz proposed a research laboratory for GE: "Charles Proteus Steinmetz had paid at least one visit to Cooper Hewitt's laboratory by mid-1900. His perception of the lighting threat it represented catalyzed his formal proposal for a laboratory focused on fundamental research, mainly in the field of lighting. His letter of September 21, 1900 to vice-president Edwin W. Rice, head of GE's manufacturing and engineering, specifically mentions mercury vapor and Nernst-type lamps as principal research targets" (Wise, 1980, p. 414).

GE's principal scientific employee had recognized the new technical threats to GE and alerted its management. This is one of the important functions of corporate research—to alert management to future technical threats (and to transform them into opportunities).

The key point in Steinmetz's proposal for a research laboratory was that the laboratory was to be kept separate from day-to-day production responsibilities. Two other GE technical leaders agreed with Steinmetz's proposal. One was a patent attorney, Albert G. Davis, and the other a consultant to GE, Elihu Thomson. Thomson had been a founder of one of GE's predecessor companies. He was a prolific inventor, and he was Rice's former teacher and long-time mentor.

Next, Edwin Rice, GE's manufacturing and engineering manager, secured the approval of GE's president, Charles Coffin. Rice and Davis then went to Boston to discuss the post of director with Whitney: "Rice recognized from the beginning that the concept of the laboratory had to be broader than mere support for GE's lighting business if he wished to recruit first-rate researchers. 'We all agreed it was to be a real scientific laboratory,' he wrote later. . . . Albert G. Davis [recalled] how anxious he had been to convince Whitney that 'industrialists . . . possessed scientific ideals' " (Wise, 1980, p. 414).

The historian Wise remarked about the importance of Whitney as a scientist in industry:

> He [Whitney] was not the first professional scientist to be employed in American industry—or even in General Electric. Nor was his laboratory the first established by that company or its predecessors. That honor must be reserved for Thomas Edison's Menlo Park. But Edison's focus was on invention. Whitney's effort marks a pioneering attempt by American industry to employ scientists in a new role—as 'industrial researchers.' . . .
> This laboratory succeeded because it created a new role for professional scientists—a blend of research freedom and practical usefulness not available before 1900. . . .
> Science and industry were not independent of one another in the United States before 1900. But their contacts then were more limited in scope, intermittent, and irregular than they are today. (Wise, 1980, p. 410)

It had been an imaginative concept—"a real scientific laboratory." Many of the firms (even in 1900) already had engineering departments to design and improve technical products. However, none had a corporate laboratory dedicated to the science behind the engineering. This organizational innovation was to change economic history. The establishment of corporate research laboratories provided the institutional basis for scientific technology. And throughout the twentieth century, the GE R&D Center succeeded in keeping GE a high-technology company: "Over the years, GE had consistently led all other companies in obtaining U.S. patents, becoming in 1979 the first firm in history to pass the 50,000th patent milestone" (General Electric, 1980, p. 22).

The first industrial research laboratories were created in the new technologies of the electrical and chemical industries. In addition to the GE example, other famous corporate laboratories created in the early twentieth century were the Bell Labs of AT&T, the DuPont laboratories, the Dow laboratory, GM's technical center, and many others. In American industry, technological innovation became an internal business function, using personnel trained in science but adapted to practical invention.

ORGANIZING THE CORPORATE LABORATORY

How should a corporate research laboratory be organized? It should be structured around the technological bases of current or future businesses of the company. The units of the organization can be formed around either fields of science and engineering or around markets and business areas.

For example, in 1982, the GE corporate laboratory was organized into four units: Chemical Science and Engineering, Electronics Science and Engineering, Energy Science and Engineering, and Materials Science and Engineering. This organization was based on the areas of science and engineering that provided the scientific base for GE technologies.

GE's corporate R&D lab was the central lab of a larger R&D effort. Each business division had an associated R&D laboratory forcused on its business lines. In GE, the corporate lab performed about 10% of GE's total R&D. There were in 1982 about 100 other labs, employing another 13,000 engineers and scientists. The difference between the corporate lab and the development labs was in a broader scope of technological expertize in the corporate laboratory and generally a longer-term business outlook. Since the central research laboratory is normally only one part of the overall R&D capability of the company, it must interact with other engineering groups and production divisions of the company. Strong and cooperative interaction is vital to encouraging practicality and implementation of corporate research.

As another example of R&D organization, in 1983, Honeywell had organized its research activities according to business areas: Corporate Technology Center, Solid State Electronics Division, Technology Strategy Center, Action Communication Systems Division, and SESA-Honeywell.

The Corporate Technology Center performed basic investigations in the disciplines related to the sensing and control functions needed for automation. The Solid State Electronics Division provided research and development of custom solid-state circuit and sensor designs, proprietary processes, and innovative packaging, along with high-volume manufacturing capacity. The Technology Strategy Center conducted research and development and demonstration of new technologies and product concepts to support businesses related to ergonomics, communications, sensors, controls, and productivity. The Action Communication Systems Division provided voice and message communications management systems. The SESA-Honeywell Communications unit was a software and telecommunications system company for the development of packet- and-message-switching technology. What can be seen in this example is that Honeywell organized its corporate research activities both into research centers and into new businesses which were research intensive as designers of custom systems.

Thus the organization of corporate research laboratories generally follows (1) disciplinary fields, (2) divisional business lines, or (3) mixtures of the two. What is the best form of laboratory organization? None, in any absolute sense, because all have advantages and limitations. The field-of-science organization of the laboratory encourages creativity but not practicality. The business-area organization encourages practicality but not creativity. What is essential is the integration of the research structure with the business divisions and activities of the company. An excellent corporate research laboratory should be both creative and practical. Major new product lines come from creativity, but only the kind of creativity that is focused on practical market needs. The problem of laboratory management is to encourage both the creativity and practicality of research.

One way to formalize this integration is in a matrix form. An example was the research organization of Dow-Corning in 1982. The personnel belonged to disciplinary units, while the research budgets belonged to business area units. To perform any R&D project thus required an agreement between managers of the personnel and business units to perform a project, in which the disciplinary units contributed people and the business units contributed money. A matrix form emphasizes the balancing of "market pull" from the perspective of the business units and "technology push" from the perspective of the disciplinary units.

OBJECTIVES OF CORPORATE R&D

Corporate research and development is the principal corporate asset for long-term technological competitiveness. Corporate research should be focused on maintaining existing businesses and on preparing the corporation for future businesses. For budgetary purposes, corporate research activities can be classified by the purpose of the research:

1. To support current businesses
2. To provide new business ventures
3. To explore possible new technology bases

The R&D projects grouped under the support of current businesses will have as objectives extending the product lifetimes of current products and lowering the costs of production of current products. In addition, other

R&D projects in this category should be creating new models of existing products. The R&D projects grouped under the new ventures will have as objectives creating new product lines which will allow the company to enter new businesses. The R&D projects grouped under exploratory research will have as objectives deepening and broadening of the existing and potentially new technology bases of the company.

FUNCTION OF
CORPORATE RESEARCH
AND PRODUCT LIFETIMES

The function of corporate research is to create and extend the lifetimes of the company's products. This is an essential function because all products have finite lifetimes (sometimes as short as two years and some as long as 100 years).

In times of new and rapidly changing technology, lifetimes tend to be short. In mature technologies, lifetimes tend to be long. A mature technology product may have a very long lifetime as long as no clearly superior technology emerges. But even in a long-lived product (such as Ivory Snow), periodic reformulations, variations in product lines, and changes in packaging provides some change in the product. To maintain a long-lived product, quality must be maintained equal to that of competing products, and cost reductions in production must be ahead or even with competitors.

An example of product lifetimes can be seen in the history of tire-cord material. Cotton thread began being used at the beginning of the nineteenth century and continued in use until market volume peaked in 1940. Cotton thread declined until 1955, after which it was no longer used in tires. This was due to the replacement of cotton thread in tires with rayon thread, beginning in 1940. For rayon thread, the market volume peaked in 1955, declining to 1970, and it was no longer used after 1975. Rayon's replacement was due to nylon thread, which was introduced into the tire market in 1948. The use of nylon thread for tires peaked in market volume in 1970. This was due to the innovation of polyester threads in tires in 1960 and to glass threads in tires in 1970. Thus as thread with superior strength and equal cost was introduced into the market, threads with lower strength lost tire market share, gradually being entirely replaced for that application. The product lifetime for tire threads averaged about 30 years, with a half-life to peak market volume from the time of introduction of about 15 years (Dewhurst, 1970).

Product lifetimes are dependent on two factors: technological obsolescence and product substitution. During the rapidly changing period of the linear portion of the technology S-curve, technological obsolescence occurs rapidly and product models have short lifetimes due to new models with improved technical performance. For example, in the 1960s and 1970s, IBM introduced new mainframe computers in 1964 (Model 360), in 1970 (Model 370), in 1977 (Model 303X), in 1979 (Models 38 and 4300 and 308X), and in 1983 (Model 4381), and each of these model generations was about a 100 to 200 per cent improvement over the previous models in terms of improved performance and price (Fraker, 1984).

In mature-technology industries (where technological change has focused primarily on process improvements), product lifetimes tend to be long—changed only by model variation to better target market niches, or by changes in fashion or packaging. Product lifetimes may be shortened by product substitution: for example, substitution of aluminum materials for iron materials or plastic materials for metals.

As product lifetimes age, changes in sales volume and profitability occur. First, sales will grow until (1) the market is saturated, or (2) competition limits market share for the product, or (3) product obsolesence occurs. At some time, sales for a company in a given product line will cease to grow and will eventually decline. At the point of decline, the firm should be planning the introduction of new products to maintain corporate cash flow.

For example, Figure 15.1 graphs an expected contribution of product

FIGURE 15.1 Products contribution to future profits.

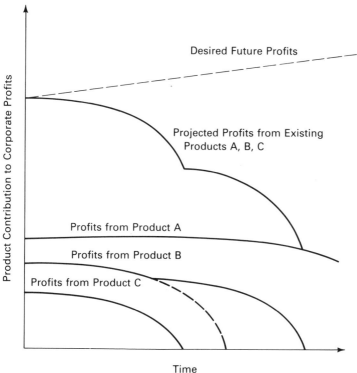

lines to the profits of a corporation over the expected lifetimes of products A, B, and C. In the chart, product C has been projected as having the shortest lifetime. Product B has been projected as having its lifetime extended by introduction of a major model improvement. Accordingly, the function of corporate research is to be creating new products to replace product C, and improving products such as B to extend their lifetimes. In addition, even with products such as A with expected long lifetimes, corporate research should be lowering the costs of production to maintain its profitability. Brian Twiss called this "gap analysis" of future profitability (Twiss, 1980, p. 40).

RELATIONSHIPS BETWEEN RESEARCH UNITS

The division of labor between the central corporate research laboratory and a research laboratory attached to individual business divisions lies in a broader technical scope and long-term business horizon for the central laboratory. This means that the category of R&D projects for the support of current businesses, or product or process improvement, will be performed principally by the divisional laboratories (attached to production divisions). Central research will become involved in these projects usually only when a business unit is confronted with a technical problem beyond the technical ability of the associated laboratory.

The corporate laboratory in the area of support of current businesses focuses on technological advance, which is common to several business units (e.g., semiconductor chips). R&D to provide new ventures that lie outside current business areas is also the responsibility of the corporate laboratory, as is exploratory research to create new technologies.

The exact balance of work between centralized corporate research and divisional research is a judgment each corporation makes and partially affects the culture of the organization—how forward looking, how technologically broad. Roland Schmitt, GE's senior vice president of corporate R&D in 1985, summarized the judgment: "The top managers of every diversified corporation must decide whether to leave the technical future of each business entirely in its own hands or to do some R&D at the corporate level. The first choice risks too much competition with the short-term demand for profits; the second, too little linkage with the needs of individual businesses" (Schmitt, 1985, p. 124). Schmitt also summarized several requirements for successful corporate research:

> A sufficiently high proportion of corporate funding to permit the centralized laboratory to define its own programs.

Close linkages with plans, strategies and programs of individual businesses as a basis of its own programs.

A thorough understanding of corporate goals and strategies to guide a balance of its programs among various businesses.

The need to hire the most outstanding people available and to link their compensation and advancement to technical performance, not to some later move into management (Schmitt, 1985, p. 124).

Schmitt also distinguished targeted research from generic research as a focus in corporate laboratories. Targeted research is goal oriented by a relatively well known market need. Generic research is goal oriented by a vision of advancing technological function and performance. In either instance, it is important for marketing personnel to be closely working with research personnel, in order to facilitate the linking of technological opportunity with market need (Schmitt, 1985). The key to successful corporate research is thus research autonomy and excellence, while being closely linked and focused on corporate businesses, goals, and strategies.

SUMMARY

The corporate research laboratory was a major historical creation by industry to maintain technological competitiveness over the long term. It has provided industry with a systematic way to continuously innovate and to maintain steady progress in technological advance. Corporate R&D in a large firm is usually organized into a central corporate laboratory and individual research laboratories attached to individual business units.

Organization of the central laboratory is based on two principles, the scientific base of corporate technologies and the business focus of research. The division of labor between the central corporate research laboratory and the research laboratory attached to individual business units lies in a broader technical scope and a longer-term business horizon for the corporate laboratory. The key to successful corporate research is research autonomy and excellence, while being closely linked and focused on corporate businesses, goals, and strategies.

The function of corporate research is to create and extend the lifetime of products. Corporate research should be focused on maintaining existing businesses and preparing the corporation for future businesses. This function can be carried out through generic or targeted research but should always be closely tied to potential market opportunities.

REFLECTION

1. **Obtain an annual report from several corporations with central research laboratories. Contact the corporations and request mate-**

rial describing their research organization. Compare corporate organizational structures with research organizational structures.

FOR FURTHER READING

FAGEN, M. D., ed., *A History of Engineering and Science in the Bell System: The Early Years (1875–1925)*. Murray Hill, N.J.: Bell Telephone Laboratories, 1975.

CHAPTER SIXTEEN
R&D PROJECTS

CENTRAL IDEAS

1. Stages of R&D projects
3. Relationship of costs to profits in successful R&D projects
3. Objectives of R&D projects

Example: Float-Glass Innovation

The activities in corporate research are R&D projects. We can illustrate an R&D project in the famous case of innovation in the glass industry by Pilkington. It was a radical process innovation which improved a major production process and expanded the market for plate glass.

In 1952, Pilkington was the major glass manufacturer in the United Kingdom, controlling 90% of that market. At that time, the world's glass industry was oligopolistic—dominated by a few large producers, with major shares of their respective national markets. The other major firms were:

In the United States, Libby-Owens-Ford (annual sales of about £187 million),
In Canada, PPG Industries (annual sales of £477 million),
In Japan, Asahi (annual sales of £265 million),
In France, Saint Gobian (annual sales of £436 million), and
In England, Pilkington (annual sales of £113 million). (Layton, 1972)

Up until 1952, flat, transparent glass was continuously manufactured in one of two ways. The first way was to draw glass upward as a ribbon from a bath of molten glass. This produced a low-cost, fire-polished glass, yet with considerable optical distortion, since the glass surface wavered as it was drawn upward. The alternate production method rolled cooling glass horizontally between rollers, which returned the glass to the right thickness. But the rollers left a marked surface, and extensive polishing and grinding was necessary to produce a transparent, polished surface. This gave flat glass with good optical properties but was very expensive, due to the labor, machine, and energy costs of the mechanical grinding and polishing.

A new production process for plate glass to reduce cost and improve quality would revolutionize the glass industry. Alastair Pilkington thought about this and had an idea for a clever invention. But invention is only one stage in research that results in technological innovation. Before continuing with the story, let us depict the general stages of R&D projects.

PROJECT STAGES

R&D projects tend to go through similar stages:

1. Basic research and invention
2. Applied research and functional prototype
3. Engineering prototype and testing
4. Production prototype and pilot production
5. Product testing and modification
6. Initial production and sales

Stages 1 to 3 are usually called "research," while stages 4 to 6 are called "development"—hence the term "research and development" (R&D).

Each stage of innovating a new product is expensive, with the expense increasing by an order of magnitude at each stage. The management decisions to continue from research to development are therefore very important. Overall, the expenses of modern industry for R&D were considerable. For example, in the United States in 1981, industrial expenditures for R&D were $49 billion. This represented about 1.7% of the national GNP in that year. Of this $49 billion, about 21% was for research and 78% for development (National Science Board/National Science Foundation, 1980).

Example: Pilkington's R&D Project

1. Invention   Alastair Pilkington was a cousin of the owning Pilkington family. He had first worked in the sheet-glass division, becoming familiar with the inexpensive method of glass production, drawing glass upward. He then became production manager of the plate-glass division and saw the very expensive process of grinding and polishing plate glass. His inventive mind began thinking of alternative ways of producing plate glass. He had the clever idea to float the molten glass out on a bed of molten metal. He chose tin as the metal, because it had a low enough melting point to remain molten as the glass solidified on it. Moreover, the tin could be kept free of oxide if the atmosphere were controlled (Layton, 1972).

The idea looked good; hopefully, it might produce plate-glass quality at sheet-glass cost. Alastair Pilkington presented his idea to his superior, the production director of the flat-glass division, who took the idea to the company's board. The board immediately saw the potentially vast economic return if the idea worked. The innovative situation was right—an inventive idea with market potential, a technically literate and strategically oriented board, and a management commitment to cut across organizational lines to get the research and development done.

2. Applied research and functional prototype   In 1952, a small project group of three people was created, Richard Barradell-Smith and two graduates, who reported to Alastair Pilkington. They built a small pilot plant, costing about £5000, that produced 10-inch-wide plates. They found, by good luck, that when glass cooled on the molten tin, it happened to be precisely 7 millimeters thick (due to a balance between the surface tensions and densities of the two immiscible liquids). Since 60% of the flat-glass trade was in 6-millimeter-thick glass, they could (by a little stretching of the glass ribbon as it cooled) reduce the natural 7-millimeter thickness to 6 millimeters.

3. Engineering prototype and testing   They then built a second pilot plant to produce 48-inch-wide plates (this was commercial size). It cost £100,000 (five times more than the first 10-inch machine). These two machines and their research took five years, until 1957. By then the research team thought they had perfected the technique enough to try a production-scale plant.

4. Production prototype and pilot-plant production   In 1957, the research team was expanded to eight people, with three graduates from different disciplines. The group was moved into the plate-glass factory and built a plant costing £1.4 million (14 times the cost of the engineering prototype).

The major purpose of research is to reduce technical risk before production-scale investment is committed. And the stages of the Pilkington project are generally true for any R&D project—invention, experimental-scale equipment, pilot-plant scale equipment, and production-scale equipment. It is also generally true that at each stage, the cost escalates by orders of magnitudes (£5000, £100,000, £1.4 million).

Problems! Solving problems is the essential feature of developmental research. For example, the researchers had to improve the control of the atmosphere to prevent oxidation of the tin. They had to flow the glass out smoothly onto the tin, then stretch it and pull it off. Never underestimate technical problems—they will always occur. Fortunately, technical problems are often solvable. For 14 months, from 1957 through 1958, 70,000 tons of unsalable glass was produced by the prototype production plant.

Then, suddenly, success! Salable glass was produced. Quickly the team refurbished the plant and were ready for production. but again, problems! Unsalable glass poured out. What was wrong? The development team analyzed the changes and discovered that the salable glass had been produced when a part of the apparatus was thought to be faulty—and, of course, they had corrected the fault. But the fault was not a fault—it had been correct! Accidents, sometimes happy accidents, happen in research. But now, at last, they understood the correct process, and they had developed the invention into a practical process.

5. Initial production and sales   In 1959, the plant went into commercial production. Another plant was built in 1962 and another converted in 1963. The total expenditure and time on the development and commercialization of the new process had cost £9 million over 10 years. Pilkington had innovated a commercial process to produce plate glass, at the inexpensive cost of sheet glass. They obtained worldwide patents on the valuable process.

What strategy should they choose for commercial exploitation of the innovation? Should they expand and try to take over the world market? Or should they license the process to international competitors, retaining their U.K. home market? The process was so radical, in improved quality and at lower cost, that no one could compete with them (without the new float-glass process). The choice was Pilkington's. We pause again in the story, to review the general form of costs and returns in R&D projects.

SALES VOLUMES AND PROFITABILITY IN PRODUCT LIFETIMES

Another important concept conerning the forms of R&D projects is the relationship of costs to profits in successful projects. The general form is similar for any successful R&D project, and has been called the R&D project lifetime chart, shown in Figure 16.1.

After commercial production of a new product or process (as in the case of the float-glass innovation), the innovative company can begin recovering its investment. Initially, cash flow in a new product line is negative because of the research and development costs. In the Pilkington example, the accumulated costs were £5000 plus £100,000 plus £1,400,000. When the new product is successful in the market, sales begin to return profits, and the cash flow begins to climb toward the positive region. After sufficient

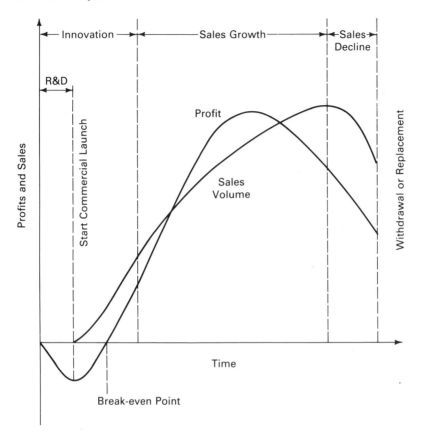

FIGURE 16.1   Product lifetime: typical pattern.

sales, profits will cross the line for a positive return on investment. This point is called the "break-even point"; the time from R&D project initiation to this point is called the "break-even time" (Twiss, 1980, p. 41).

Financially, the break-even time is important, because the time to break even multiplied by the average negative cash flow represents an income loss to the company. In the case of the Pilkington float-glass process, the break-even time was 10 years and the accumulated R&D and plant construction costs to reach that point were £9 million.

Example: Pilkington Profits

After the break-even time is attained, further profitability can be estimated. It was these kinds of estimates that influenced Pilkington's strategy.

Pilkington decided to license the new process to competitors in other countries, rather than trying to expand internationally. Several reasons went into that decision: the very great amount of capital required for worldwide expansion, the location needs for plants (near supplies of iron-free sand, sources of soda ash, quarries for dolomite and limestone, and cheap fuel), and the oligopolistic traditions of nationally oriented industries.

Thus in 1959, Pilkington informed all major glass producers in the Western world that it was prepared to license the process. All producers purchased licenses, including Czechoslovakian and Soviet manufacturers. In the 10 years from 1959 to 1969 following the commercial introduction of the float-glass process to Pilkington, the license revenue exceeded £25 million. It provided Pilkington with a third of the company's profits, with the other two-thirds coming from their production and sale of plate glass produced by the new process.

OBJECTIVES OF R&D PROJECTS

R&D projects in corporate research create and extend the lifetimes of corporate products, avoiding technological obsolesence of businesses. Extending product lifetimes can be done by:

1. Improving the production processes to lower production costs and increase quality
2. Upgrading and improving current product models
3. Creating next-generation product models

We have seen in the Pilkington example an R&D project that improved the production process. Although the product model was not altered, the lowering of production costs allowed expansion of the plate-glass market by substituting for glass of inferior optical properties.

SUMMARY

R&D projects, either for process innovation or for product innovation, tend to go through similar phases. Each phase increases in cost by an order of magnitude. When initial sales begin, profitability of the new product or process begins to turn positive. R&D projects in corporate research create and extend the lifetimes of corporate products, avoiding technological obsolesence of businesses. Extending product lifetimes can be done by improving production processes, improving product models, and creating next-generation product models.

REFLECTION

1. Find case studies of R&D projects and list the problems and costs as the research progressed into a commercial product. How long did the project take?

FOR FURTHER READING

TWISS, BRIAN,   *Managing Technological Innovation.* Harlow, Essex, England: Longman Group, 1980.

CHAPTER SEVENTEEN
PRODUCTION
COSTS AND R&D

CENTRAL IDEAS

1. Production learning curve
2. Market share and profit margins
3. Production costs and pricing strategy

Example: Demise of Texas Instruments' Home Computer

Timely and continuous lowering of the costs of production is essential for survival against competition. An example of losing a whole business line through failure to lower production costs rapidly enough can be seen early days of the home computer industry. In the beginning of the 1980s, a competitor's learning curve killed Texas Instruments' first foray into the home computer market—the ill-fated TI 99/4A.

In the 1970s, Texas Instruments was a leading producer of semiconductor chips. It had produced a microprocessor on a chip and created one of the early home computers, which had been improved and sold in 1980 as the model TI 99/4A. TI thought it had a technically better home computer than competitors since it had a 16-bit processor compared to the competition's 8-bit processors. By 1981, the first set of major competitors in the new home computer market were lined up as follows: Apple, Commodore, Tandy, Texas Instruments, Atari, and Sinclair Timex. The market had divided by 1981 between Apple as leader, Tandy second, Sinclair Timex third, with Atari fourth, Texas Instruments fifth, and Commodore a weak sixth (Nocera, 1984).

At Texas Instruments, the head of marketing in TI's home computer division had been aggressively expanding TI's retailing network for the 99/4A. But he saw the 99/4A sitting on retail shelves beside the Vic 20 (the 99/4A was priced at $300 against the Vic's price of $250). Moreover, since the average consumer then did not appreciate the difference between 16- and 8-bit processors, they bought the cheaper product.

The Vic 20 was a product of Commodore. Jack Tramiel had founded Commodore Business Machines in 1955, making typewriters and adding machines. In the late 1960s, Commodore began manufacturing the then new electronic calculators. By 1977, calculator prices had dropped from the thousand-dollar range to the few-dollar range. Commodore began making personal computers (Mace, 1984).

Tramiel observed the price sensitivity of the home computer market by watching the rapidly growing sales of the Sinclair at $100 (far below the $1000 price of other home computers). The learning-curve strategy was clear to him. Produce a product equivalent to the leaders but priced down toward $100 rather than $1000. To do so, he would have to greatly reduce production costs. This could be done by creating new models, designed to be cheaply produced. Earlier, Tramiel had purchased a troubled semiconductor chip maker, MOS Technology. Since Commodore now manufactured its own computer chips, Tramiel had a cost advantage in vertical integration (which at that time, only Texas Instruments also had). In 1981, Tramiel had attacked, launching the Vic 20, a small memory home computer with a real keyboard. It sold well. Tramiel knew that he was on the right marketing track (Nulty, 1984).

What was Texas Instruments to do to respond to Tramiel's aggressive pricing of the Vic 20? It would take TI at least a year to design a new computer that could be produced to sell for less than the Vic 20. Commodore had a year's lead time. TI's management decided to take a gamble. On September 1, 1982, TI announced a rebate which effectively priced the 99/4A at $199—$50 less than the Vic 20. This cut TI's profit margins on the 99/4A in half. A price war began.

Initially, the gamble worked. From September through December, the 99/4A sold like hotcakes. TI assembly lines produced 150,000 computers a month. The retail network was up to 12,000 stores. The 99/4A was outselling the Vic 20 by three to one. By December 1982, the TI 99/4A was the best-selling home computer in the country. Within four months, the TI home computer business had been transformed from a $20 million business to a $200 million business. Texas Instruments' managers felt good. They had started a crash program for an even cheaper computer (the TI 99/2) to wipe out Commodore's advantage and an advanced computer for the range $500 to $1000 (the TI/8).

However, back at Commodore new product development was moving even faster. In 1981, Albert J. Charpentier headed the LSI (large-scale integration) group of Commodore's MOS Technology division. He had proposed to produce "state-of-the-art video and sound chips for the world's next great video game." Charpentier's boss, Charles Winterable, said to go ahead. In November 1981, the new chip was ready and they showed it to Tramiel (Perry and Wallich, 1985, p. 48).

Tramiel liked it but told them to put it, instead, into a new home computer. He wanted it to have a 64K memory (since these new chips were on the market), and he wanted it ready for announcement at the Consumer Electronics Show in Las Vegas, January 1982. It was a gamble that worked: "What surprised the rest of the home computer industry most . . . was the introductory price of the Commodore 64: $595 . . ." (Perry and Wallich, 1985, p. 48).

That January, the TI personnel went to Las Vegas for the trade show. They felt good, not seeing anything with a 16-bit processor to technically challenge the 99/4A (or its successor, the 99/8), yet not appreciating the pricing significance of the Commodore 64: "On the last day of the show, the TI crew went out on the town and wound up in a Las Vegas bar, where they started drinking tequila. They talked about the show and the products and how it looked like there was nothing on the horizon that might stop the 99/4A or 99/8 and the 99/2 when they were ready. 'Some guy from Apple told me they've sold 200,000 computers in schools,' one man said. 'I told him we put out more than that in a month.' Everybody roared" (Nocera, 1984, p. 64).

Then the cruel blows began. After the show, Commodore cut the price of the Vic 20 to $125. TI had to match that price, but by then the 99/4A profit margin was zero. In April, Commodore lowered the price to $99 (at which Commodore could still make money). Sales of the 99/4A again dropped. TI also cut the 99/4A price to $99 to get the sales going again. At that price, the 99/4A lost money: "Prices of home computers—those toylike electronic boxes that hook up to TV sets—have fallen 75% in 18 months. The shock wave has shaken the industry's pecking order. Texas Instruments and Warner Communications, Atari's owner, have suffered stunning losses. But Commodore International's first-half profits should more than double" (Uttal, 1983a, p. 105).

Throughout 1982 and 1983, TI's home computer division lost money. In the second quarter of 1983, the TI home computer division lost $119 million. TI canceled the 99/2, for it was too expensive for the $99 price. The only hope left was the 99/8 model to succeed the 99/4A. TI took it the summer 1983 consumer electronics trade show, to show it off. But they didn't show it. They looked at the competition. The price of the Commodore 64 was declining. Rumors about Apple's new computers and an IBM PC Jr abounded. After the show, meetings were held at TI to discuss the future of the TI 99/8: "At the last of them, Fred Bucy got in front of everyone and said, 'I don't think this product can make any money. Does anyone disagree?' No one did. The 99/8 was dead" (Nocera, 1984, p. 65).

Texas Instruments announced that it was withdrawing from the home computer market and left. All through 1983 and on into the 1984 and 1985,

Commodore made money and came to dominate the home computer market in the middle 1980s. They had won the dominant market share in that price war because they had designed a second-generation product line with improved performance but at a lower production costs. At introduction, the Commodore 64 had a production cost of $135, then two or three times below competitors' costs. By 1985, the long-running product had production costs reduced to between $35 and $50 (Perry and Wallich, 1985).

THE PRODUCTION
LEARNING CURVE

This example illustrated a general and important lesson. Production costs of new products usually decline over time, due to process and product improvement. In any new product line, initial production costs are usually much higher than later production costs. This is due to the corporation learning how to make the product better and more cheaply. The effect of this on production costs has been called the "production learning curve." The typical pattern of cost reduction is shown in Figure 17.1: beginning high and decreasing exponentially, then leveling off.

For example, TI's home computer was priced high because of the high cost of using many chips to make up the computer. Chip cost, board size,

FIGURE 17.1
Learning curve in production processes. (Unit costs of production decline from learning how to make the product better, more cheaply.)

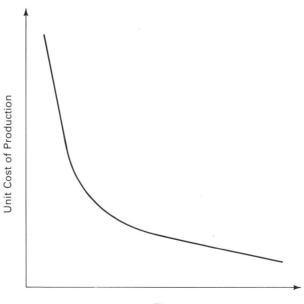

assembly costs, and peripheral costs—all went into the cost of the computer. Commodore decreased the number of chips in their new computer (through a new VLSI chip which integrated several of the older chips). In addition, Commodore used a newer 64K chip for memory, thus also reducing the number of memory chips. Commodore could sell their new computer for less because it was designed to be produced at lower cost, using far fewer chips.

All new products based on new technologies have initially high per unit production costs because of (1) large R&D and plant investment costs, (2) small volumes of initial production, and (3) inefficiencies in the production processes and in product design. For a successful product, over time, these factors improve. Investment capital becomes amortized over larger production volumes. The increasingly larger volume of production also lowers per unit overhead charges. Innovations and improvements in production processes create more efficient production procedures. Later-generation product models are designed to lower production costs.

MARKET SHARE AND
PROFIT MARGINS

In addition to productivity improvement, lowered production costs are attained by economies of scale in manufacturing. However, large market share may not always translate into large profits if the profit margin of the sales is small. Many corporations have examined their businesses in light of their return on investment and market share. They plotted these factors in a graph, which showed a general "U" shape, as illustrated in Figure 17.2. Business strategy was then expressed as being in one of three positions on the graph: at the right, center, or left (Kiechell, 1981).

The most desirable position would be on the right side with high volume and large profit margin—together producing large profits. However, only a stongly protected patented product (such as the early Xerox patent monopoly) can create such a position or an industrial cartel. The center position is known as the "commodity" position. In this position, many competitors compete with similar products at the lowest possible price, which keeps margins low and market shares small. Generally, older technology industries create commodity markets because technical knowledge is widespread, and this allows many competitors to enter the industry (limited only by the costs of entry). Moreover, the volume of the market is large enough to encourage entry. The left position on the curve is characterized by low volume but a large profit margin. It is attained with products that are (1) luxury or (2) high technology.

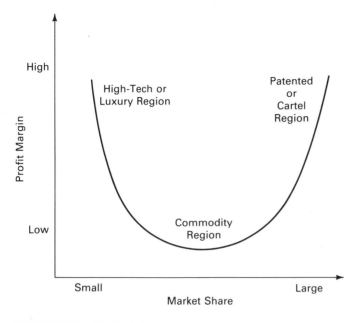

FIGURE 17.2   Market niche strategy curve.

PRODUCTION COSTS AND PRICING STRATEGY

As a kind of "strategic planning" in the 1970s, many companies sought the high-tech, low volume, high-profit-margin corner. However, that strategy began to be seriously challenged in the same period. There was a different price strategy—high technology but quickly lower prices, by lowering production costs in anticipation of large market volumes.

Figure 17.3 compares two pricing strategies, conservative and aggressive, superimposed on the cost-reduction learning curve. The conservative pricing strategy is to keep prices up, restricing sales growth but rapidly recovering R&D investment costs. Then competition enters and cuts prices. In contrast, the aggressive strategy is to lower prices in anticipation of lowered production costs, thereby discouraging future entering competition and eventually locking others out of the market.

Commodore had used this pricing strategy in their Vic 20 and Commodore 64 models. Others have used this aggressive strategy: "Japan adopted the concept as a basic strategy . . . and targeted steel, automobiles, consumer electronics microchips, and so forth, as priority areas. . . . This is a very astute strategy . . . it is limited to areas where there are large volume markets, and where there is long enough time period to recapture . . . nega-

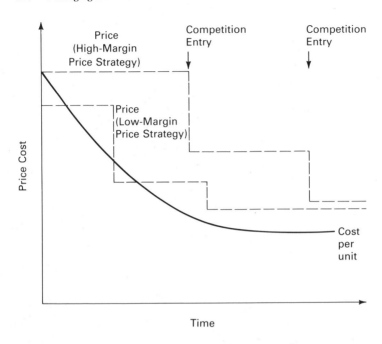

FIGURE 17.3 High-tech and margin price strategies.

tive cash flow. . . . Economies of scale then become the dominant factor, even over the best technology" (Merrifield, 1982).

The entry into a new high-technology market is restricted because knowledge is new and not widely known. Products then are high priced because sales volume is small and production costs high. Yet if the price is held there too long, other competitors can enter with "me-too" technology products, since high profit margins and growing markets provide the competitive incentive. However, if prices are reduced in anticipation of production costs being reduced (through the learning curve of industrial production), (1) competition has less incentive to enter, and (2) competitors who have not moved down that learning curve will incure losses. The strategic trick is for the technology innovator to move down the production learning curve faster than competitors.

SUMMARY

The production learning curve summarizes the general knowledge that experience in production lowers costs of production over time and improves product quality. Pricing strategies should take the learning curve into strategic consideration. A conservative strategy will maintain high prices and a large margin to recover investment more rapidly. An aggressive strategy will decrease prices in anticipation of production costs falling. The conservative strategy invites competition to enter under the shelter of the high margins and invited by the growing market. The aggressive strategy forces competitors to pay a higher price for entry and limits competition.

REFLECTION

1. Choose a major device (such as automobiles or computers), and chart the production costs of one of its product lines over time. What is the shape of the curve? How long did it take to slow to a gradual decrease? Has it flattened off?

FOR FURTHER READING

ABERNATHY, W. J., *The Productivity Dilemma*, Baltimore, Md.: Johns Hopkins University Press, 1978.

CHAPTER EIGHTEEN
MANAGING RESEARCH
PROJECTS

CENTRAL IDEAS

1. Performance parameters of research projects
2. Monitoring performance, cost, and time
3. Project structure
4. Project personnel

Example: Managing the Development of the Wang Word Processor

Creating new products and lowering production costs occur in R&D projects. Management of R&D projects requires attention to several aspects: objectives, tasks, schedule, and personnel. We can illustrate these aspects through an example of a successfully managed R&D project which innovated the modern word processor. The first word processors were awkward things, recording on magnetic tape and displaying only a few words. This required a typist to be very clever and calculating. One had to be clever to calculate where to find a sentence to be corrected. The makers of these first-generation word processors were big companies such as IBM and Xerox, and a small company named Wang.

On September 28, 1975, An Wang held a strategy meeting with three of his employees at Wang Laboratories. He said he was worried that their current word processor, which they had introduced in 1971, was facing stiff competition from big firms: IBM, Burroughs, and Xerox. He pointed out that the Wang word processor had captured only 3% of sales, whereas IBM had 75% of sales. The problem was how to fight, survive, and prosper in the word-processor market (Shackil, 1981).

IBM and Xerox dominated the office markets with their typewriters and copiers. Wang wanted to look into the future, gazing on the second generation of word processors (even though the first generation was only four years old). Wang understood that in a radically new product generation, a small company has a chance to compete with big companies if the small company offers a technologically superior product at a competitive price. In the time required for competitors to "catch up" the small company can establish significant market share and become a bigger company.

At his strategy meeting, Wang announced that the time was ripe for a major technological advance in word processors. They would focus on performance—a word processor that would be easy to learn and use: "As ideas bounced from one specialist to another at the meeting, the broad outlines of a new word processor began to take shape. . . . It should have greater memory. . . . It should be simpler to use. The key to meeting these needs, the participants agreed, would be the [new] microprocessors" (Shackil, 1981, p. 29).

PROJECT OBJECTIVES, TASKS, AND BUDGETS

In managing an R&D projet, the first steps are to define the objectives of the project and schedule the tasks. Objectives are defined in terms of performance parameters. R&D projects are intended to create new products or processes that provide function and performance superior to those of existing products or processes. Function means what a product can do. Performance means how well the product does it. All products and processes can be viewed as types of tools; and in evaluating any tool, one can measure how effectively and efficiently the tool accomplishes the end.

The first managerial task in any R&D project is thus to define measures of performance for the intended product (or process). R&D progress can then be measured in terms of the degree of attainment of desired performance. For example, in Wang's new word processor, the performance parameters were the speed and easiness with which secretaries could type and alter letters and manuscripts on the word processor.

After defining goals and performance parameters for an R&D project, the next thing is to lay out project tasks and targets for completion—structuring the project. The task schedule can then be presented as a Gantt (or milestone) chart or as a PERT chart. A Gantt chart is a list of tasks to be accomplished, arranged vertically, with the time to completion listed horizontally (see Figure 18.1a). A PERT chart also depicts the types of tasks to be accomplished (and the order and schedule for their completion, as in the Gantt or milestone chart), but it adds information about the probability of success for each task (see Figure 18.1b).

Some research tasks are more familiar than other research tasks, be-

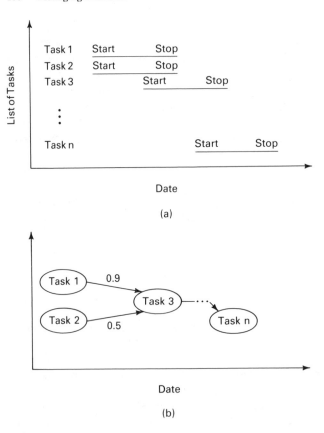

FIGURE 18.1 (a) Gantt chart: (b) PERT chart.

cause they have been done before on other projects. For example, adapting previously written software from an earlier project to a new project is a more familiar task than writing a wholly new piece of software. Consequently, the probability of completing the task successfully in the time scheduled will be higher for the more familiar task than for the unfamiliar task. The PERT chart lists the probabilities of completing the tasks as scheduled. Thus tasks of potentially greater problems can be identified and monitored in a PERT chart description of a project. This can be a great advantage in a complex project, having many tasks of varying degrees of novelty to be completed.

As an accompaniment to any task schedule for an R&D project, it is also important to create a planned budget. The budget should be detailed as to personnel costs, equipment and materials, and overhead costs, laid out according to the schedule.

Example: Timing and Costs in the Wang Project

Technology leadership would create the competitive advantage for Wang; and correct timing was imperative for the company to benefit. Wang set the goal of developing the new machine in time to introduce it at the next International Word Processing Show in New York on June 21, 1976. This gave them nine months in which to design and create the machine. It was a very short time.

Wang's plan was to put the new microprocessors into the different parts of a word processor—entry keyboard, memory, printer—in order to distribute intelligence and increase performance. The inexpensive microprocessor on a chip provided the ability to program sophisticated control in any part of a complicated system. Wang's product would consist of several workstations, using a common memory storage device and a common printer. Each workstation would be a smart terminal, that is, a video display with keyboard, incorporating a microprocessor, for entering and editing text. The microprocessors also provided the individual workstations with a shared memory and printing system. In computer jargon, this use of microprocessors is called "distributed intelligence."

Wang's project was primarily a system design problem—distributed intelligence applied to word processing. Wang planned on purchasing components and assembling them into a word-processing system. Therefore, the central tasks of the R&D project were system design and creation of controlling software for the system. The cost of the project was primarily in personnel, and such talents already existed in the company. Wang had the cash flow to carry the project to completion. The schedule was aimed toward the New York show.

MONITORING R&D
PROJECT PROGRESS

Monitoring the progress of R&D projects requires attention to progress in performance, meeting deadlines, and cost. As illustrated in Figure 18.2, progress in R&D projects can be watched by graphing (1) performance parameters against time, (2) performance parameters against cost, and (3) cumulative cost against time (Twiss, 1980).

Performance can usually be improved by putting more research effort into a problem (as long as one is not in the natural-limits region of the technology S-curve). Therefore, in any R&D project, the level of performance attained is partly a function of the level of effort and length of time. Following the progress in performance as time elapses allows the manager to judge (1) whether sufficient performance will be attained by the targeted date, and (2) when to cut off development.

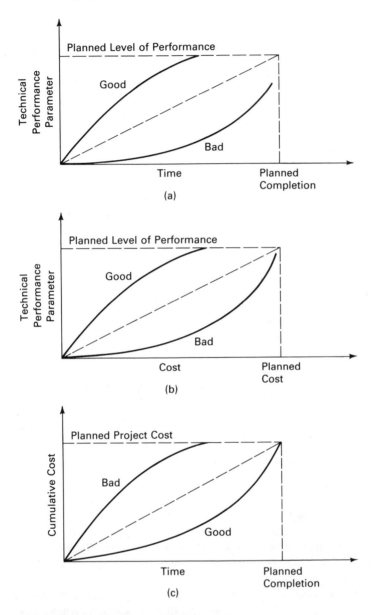

FIGURE 18.2   Monitoring R&D projects.

   Attaining higher levels of performance also costs more in resources as well as time. Charting the performance improvement against cost allows the manager to judge whether further performance improvement will be worth the cost to get it. Since each R&D project has a research budget, it is also important to watch the cumulative costs against time, to see if the project can be completed within budget. Perfection may be wished but at some point performance matching the desired markets will be attained, and at this point, the project should move into a product. It is an important management judgment about what level of performance is desirable and competitive for a given market.

Example: Personnel in the Wang Project

An Wang provided both technical and managerial leadership. Wang had once been a professor at the Massachusetts Institute of Technology. He had invented an important advance in computer memory which made larger computers possible in the 1950s—the magnetic-core memory. Wang later established his own company to manufacture calculators, using transistors. After the Japanese invaded this market, Wang began to build word processors. Wang is one of those scientist-inventor-entrepreneurs, such as Alexander Graham Bell, who occur in the history of technology. Such people have a keen insight for both technical opportunities and market needs.

Wang worked hard and expected his employees to work hard. They worked to meet the deadline. One of the project members, Edward Wild, remembers: "We worked until 10 o'clock almost every weekday, many Saturdays, and some Sundays. I can remember eating lots of McDonald's hamburgers during those long hours" (Shackil, 1981, p. 30).

Problems abounded in the R&D project. In fact, the experience in any R&D project can been seen as a series of problem-solving activities. For example, one of the first designs the Wang project team considered used a single memory shared by two workstations. But a problem occurred in trying to assign priorities for access to the memory by either of the stations. Information could not be transferred quickly enough from microprocessors to the shared memory to avoid tying up one or the other workstations. How to solve that problem? Redesign! A second design provided local memory together with a local microprocessor for each workstation.

New ideas are never exactly right, and researchers in R&D projects must try and try again. Hard work, problem solving, creativity, and persistence—the ingredients of a successful R&D team. All through the difficulties, the project leadership must keep the focus on innovative ideas: "Discouraged by their first attempt at a distributed processing scheme, the designers turned to a system with all the microprocessors housed in one unit, which would do all the processing for the work stations that would surround it. But Dr. Wang rejected the idea. 'I realized at that time that a distributed-data-processing configuration would be more powerful and flexible from a system point of view" (Shackil, 1981, p. 31).

In any technological system, certain design principles are fundamental to distinguishing one generation from another. It is design principles of this sort that eventually lead to dominant designs that characterize a product generation—in this case, distributed intelligence. In fact, this idea was the key concept in the new office automation technology.

There were lots of problems for the Wang team:

> Every new design has its share of 'war' stories, and even though this system's architecture was relatively simple, the designers' unfamiliarity with microprocessor-based designs did generate some new headaches.
> There were microprocessor documentation problems. . . .
> There were elusive system problems. . . .
> Another problem that arose later on concerned the allocation of space on the rigid disk while a read or write was going on . . . (Shackil, 1981, p. 31).

Successful R&D project stories have the same plot: a good idea for an innovative product to beat out competitors; creation of the project team; problems, blood, sweat, and tears; problems and more problems; and finally, success: "The opposition was caught flat-footed. Wang leapfrogged IBM in word-processor sales. From being a nobody, the company shot up to capture more than 50% of the dedicated word-processor market" (Shackil, 1981, p. 29).

Introduced in 1977, sales began at $12 million, rose to $21 million in 1978, then to $63 million, $130 million, and $160 million. Wang had used technological leadership to leapfrog the competition with a second generation of word processors, using significantly new design principles in distributed processing, thereby capturing the market and transforming a small company into a large company. Technology leadership linked to market leadership is a powerful business combination.

PERSONNEL IN AN R&D PROJECT

Technical excellence and creative ability for invention and problem solving by technical personnel are the essential and most important features of any R&D group. R&D projects and technical progress are only as good as the ideas and technical skills of the personnel. While it is important to keep technical creativity focused on business goals and aimed toward meeting performance goals toward time and cost constraints, no decisions by management should ever discourage the primary emphasis of R&D personnel toward technical excellence and creativity. An R&D project, although meeting its time and cost constraints with but mediocre technical performance, is not worth the time and cost.

Since an R&D project is a team effort (composed of a project leader and technical personnel), the project leader must provide both technical and managerial leadership. Accordingly, R&D project leaders are technical personnel who have first demonstrated outstanding technical ability and then demonstrated managerial ability.

For example, in a study on management control of projects, McDonough and Kinnunen compared formal and nonformal monitoring of project progress and found that some personal monitoring of projects by management was important in order to learn quickly about any problems that may have arisen. They emphasized the importance of having project leaders who were not only technically competent but also had a strong business sense, in order to judge the importance of balancing technical refinement against commercial focusing of the projects (McDonough and Kinnunen, 1984).

Some R&D organizations use matrix management to organize projects, with project budgets under business area management and personnel under scientific and engineering discipline management. William Wall, in studying this form of project management, emphasized the importance of using monitoring information to integrate the two managements from the business areas and technical disciplines (Wall, 1984).

An important attitude for management to cultivate in R&D projects is esprit—group enthusiasm and commitment to achieving technical success (within the time and budget constraints of the project). A good leader generates a commitment to both hard work and to quality, creative work—the pride of the research group.

SUMMARY

Managing R&D projects requires attention to performance, timing, cost, and personnel. Performance is the measure of a product or process to accomplish a specific function or application and how well it accomplishes the function or application. The performance parameters must be defined for an R&D project in order to determine how successfully the goals of the project are attained.

Progress in R&D projects can be watched by monitoring: (1) technical-performance parameters against time, (2) performance parameters against cost, and (3) cumulative cost against time. Timing is important to the success of a project, since lead time created from timely innovation provides a competitive advantage. Milestone and PERT charts are useful in identifying the necessary tasks and sequencing to accomplish the R&D project. Costs of the project are essential to its commercial success, for R&D costs must be recovered as part of the investment costs in the new product or process. Personnel are also critical parts of any R&D project, since the talents, creativity, dedication, and problem-solving ability of the personnel are essential to the success of any R&D project.

REFLECTION

1. Examine some of the R&D administration literature and try to find case studies in the management of R&D projects. A good journal to try is *IEEE Spectrum.* Write up a summary of the project tasks and problems in completing the project.

FOR FURTHER READING

BEATTIE, C. J., and R. D. READER,   *Quantitative Management in R&D,* London: Chapman & Hall, 1971.
KIDDER, TRACY.   *The Soul of a New Machine.* New York: Avon Books, 1981.

CHAPTER NINETEEN
RESEARCH PERSONNEL

Central Ideas

1. Careers of research personnel in industry
2. Industrial research values and academic research values

Example: William Coolidge as an Industrial Scientist at GE

As people in any part of a business make the organization, so do research people make the laboratory. In corporate research, the personnel are scientists, engineers, and technicians. What makes managing these people a bit different from managing other personnel in the corporation is the need to balance the processes of business against the processes of research. An example of an outstanding industrial scientist was William Coolidge, who became the second director of the General Electric Research Laboratory.

As a young scientist at GE, Coolidge made major contributions to GE's survival and business future. Later he headed the laboratory during some of its most difficult years, the depression of the 1930s. Coolidge exemplified the nice balance that makes a good researcher—creativity in research but focused on business.

Coolidge had grown up as the son of a farmer and a shoe factory worker. He had attended a one-room elementary school and a small high school. An outstanding student, he had gone on to college, which was very unusual in the late nineteenth century. In 1891, Coolidge enrolled in the new electrical engineering program at MIT (Wolff, 1984).

In the late nineteenth century the electrical industry comprised electric lights, telegraph, and telephone, and these were high tech. Engineers who knew how to work with electricity were a new kind of technical person, and they had to be trained. In 1882, MIT had begun the first electrical engineering program in America. Coolidge graduated from this program and decided on a scientific career.

But science required a research degree. In the late nineteenth century few Ph.D. programs existed in America, and most of the early American scientists went to Europe for their graduate training. Coolidge went to Germany and returned in 1905 with a doctorate from the University of Leipzig. He was $4000 in debt for his graduate education. He took a position at MIT as an assistant to Arthur Noyes (a notable American scientist). The pay was $1500 a year.

We recall that the GE laboratory was one of the first of the new corporate research laboratories and that Whitney, hired from the Massachusetts Institute of Technology, was the first director. When Whitney was a chemistry professor at MIT, he had taught chemistry to the young Coolidge. Afterward, Whitney remembered the promising student and offered him a job at GE at a salary of $3000. This was double Coolidge's salary at MIT. The money eased Coolidge's mind about his debts, yet he worried whether he could conduct scientific research in industry. Coolidge went to work in a three-story brick building at GE's facility in Schenectady, New York. His fears about not being able to do exciting research were quickly laid to rest: "Dr. Whitney had already successfully transplanted a lot of academic atmosphere from MIT to the new laboratory. . . . The misgivings I had about the transfer all proved to be unfounded" (Wolff, 1984, p. 81).

We recall that General Electric's main business then was producing electric light bulbs. In 1905, GE's technical design still depended on the original Edison invention of the carbon-filament lamp. However, other inventors and companies had made technical progress toward lamps with improved performance, higher efficiency, and longer life-times. Whitney, as director of the new GE laboratory, tried to jump the competition by inventing an improved carbon-filament lamp. But a German company developed a better lamp using a tantalum filament. Then Whitney fought back with a broad (but targeted) research strategy. He assigned to each of his researchers the responsibility for exploring each of the elements in the periodic table which had a melting point equal to or higher than tantalum.

Whitney assigned Coolidge the element of tungsten to explore as a new lamp filament. Coolidge wrote to his parents: "I am fortunate now in being on the most important problem the lab has ever had. . . . If we can get the metal tungsten in such shape that it can be drawn into wire, it means millions of dollars to the company" (Wolff, 1984, p. 84).

The problem was the ductility of tungsten. It had a high melting point but was brittle. It could not be made into wire. Coolidge researched the problem. The first research break came in June 1906. Coolidge observed that mercury was absorbed into the hot tungsten, making an amalgam. Next he found that cadmium and bismuth absorbed into tungsten made an amalgam that could be squeezed through a die to make a wire. Then on March

1907, Coolidge discovered that by heating this tungsten amalgam to about 400°, it could be bent without cracking.

By the fall of 1908, Coolidge knew he was on the right track. He began looking for mechanical ways of working the amalgam. He went to New England and visited the wire- and needle-making factories. He saw there a swaging technique which these factories used for wire making. Swaging was a process of gradually reducing the thickness of metal by repeated blows of hammers and the use of dies.

Back in Schenectady in May 1909, he purchased a commercial swaging machine and redesigned and altered the machine so that it could swage the tungsten amalgram into wire. It made tungsten wire, but when the wire was heated in a lamp, the tungsten filament broke. Coolidge examined the failure and learned that it was due to crystallization of the tungsten wire upon heating.

This problem was solvable. Coolidge knew that in a similar problem of making ice cream, glycerine was added to prevent the forming of ice crystals as the milk freezes. So he tried adding another substance to the tungson amalgam, thorium oxide, to prevent crystallization. It worked. On September 27, 1910, Coolidge had achieved success. He had developed a manufacturing process for producing tungsten wire.

GE immediately innovated the new process. By 1911, GE had thrown out all the earlier lamp-making equipment and was producing and selling lamp bulbs made with the new tungsten filaments. The research effort cost GE five years and $100,000. By 1920, two-thirds of GE's $22 million profit came from the new lamps. In 1911, Whitney and Coolidge, scientifically creating new technology in the new corporate research laboratory, had saved General Electric's principal business.

CAREERS OF RESEARCH PERSONNEL

Coolidge's story exemplifies one of the most important lessons in managing the research laboratory—that the career of an industrial scientist involves a creative tension between research and management. The key personnel in the corporate research laboratory are scientists in industry, and they must be specially recruited, motivated, and integrated into the corporation for the investment in R&D to pay off.

Research can be for scientific or for technological purposes. Science is the pursuit of fundamental knowledge, and technology is the application of knowledge to solve problems. The balancing of business with research is therefore (1) the focusing of fundamental knowledge on (2) invention and technical problem solving, which (3) increases the productivity of the corporation.

Universities train new scientists. The transition from a university-trained scientist to an industrially creative scientist is not easy. In industry, scientists follow different career paths from academic scientists. They develop different values, goals, and research styles.

In academia, the career path for a scientist is focused on a combination of teaching and basic research. A new assistant professor is expected to perform research and publish in order to attain tenure. After that, the associate professor is expected to continue actively in research and publication as a complement to teaching and as essential to graduate education. In contrast, the new industrial researcher is expected not only to perform research but also to invent and improve technologies. The industrial researcher is expected to remain scientifically competent but to become an inventor and technical problem solver. Demands on the industrial researcher are therefore broader than these on the academic researcher—pulling the industrial researcher in two directions, science and technology.

Due to the other job opportunities available in the corporation, most industrial scientists will eventually leave active research altogether, becoming managers or technical personnel in other parts of the corporation. In summarizing the studies of research productivity of scientists, Albert Goldberg and Yehouda Shenhav emphasized that scientists tend to diverge in two different paths. The first group has an early research productivity peak within about 10 years after their degree (usually by the age of 40), and thereafter their research output declines sharply. The second group has an equally early research productivity but instead of declining after 40, it continues strongly through the next decade (usually through the age of 50). Goldberg and Shenhav called this second group the "veteran group of highly productive researchers." They saw this group as expressing a concept of cumulative advantage in research capability. This group makes an even more impressive start in their research than average, gaining early recognition and access to resources to produce research. This in turn both reinforces motivational commitment to research and improves a continuing ability to acquire facilities and to attract younger researchers to help them maintain research productivity (Goldberg and Shenhav, 1984).

To take advantage of this kind of natural grouping in research productivity, many industrial research laboratories have created a dual career ladder in the laboratories—a managerial ladder and a technical ladder. With this, the career paths of researchers take one of three paths: (1) leaving the laboratory, (2) becoming a research manager, or (3) becoming a senior scientist.

The first path leaves from the laboratory to other parts of the corporation. There they become managers in production, service, sales, or other divisions. This group corresponds to the scientists whose research productivity declines after an initial level.

In the second path, after an initial period of research, the researchers remain in the laboratory but move into managerial positions, becoming research managers. This group corresponds to part of the second group—highly productive, able to gain recognition and research resources, but choosing to become managers of research groups.

In the third path, the researchers remain in the laboratory as senior researchers. These researchers are the other part of the second group, continuing as highly productive researchers but with either little interest or skill in management. The dual career ladder in the laboratory accommodates this last group, rewarding scientific skill without forcing them to become managers. These last two groups become the veteran R&D professionals: research managers and senior scientists.

In number, by far the largest group is the first. Few researchers entering the research laboratory remain in the laboratory. The average annual turnover in a large, stable research laboratory is about 10% a year, so that within 10 years, most of the researchers will have departed the laboratory (say, about 90% of the researchers). Most of the 10% of entering groups of researchers who remain on as veteran R&D personnel will become research managers, and a few, senior scientists. These veteran R&D people provide the corporate laboratory with its research leadership.

An example of a senior industrial researcher was Jack Preston at Monsanto Co. In 1985, Preston was an industrial scientist advancing on the technical career ladder. Preston had received a Ph.D. in chemistry from the University of Alabama in 1957. He then joined the Research Development Section of Chemstrand Corporation. In 1963, he was promoted to senior research chemist at the Chemstrand Research Center, and in 1965, he was advanced to associate scientist. Preston then joined Monsanto and advanced to scientist in 1966. In 1974, he was appointed Monsanto senior fellow. Preston's research interests had been "in tailoring condensation polymers for specific uses, particularly heat resistant polymers for films and fibers and rodlike polymers for high strength, high modulus fibers" (Preston, 1985).

INDUSTRIAL RESEARCH VALUES

The transition from academic science to industrial science and research management is the first step in the career paths of industrial scientists. For this transition, the industrial researcher must learn to refocus the style of academic research into the style of industrial research.

The academic researcher is institutionally encouraged to become a narrowly focused disciplinary specialist, teaching and looking toward other peer specialists for communication and rewards. Depth in science, not breadth, is valued in academia and perceived as the most efficient means of advancing science. In contrast, the industrial researcher is encouraged to become broader in scientific perspective, working in multidisciplinary teams, and focused on technical problem solving in a managerially oriented organization (where the bottom line is neither knowledge nor education but sales, service, and profits).

Differing values arise from the different research styles of academic and industrial scientists. Information for the academic researcher is predominantly valued as public, whereas information for the industrial researcher is predominantly valued as proprietary. Proprietary information includes patented and unpatented inventions and trade secrets. Accordingly, industrial researchers learn to be guarded about the exchange of information. Information is exchanged, but formal and informal rules govern this exchange. Confidentiality statements and patent ownership agreements are signed when beginning employment. Research publications are examined for patentability or disclosure of confidential information before publication. When technical information is published by industry, it is either patented or less current or information unrelated to current production (Larsen, 1983). Thus it is more difficult for industrial scientists to gain scientific recognition through publication than for their academic colleagues. Management must offer the industrial scientist a mixture of incentives and rewards to compensate for lost professional recognition, while encouraging them to remain scientifically active and creative.

As attitudes toward the value of information differ between industrial and academic researchers, so do attitudes toward research management: the academic favoring a less planned, less tightly supervised style, and the industrial researcher valuing more targeted focus, supervision, and scheduling. In academia, research projects are conceived as advancing a frontier of basic knowledge and performed as a part of graduate education. In industry, research projects are conceived as (1) leading toward improvement of current products and production processes, or (2) leading toward new products or production processes.

Research in industry thus tends to be (1) targeted (whether basic or applied), (2) multidisciplinary, (3) team performed, and (4) scheduled. The problem of the modern industrial manager in keeping the corporation technologically competitive is:

1. How best to employ scientists in the advancement of technology
2. How to effectively integrate the attitudes and activities of scientific personnel with those of engineering, production, sales, and finance

SUMMARY

The corporate research laboratory is a place for applying the methods of science to the pursuit of technological knowledge. It is staffed with scientists hired from academic training areas. The first step is to transform the academic attitudes of scientists into industrial attitudes while preserving dedication to research and encouraging creativity focused on technological innovation. Attitudes toward research management differ between academic and industrial scientists. Management must offer the industrial scientist a mixture of incentives and rewards to compensate for lost professional recognition. The career paths for the industrial scientist diverge after an initial period into R&D veterans or into positions in other parts of the corporation (production, sales, service, etc.).

REFLECTION

1. **Using the biographies of an academic scientist and an industrial scientist, compare their careers and accomplishments.**

FOR FURTHER READING

KORNHAUSER, WILLIAM, *Scientists in Industry*. Berkeley, Calif.: University of California Press, 1962.

CHAPTER TWENTY
RESEARCH LEADERSHIP

CENTRAL IDEAS

1. Boundary spanning role of research leadership
2. Leadership style

Example: William Coolidge as a Research Manager at GE

As an example of management in an industrial laboratory, we will describe some experiences of William Coolidge after he moved into management. We recall that he succeeded with his first assignment in 1900 to develop a tungsten filament for light bulbs. He then became one of the R&D veterans at GE, continuing to perform research. He turned his attention to x-rays.

X-rays had been discovered in 1895 by William Roentgen. The potential application of x-rays to medicine and other areas were known, but early x-ray tubes were impractical and undependable. Coolidge thought of trying tungsten as a target material. With the help of another GE scientist, Irving Langmuir (Langmuir later received a Nobel prize in physics), Coolidge invented the first practical x-ray tube in 1913. Over the course of the next 15 years, Coolidge continued to make technical contributions to x-ray applications. Then in 1928, he was promoted to associate director of the laboratory, beginning a management career (Wolff, 1984).

The depression of the 1930s severely stressed GE, as it did other firms. By April 1932, Whitney had decided to retire, his health suffering from worry about keeping the GE lab going and fears that it might be shut down in view of the bad economic conditions. Coolidge succeeded him as director on November 1, 1932, and took immediate action to save the lab. He put the laboratory on a four-day workweek and cut the work force from 555 people to 270. In taking this reduction, he was careful to prune, keeping the best researchers and maintaining the emphasis on fundamental research for new technologies. It was a tough task.

It was tougher even to maintain morale and to continue the search for new products. Yet by December 1933, he was permitted to add five new chemists to develop chemical-based products. Research continued at GE, and the 1930s turned out to be one of great technical advance, laying the base for some of the war effort in the 1940s and the economic expansion thereafter.

In terms of management style, Coolidge combined the firmness of expense control with the leadership of technical excellence. He interacted with the staff and was accessible. He walked around the lab, looking "more like a scientist than a laboratory manager." Because Coolidge maintained his interest in research, he inspired his researchers. He encourged them with words like: "This is fascinating, anything we can do to help?" (Wolff, 1984). One of his colleagues was quoted as saying of Coolidge: "That man oozes optimism of an inspiring brand. You feel in his presence that if all things are not possible, many are. Yet he has plenty of circumspection, with a verifying, sagacious mind that readily isolates what is either impossible or extraneous" (Wolff, 1984, p. 84).

BOUNDARY SPANNING BETWEEN THE RESEARCH LABORATORY AND THE CORPORATION

Collidge's career exemplifies the role of the research manager, focusing on business, controlling costs, encouraging and inspiring technical excellence, and separating the technically feasible from the infeasible. Research leadership provides the technological vision for the corporation. The research manager must thus span the boundaries between the worlds of business and technology, managing the interface between the economic and technical aspects of the corporation. Within the corporation, research management must contribute (1) to product creation and maintenance, and (2) to productivity improvement and cost reduction. Outside the corporation, research management must contribute (1) to the corporation's competitive ability, (2) to corporate safety and environmental responsibilities, and (3) to the corporate ability to respond to changes in the availability and costs of resources.

One way in which people have examined the nature of research leadership has been through the concept of "boundary-spanning activities." For example, Warren Brown and Robert Schwab summarized many of the kinds of boundary-spanning activities that have been discussed in the literature on research leadership. They classified these activities as scanning, monitoring, acquiring, linking, gatekeeping, representing, distributing, and protecting (Brown and Schwab, 1984). In illustrating these terms, it will simplify matters to reclassify them as (1) obtaining, (2) implementing, and (3) communicating technical information.

Obtaining Technical Information

The boundary-spanning activities of research management in "scanning," "monitoring", and "acquiring" are all important in generating the technical knowledge base for corporate productivity. "Scanning" means to search for changes in the external environment, particularly technological, which might provide an opportunity or a problem for the corporation. "Monitoring" means to follow trends, scientific or technological, which have strategic implication for the corporation. "Acquiring" means to obtain scientific and technical skills, tools, and information from the environment for improving the corporation's technical capability.

For example, in the GE laboratory, technical management had been scanning the changing technology in lighting bulbs, which led to their worry that GE's lighting business was threatened by technical advances by competitors. The establishment of the GE laboratory was itself a corporate response to this worry. Coolidge, in searching for ways to make tungsten ductile, visited German and American factories, wherein he became aware of the swaging technique.

Implementing Technical Information

By "linking" Brown and Schwab mean the establishment and maintainance of communcation between the laboratory and the other parts of the corporation. "Representing" means the presentation of technical opportunities to other parts of the corporation to shape the purpose and productivity of the corporation. "Protecting" means to maintain the technological capability of the corporation in its competitive environment.

In implementing technical information into corporate products and processes, the research manager plays an essential linking and representational role between the researchers and the production, marketing, and financial people. The research manager must understand the technical aspects of innovation in order to match it to the economic aspects. For example, Coolidge implemented the processing of tungsten into a machineable process that was introduced into GE's production processes. Coolidge worked closely with both the production personnel and financial personnel in planning and implementing the conversion.

Communicating Technical Information

By "gatekeeping" Brown and Schwab mean the translation, interpretation, and selective communication of technical information on the scientific and technical environment to managers in the corporation. "Distributing" means facilitating the understanding of the applications of the technology to products and services from the corporation to its environment.

The leadership role of the research manager in communicating the technical aspects of corporation actions is vitally important both to the innovation of new products and processes and to the development of new applications for these products. The research mananager provides the technical channel of information for the corporation. Most major corporations have a vice president of research and development.

In the GE example, it was explicitly planned that the laboratory would do "real scientific research." Furthermore, when Coolidge was forced to reduce the laboratory by half in order to accommodate the reduced corporate profitability during the depression, he continued the scientific research (although at a reduced and less expensive level) and maintained research morale. Accordingly, GE continued as an innovative company through the 1930s.

Example: Mervin J. Kelly of Bell Labs

Another example of an industrial manager who effectively spanned the boundaries between science, technology, and business was Mervin Kelly. Moreover, in performing his research leadership for Bell Labs, Kelly also provided leadership for the nation; Kelly created the research group that invented the transistor.

Mervin Kelly was born in 1894 in Princeton, Missouri; his father was the principal of the high school of that small town. When Kelly graduated from high school, he enrolled in the Missouri School of Mines and Metallurgy. There he decided that physics and mathematics were more interesting to him than mining. In 1914, he graduated and enrolled for graduate work at the University of Kentucky. He also taught for two years to support himself, leaving with a master's degree and a new bride. In 1916 they went to the University of Chicago, where Kelly worked as an assistant to Professor Robert Millikan. Millikan was measuring the charge of the electron, and Kelly participated in Millikan's famous "oil drop" experiment (which showed the electron's charge to be discrete and for which Millikan received a Nobel prize) (Wolff, 1984).

In 1918, Kelly received a Ph.D. in physics from the University of Chicago and went to work for the Western Electric engineering department of the Bell system. He was hired by Frank Jewett (who had been a student of Millikan and who became the first president of Bell Labs when it was created in 1925). Kelly first worked on projects to improve the new electron vacuum tube that made long-distance telephones possible. Kelly received seven patents for his technical work.

In 1936, Kelly was made director of research of the Bell Labs. He decided to increase research in fundamental areas of science. He hired William Shockley in 1936, a Ph.D. from MIT in the new field of solid-state physics. Shockley later recalled: "Kelly gave me an eloquent pep talk. . . . He pointed out that relays in telephones exchanges caused problems. . . . He felt electronics should contribute. . . . Dr. Kelly's discussion left me continually alert for possible applications of solid-state effects in telephone-switching problems" (Wolff, 1983, pp. 72–73).

Kelly's support and Shockley's alertness paid off—but after World War II. During the war, Kelly was responsible for the military programs at Bell (of which there were about 1200). After the war, Kelly reestablished the solid-state physics research program at Bell and invited Shockley back to Bell. Shockley had spent the war in the Pentagon working on military problems. Kelly then made James Fisk assistant director of physical research at Bell and told him to make a major and broad research effort in all aspects of solid-state physics and the underlying quantum mechanical theory.

Fisk set up three research groups: physical electronics, electron dynamics, and solid-state physics. William Shockley and Stanley Morgen led the solid-state physics group. As part of that group, they hired Bardeen and Brattain. Shockley, Bardeen, and Brattain invented the transistor, for which they received Nobel prizes, and AT&T, a basic patent.

Kelly showed research leadership in supporting basic research and in forming the first solid-state research group in industry. He hired the best young scientists for the group and ecouraged them to be creative while keeping in sight what AT&T's business was about—communications. His vision and leadership created the organizational conditions for a technological revolution. Later Kelly became chairman of the board of Bell Telephone Laboratories, retiring in 1959. In that year he was awarded the John Fritz Medal for "his achievements in electronics, leadership of a great industrial research laboratory, and contributions to the defense of the country through science and technology." The medal was an award from the American professional engineering societies (other recipients included Edison, Marconi, Wright, and Westinghouse). Kelly died in 1971.

LEADERSHIP STYLE IN R&D MANAGEMENT

The role of the research manager is:

1. To set research objectives and determine research areas
2. To find, hire, and encourage creative researchers to pursue new technical knowledge and to make technical inventions

3. To ensure that the free and creative atmosphere for research is focused on ultimate economic benefit

4. To implement research results in product and process creation and improvement in the business of the corporation

Because research managers must maintain and integrate two cultures, the corporate economic culture and the scientific technical culture, the research manager must exhibit a style of research leadership that balances managerial and technical values. In a study of management in high-technology research projects, Zachary and Krone made suggestions about research management style. First they suggested that research managers avoid assigning research tasks arbitrarily, making sure that researchers understand the purposes of the assignment. Second, they suggested that research tasks be structured to provide opportunities for researchers to exercise and develop their technical and research expertise. Third, they recommended equitable distribution of work, so that the work load was seen as fair. Fourth, they suggested that the research manager be a good listener, seeking to stimulate and encourage the creativity of the researchers. Fifth, they suggested that the project goals be clear and that there be specific performance standards against which to measure research progress (Zachary and Krone, 1984, p. 39).

In the example of GE, Coolidge ecouraged the creativity of researchers and their particpation in the decisions about the directions of research. As an example of GE's research morale under Coolidge, Charles Reed (when retiring from GE in 1978 as senior vice president of technology) was quoted about the laboratory when he joined it in 1942: "There was the greatest amount of freedom—and encouragement—to go ahead and do your own thing, and do it in some radically different way" (Wolff, 1984, p. 84). In the example of Kelly's leadership at Bell Labs, a former AT&T board chairman, Frederick R. Kappel, said of Kelly: "Every place needs a fireball or spark plug, and he was it" (Wolff, 1983, p. 74).

In another study of engineers' attitudes toward management, Hans Thamhain listed a set of values in priority order of expressed professional interests. The highest priority expressed by the engineers was for work opportunities that provided (1) interesting and challenging work, (2) a professionally stimulating work environment, and (3) professional growth. Next in order of importance to the engineer's expressed values were conditions of leadership and groups which provided (4) overall, complete, and capable leadership for research groups, and (5) tangible rewards. Then in order of importance were desires for (6) technical expertize of all necessary kinds in research groups, (7) management assistance in solving administrative problems, (8) clearly defined objectives, (9) capable management controls on projects, and (10) job security. Then of value were provisions for (11) senior management support, (12) good interpersonnel relations, (13) proper planning, (14) clear role definition, (15) open communication, and (16) minimizing changes (Thamhain, 1983).

One can see from these expressed values that engineers first value technical challenges and growth. Technical personnel are concerned primarily with technical matters—no surprise, but worth keeping in mind. People with skills and ideas want conditions in which to develop and use their skills and ideas and to be rewarded for it. Engineers and scientists are no different from other people who value most things that are dearest to them.

Thamhain concluded that it is important for management to provide the following leadership for its technical personnel:

> Clarity of management direction;
> Understanding of the technology they are working with;
> Understanding of the organization and their interfaces;
> Understanding of the professional and personal needs of their personnel;
> Planning and administrative skills;
> Credibility within the organization . . .;
> Written oral and communication skills;
> Delineation of goals and objectives;
> Methods to aid group decision-making;
> Assistance to problem solving;
> Conflict management skills. (Thamhain, 1983, p. 235).

To summarize these points: Engineers value technical work and expertise and expect certain things from management—general leadership, research directions, resources, and administrative support.

SUMMARY

The research manager must span the boundaries between the technical and the business worlds. The research and engineering functions in a modern corporation cross boundaries both within and outside the organization. Because research managers are trying to maintain and integrate two cultures, the corporate economic culture and the scientific technical culture, it is important that the research manager exhibit a style of research leadership that balances managerial and technical values. Research and engineering personnel value technical work and expertise and expect certain things from management—providing leadership and support for technical creativity.

REFLECTION

1. Compare research management to management of another business function, such as finance, marketing, or personnel. How does the content of the functional area affect the forms and styles of management?

FOR FURTHER READING

WHITEHEAD, DON, *The Dow Story: The History of the Dow Chemical Company*. New York: McGraw-Hill, 1968.

CHAPTER TWENTY-ONE
EVALUATING R&D
PROJECTS

CENTRAL IDEAS

1. Classification of R&D projects according to business function
2. Criteria for evaluating R&D projects
3. Importance of superior technical performance as goal of R&D projects
4. Use of discounted futures in evaluating R&D projects
5. Organization of evaluation process

Example: The RCA Videodisc—The Product That Could and Couldn't

Successful R&D projects must ultimately be evaluated on their contribution to profitability. R&D projects may be thought to succeed technically but fail commercially, since the criteria of success for technical factors and commercial factors may be considered independently. However, technical and commercial success are more often critically interdependent in successful innovation. The subtle interdependence of technical and commercial goals of R&D projects makes their initial evaluation tricky business. An example of this trickiness was provided by RCA's venture into the videodisc market.

In the late 1970s, recording of video images was clearly going to be a hot new technology and a big market. It started with a commercial videotape recorder innovated by Ampex Corporation in 1956. RCA began producing videotape machines in 1959. In Japan, engineers of several electronics companies examined the Ampex machine and read the equipment manuals. Japanese government officials at the Ministry of International Trade and Investment (MITI) encouraged this interest by providing a small grant to one firm to develop videotape technology. Improvements in the technology continued at Ampex and independently in Japan. Finally, in the 1960s it became clear that a consumer version of the machine could be built, but only the Japanese were interested. Sony and Matsushita were the first to introduce a consumer videotape recorder in 1965. In 1970, the first generation of videocassette recorders (VCR) was introduced by Philips in Europe and by several companies in Japan. By 1975, the first successful consumer VCR, the Betamax, was introduced by Sony. After 1975, the consumer videodisc player market began.

VCRs were costly, about $1000 a machine, and tape was expensive, yet the market for home playing of movies was demonstrated. RCA decided to innovate the video equivalent of the audio record player—the videodisc. The technical path to the videodisc player began in the RCA Sarnoff laboratories with work on holographic tape to create three-dimensional images. Technical difficulties in this led to the idea of developing a laser device that could play through a TV set—the video laser disk (Nulty, 1981).

But at that time laser-disc technology looked expensive, as expensive as the VCR. RCA managers wanted a cheaper product. They decided to try capacitance recording rather than laser recording. They planned on marketing a device that cost in the range of $500 compared to the VCR price of $1000 and disks that could be sold at $25 compared to taped movie prices of $50. Choosing capacitance recording over laser recording was a sacrifice of performance in the machine for lower cost of development and production. Sacrificing performance for cost early in an R&D project is a serious choice which may turn out to be irreversible.

At the time, that choice looked reasonable. The capacitance approach meant serially recording and playback like a tape (since the capacitance stylus actually touched the disc), whereas the more expensive laser disc could be jumped and skipped around for random access to information on the disc. The laser beam read the disc and nothing mechanical (like the capacitance stylus) touched the disc. What did random access matter in showing movies? Nothing. So RCA chose the cheaper technology with the lower technical performance—capacitance recording rather than laser recording. It was an error: " 'It was a technological success but a commercial failure." That epitaph, pronounced early in April by Thornton F. Bradsaw, RCA Corp.'s chairman and chief executive, marked the demise of the company's home-grown $580 million gamble on videodiscs" (*Business Week*, 1984c).

The capacitance videodisc turned out to be a classic business failure. By 1981, RCA had spent $200 million developing that product. During the next three years, they spent another $300 million launching the product. But in 1984, they closed down the videodisc business—writing off a $500 million loss (*Business Week*, 1984c).

What had happened? First of all, the Japanese VCR manufacturers had reduced their manufacturing costs from 1975, so that by 1981, they could sell VCRs at $500. Consumers choose the VCRs over RCA's videodisc, since they could record movies as well as show movies—superior functionality at the same price. Also, videotape had dropped in price by 1981 to about $10 a cartridge (Meadows, 1981; *Business Week,* 1984e). Fighting back in 1983, RCA dropped the price on video disc players to $300, then to $200. No good. Consumers bought VCRs by the millions from 1981 through 1984 at prices from $300 to $500—superior functionality.

RCA managers had not anticipated the ability of the VCR makers to move down their production learning curve, dropping costs as market volume expanded. When RCA chose to develop the videodisc, it did not envision that the machinery needed to mass-produce pickup heads on tape recorders could be dramatically improved. The standard tolerance then for U.S. precision machinery was 0.5 millimeter. Yet the Japanese improved the machinery to 0.2 millimeter. Jack K. Sauter, an RCA group vice-president, said: "We had estimated that $499 would be the lowest VCR price by now (1984). We did not see the opportunity for mechanization and miniaturization to lower costs" (*Business Week* 1984d).

The killer of the RCA videodisc, however, was the choice of capacitance over laser recording. Since RCA had chosen to have a needle-like stylus following a groove, this inherently made random access (going quickly to any place on a disc) slower than with a laser videodisc. The laser never mechanically touches the disc and so can be easily and swiftly moved from one spot on the disc to another. While the RCA capacitance video disc was bombing in the home consumer market, another kind of videodisc player, the laser disc, was taking off. Laser, videodisc players of Sony and Pioneer and Phillips were selling. The videodisc player had a future, but with computers, not with home movies. By the middle of the 1980s, laser videodiscs coupled with personnal computers were beginning a revolution in industrial instruction. Surprise—the RCA engineers had developed the wrong machine for the wrong market (*Videography,* 1984).

The lesson from this example is very general. In a new technology, sacrificing performance is probably a wrong choice, since performance is the competitive edge in new technologies. In evaluating high-techology R&D, always go for the clearly superior technology. Cost problems might be solved later, but performance problems can never be righted if the inherently inferior technology is chosen.

TECHNICAL AND FINANCIAL CRITERIA FOR EVALUATING R&D PROJECTS

In any corporate research laboratory with good management and talented researchers, there will usually be more ideas for projects than there will be funds and personnel to perform all of them. Accordingly, it is an important management function to select the research projects that will be carried into innovation. The selection of research projects should be based on both technical and business criteria:

1. Is the project technically feasible and exciting in creating new functionality and advancing technical performance?
2. Will the project contribute significantly to corporate profitability?

As we saw in the RCA example, the technical and financial criteria are interdependent because commercial success requires providing the right performance at the right cost to the market. In the case of the videodisc, performance required recording capability or random-access capability for the market to accept the product at the competing price of videotape recording equipment.

Financial Criteria

Research and development is a capital investment in the future productivity of the company. Like any investment, the principal management criteria for evaluating R&D projects are cash flow and return on investment. Cash flow tells whether or not a company can afford an investment on a current basis. Return on investment tells how valuable the investment is to the company. Thus evaluating R&D projects requires applying traditional concepts of finance to potentially new products.

Initially, cash flow in a new product line is negative from the research and development costs accrued in inventing, developing and designing, testing, and creating production capacity. Each stage of innovating a new product is expensive, with the expense increasing by an order at every stage. Invention is much cheaper than development and design. Testing and setting up production capacity are much more expensive. When the product finally begins production and sales begin, profits turn the cash flow from a steady decline toward a positive flow. After sufficient sales, profits will cross the line for a positive return on investment.

We recall that this point is called the break-even point, and the time from R&D project initiation to this point is the break-even time. Financially, the break-even time is important, because the time to break even multiplied by the average negative cash flow represents an income loss to the company. The basic reason why all new enterprises require capital is this negative cash flow in the beginning of any new enterprise. The immediate reason for any business failure is a cash-flow crisis. Therefore, the most important business factor to watch in R&D projects is the cash-flow estimate to break even.

Provided that the company has capital to bear the negative cash flow on an R&D project until break even, the next financial consideration is the projected return on investment. For a successful R&D project, sales will eventually grow until either (1) the market is saturated, (2) competition limits market share for the product, or (3) product obsolescence occurs. It is important to try to estimate potential sales in order to estimate a return on investment for the product. Of course, in such estimates the goal is to get "into the ball park," to get a correct order-of-magnitude estimate of the size of the market and the market share the company can capture.

Technical Robustness in Market Strategy

The difficulty of applying financial concepts in high technology is the difficulty in guessing how a future market will look. The largest markets for radical innovations have often turned out to be in markets other than those originally envisioned by the innovator. Accordingly, the concept of robustness in R&D strategy is important. A robust R&D strategy selects innovation that provides the highest envisioned superior performance and flexibility of function. Then, even if the correct market had not been guessed, the technical superiority of the product may be applied to the creation of other, unexpected markets.

Therefore, one should be cautious in taking too literally market estimates for new technology markets. The more radical and innovating the technology, the more likely the market estimates are to be wrong. Really new technology eventually finds new applications undreamed of and markets unforeseen. Accordingly, market estimates should only be considered accurate for me-too technologies or incrementally advancing technologies.

Discounted Future

This caution about market estimates in new technologies applies particularly to the use of discounting techniques. In projecting return on investment, one should also take into account the time to introduction of product when comparing two projects. The standard way to compare the current value of future financial returns is the "discounted future value." The cost of the R&D project and initial production can be compared to interest received from an investment of a like amount accruing an estimated rate of interest.

The discounted future value of a new product line is thus the amount of equivalent principal that could have been invested at the beginning of the R&D project in an account, such that accrued interest would create a return equal to the product's return on investment. Comparing this equivalent principal to the cost of the R&D project is useful when comparing the financial returns between R&D projects. For example, two projects might provide similar estimated returns on investment, but one may bring the return earlier, in which case its discounted future value would be higher than the project with the later return.

Yet because of uncertainties in estimating future markets, too liberal a use of this technique in evaluating R&D projects may undervalue the corporate future. This is particularly true when inflation is high, and it is difficult to plan any future. For example, in 1982, Robert Hayes and David Garvin cautioned about misusing discounting techniques:

> Highly sophisticated analytic techniques now dominate the capital budgeting process at most companies. . . .
> As these techniques have gained ever wider use in investment decision making, the growth of capital investment and R&D spending in this country has slowed. We believe this to be more than a simple coincidence. We submit that the discounting approach has contributed to a decreased willingness to invest. . . .
> Bluntly stated, the willingness of managers to view the future through the reversed telescope of discounted cash flow analysis is seriously shortchanging the futures of their companies. (Hayes and Garvin, 1982, p. 71)

Inflation is a vicious factor in eroding confidence in long-range futures. Any significant level of inflation applied in a discounted cash-flow technique will always produce the same conclusion—go out of business—for no legitimate business can beat a highly discounted future. Consequently, one should always use analytical techniques intelligently. While discounted future value is a useful technique for comparing R&D projects, it must not be used in an absolute sense. The function of corporate research is to prepare the corporation for the future—both inflationary and noninflationary futures.

R&D EVALUATION AND ORGANIZATION

Evaluation of R&D projects occurs within the formal processes of planning and budgeting in the research laboratory. Essential to this is both vertical and horizontal communication, vertically within the laboratory and horizontally between the laboratory and the production and marketing functions of the company. We recall that for budget purposes, the objectives of R&D projects can be classified as (1) to support current businesses, (2) to create new ventures, and (3) to explore new technologies. Financial evaluation of projects in these different categories should use the following approaches:

A.   R&D projects in support of current business:
    1.   The current products are projected as to lifetimes.
    2.   This product mix is then projected as a sum of profits.
    3.   The current and proposed R&D projects in support of current business

are evaluated in terms of their contribution to extending the lifetimes or improving the sales or lowering costs of the products.
B. R&D projects for new ventures:
   1. Projects that result in new ventures are charted over expected lifetimes.
   2. Cash-flow requirements and return on investment are calculated.
C. R&D projects for exploratory research:
   1. These projects are not financially evaluated but chosen for their potential for dramatic impact on technological performance parameters.
   2. Project costs are treated as an overhead function in corporate R&D.

Example: Communication in the GE Laboratory

As an example of the layers of vertical communication within the laboratory, let us recall the organization of the GE central corporate lab in 1982. It had four divisions (Chemical, Physics, Electronics, and Materials) reporting to a senior vice president for research. In each division there were three more layers of organization in the research projects. For example, in the Physics lab, there were three units (Automation Systems, Engineering Systems, and Information Systems). In each unit there were branches (for example, in the Engineering Systems lab, the branches were Thermochemical Processes, Electromechanics, Solid Mechanics, and Fluid Mechanics). Finally, there were several research programs in each branch (Morone and Alben, 1984).

Decisions of R&D projects occurred in a continuous stream of communication up and down the chain of command. Project managers were influenced by signals received from above about the range of technological applications and markets in which the company was interested. In turn, upper levels of management were influenced by the technological opportunities and visions communicated from below. Annual, formal processes of budgeting and program reviews systematized the up–down communication.

Horizontal communication also occurred within the laboratory, concerning technologies in other disciplines which synergistically interacted with technologies of concern to a given unit. Much technological advance resulted from transfer of use from one area of technology to another.

Decisions to move an R&D project from exploratory to applied research could be taken within a branch. Decisions to proceed to the more advanced stages of engineering prototype and production prototype required horizontal communication—participation and approval with production and marketing.

Even in the early stages of exploratory research, it was important for researchers to have ideas about market needs (market pull), which they obtained from interacting with production and marketing people in the businesses of the corporation. We had earlier identified the roles of Product User or Process User Gatekeeper in the innovation process as indicating the importance of horizontal communication to the creation of innovative ideas. Research personnel are technically expert, but making them user expert is a major problem and is the goal of horizontal communication between the research labs and business units.

OPERATIONS RESEARCH TECHNIQUES FOR R&D PROJECT SELECTION

There is a vast literature on project selection techniques, using different kinds of scoring techniques. For example, projects are scored on several criteria: technical performance, financial cash flow and returns, and likelihood of technical success. This last criterion is difficult to measure. Usually, a subjective probability is assigned to judge the likelihood of technical success. The maximization of scores then depends critically on the subjective criteria and provides the largest source of error in the procedure.

These procedures are useful only when a larger number of projects are to be compared to each other. But it has in practice turned out to be most effective in dividing the R&D programs so that smaller numbers need only be compared. Then elaborate scoring techniques are not useful; accordingly, there has not been widespread adoption of such techniques. A summary of such techniques is given in Dean and Goldhar (1980).

SUMMARY

Selection of R&D projects to carry through to commercial innovation is a critical R&D management decision. Projects should be selected on both technical and financial criteria. Technical criteria should select R&D projects that create clearly superior functionality and performance. Financial criteria should select R&D projects based on positive cash flows in reasonable break-even times and adequate returns on investments. However, the technique of discounting should not be used rigidly to rule out all R&D projects, since in times of large inflation very few projects can beat a highly discounted future.

In evaluating R&D projects, each category of R&D in support of current businesses, new ventures, and exploratory research requires a different evaluation emphasis. Evaluation of research projects is a series of go–no go decisions involving estimates of technical performance and business performance at each stage of an R&D project. Vertical and horizontal communication within the research lab and between the research lab and business units is important at all stages of a research project and becomes increasingly important as the stages advance.

REFLECTION

1. Choose a major product innovation, such as computers, and chart the volume of sales over its history. Divide the markets into applications and segments. What was the original market envisioned by the innovators? How did the applications grow and markets segment? Were that growth and segmentation envisioned by the innovators? Could they have been?

FOR FURTHER READING

GEE, EDWIN A.,   *Managing Innovation*, New York: Wiley, 1976.

CHAPTER TWENTY-TWO
CORPORATE RESEARCH
STRATEGY

CENTRAL IDEAS

1. Acquisition and generation of corporate technologies
2. Determination of areas for corporate research
3. Morphological analysis of technologies
4. Phenomena and materials underlying technologies that provide other areas for research
5. Funding of corporate R&D—an assembled budget from several levels of research needs

Example: GE's Changed Research Strategy in the 1980s

Corporate research is performed in areas of science and technology underlying the current or future businesses of a company. How can a corporate manager decide on the appropriateness of the areas for corporate research? An example of major changes in research strategy occurred in General Electric in the early 1980s. These changes arose from business problems and technological opportunities.

General Electric has traditionally been a strong technology company, but even strong companies have occasional problems. In the 1960s, General Electric tried to develop three new businesses at the same time: computer, nuclear energy, and commercial-jet engines. Each required enormous investments in research and resources. The computer business was dominated by IBM, and the nuclear energy business was in trouble both environmentally and financially. In 1970, Reginald H. Jones, a new GE president, set out to strengthen GE's financial position. He sold the computer business to Honeywell, which eased the principal cash problem (but it also took GE out of the integrated-circuit business). Jones tightened operations, generating cash, and by 1980 had GE back into a strong financial position (Morrison, 1982; *Electronics Week*, 1984).

During this time, Jones also realized that chip-manufacturing capability had been essential to GE's productivity and to the quality and innovativeness of its other product lines. Accordingly, in 1975, he ordered a corporate study, and it concluded that GE had begun to lag in electronics. Jones then began a long-term strategy to reposition GE in electronics. This came to fruition under his successor, John Welch. Jones had begun at GE as an auditor and rose through the financial side, whereas Welch was a chemical engineer with a Ph.D. from the University of Illinois and came up on the production side. Yet they were in agreement on the long-term strategy: "Welch . . . is not about to repudiate Jones' legacy. 'You've got to understand,' he [Welch] says, 'Reg hired me for this job' " (Morrison, 1982, p. 51). Jones and Welch both agreed that despite the need to have pulled out of mainframe computers, GE had to get back into the electronics business. Welch commented: "In terms of fighting IBM in big computers, [pulling out] was probably the right decision at the time" (Banks, 1984, p. 102).

Yet what was missed were (1) the minicomputer revolution [that Digital Equipment Corporation had begun around that time (Banks, 1984, p. 102)] and (2) the second wave of semiconductor chip innovation (based on large-scale-integrated technology). In 1984, James Dykes, GE's manager of the new Semiconductor Business Division, commented: " 'That was a mistake, as the IC market subsequently exploded. . . . We simply had to get back into the technology to keep our products competitive" (*Electronics Week*, 1984, p. 51).

Acquisition of Technology

Research strategy involves decisions to create or to acquire new technology. A laboratory will invent some of the corporate technology, and some must be acquired from outside, since no corporation is a technological island unto itself. One means of acquiring technology is licensing technology developed and patented by another firm. Another way of acquiring technology, patented or not, is by acquisition. Many small high-technology companies, which develop a successful new technology, become acquired by a larger firm which desires to gain the new technology as a part of its research and product strategy.

Example: GE's Semiconductor Business Division

GE did get back into electronics. By 1985, GE had caught up. In 1981, GE purchased Intersil, a medium-sized semiconductor manufacturer, for

$235 million. GE also purchased Calma, a manufacturer of computer-aided design (CAD) equipment, for $100 million. Four small software firms were purchased for $50 million, and Great Western Silicon was purchased for $7.7 million. GE also bought the ceramics division of 3M Corporation for $100 million and paid the Communications Satellite Corporation $14 million for its computer-aided engineering business. In addition to these technology acquisitions, GE doubled the size of its GE research laboratory in Schenectady by adding a new $90 million microelectronics center. The new center and the acquired businesses were intended to service GE's core businesses and then to supply outside services and products.

In 1984, Dykes was vice president and general manager of GE's new presence in semiconductor technology—the Semiconductor Business Division. Built up from some of the acquisitions, the division had five departments, employed 6000 people, and provided three product lines: custom chips, high-voltage power chips, and hybrid data-acquisition components. From 1981 until 1984, the new division ran annual startup loses of $5 to $10 million on sales of $200 to $250 million. In 1984, however, Dyke produced a $5 million pretax profit on $300 million sales. It took time and a very large investment to modernize GE's electronics technology. In 1984, Jack Welch's strategy for GE was to be only in businesses in which it would be a dominant player: " 'The third or fourth player in a game today is in a tough world, a very tough world,' says Welch" (Banks, 1984, p. 98).

MORPHOLOGICAL ANALYSIS

Corporate research strategy is a set of areas of research which underpin the technologies and businesses of the corporation. As the nature of the corporation's businesses changes, so the research areas should change. How does one choose the research areas given the choices of businesses? A technique for systematically analyzing technological structures is called "morphological analysis." "Morphology" is a synonym for "structure." All technical systems embody some form of physical reality and so can be analyzed structurally, based on the phenomenon of the reality.

F. Zwicky, who introduced the technique of structural analysis in technology planning, stated: "An exact statement is made of the problem which is to be solved. For instance, we may wish to study the morphological character of all modes of motion, or of all possible propulsive power plants, telescopes, pumps, communication, detection devices, and so on. If one specific device, method or system is asked for, the new [mophological] method immediately generalizes the inquiry to all possible devices, methods, or systems which provide the answer to a more generalized request" (Jantsch, 1967, p. 175).

Zwicky's procedure was to identify the logical structure of a technology and to generalize to all possible structural variations. The generalization constituted the mophological analysis. An example Zwicky used was a morphological analysis of jet engines. Zwicky identified the logical elements of jet engines as having the following structural features:

1. Intrinsic or extrinsic chemically active mass,
2. Internal or external thrust generation,
3. Intrinsic, extrinsic, or zero thrust augmentation,
4. Internal or external thrust augmentation,
5. Positive or negative jets,
6. Nature of the conversion of the chemical energy into mechanical energy,
7. Vacuum, air, water, earth,
8. Translatory, rotatory, oscillatory or no motion,
9. Gaseous, liquid, solid state of propellant,
10. Continuous or intermittent operation,
11. Self-igniting or non-self-igniting propellants.
    (Jantsch, 1967, p. 176)

Having identified the main structural features, the next step in a morphological analysis is to take all possible combinations of these features. In the jet engine example, the number of different possible structures of jet engines is 36,864 possible combinations. The next step is to eliminate combinations that are not technically interesting. In Zwicky's example, his first evaluation, performed in 1943, used fewer parameters and reduced the cases to 576 possibilities.

A historical annecdote: In his analysis Zwicky correctly anticipated five possible combinations, which were later developed. In fact, at that time, in 1943, two of Zwicky's combinations were the secret German pulse-jet-powered aerial bomb (V-1) and the V-2 rocket: "One may recall, in this context, that the fatal failure of Lindemann, Churchill's scientific advisor, to recognize the potential of the V-2 even when he was shown photographs ("It will not fly") is plausibly explained by his exclusive preoccupation with solid propellants, stubbornly rejecting the idea of liquid propellants" (Jantsch, 1967, p. 178).

Technological search is not blind. The search for new structural conceptions in technological change is the basic logic behind R&D strategy. The technical personnel in a research laboratory are hired precisely for their ability to understand and perform logical searches for technological improvement. Morphological analysis provides a systematic way for determining the research areas to be explored in improving a technology. It also provides a useful way to communicate the reasons for research strategies between the research laboratory and other divisions of the corporation.

Example: Advances in Vacuums Due to Structural Changes

By examining the structures of technologies, possibilities of technological innovation arise by implementing changes in the structures. New energy sources or new motive power may be utilized. New materials or new processes may be used. Major devices or components may be used. The system architecture may be altered. Any of these structural changes in a technology may make significant changes in the technology. As an example of the structural change as a source of innovation progress, Jantsch listed the advances in the technology for creating vacuums. High vacuums are very important both for scientific research and for many industrial processes, such as semiconductor chip production (Jantsch, 1967).

The invention and development of vacuum technology began with the invention of the mechanical vacuum pump. This was a tightly sealed cylinder with a motor pulling the piston in and out to evacuate air from a lower-pressure area to a high-pressure area. The battery-operated tire pumps one buys in stores to pump up an automobile tire works on this principle. But there is a limit to the best vacuum that one can create with the mechanical pump (-8 millibar pressure), due to the sealing properties of the materials used in making the pump.

The diffusion pump of the 1950s was followed by the ion pump in the 1960s and the cryogenic pump in the late 1960s. Each of these different kinds of pumps operate on different physical principles and attain purer forms of vacuum. Consequently, each structural change in vacuum technology was necessary to increase vacuum performance, that is, to reach lower and lower vacuums:

Mechanical pump: 10^{-8} millibar pressure
Diffusion pump: 10^{-9} millibar pressure
Ion pump: 10^{-11} millibar pressure
Cryogenic pump: 10^{-13} millibar pressure

In the development of these succeeding devices, several other devices had to be invented to make them possible. Important to the ion pump was the invention of the ion gauge and the development of elastomer sealants and impermeable helium glass. The cryogenic pump required the development of low-temperature technology and the mass spectrometer gauge. The use of morphological analysis to search for technical improvement would have required this kind of expansion of strategy away from the basis of the first device by generalizing the structural features of the pumping system.

EXPERT CONSULTATION
ON MORPHOLOGY

In examining alternative research strategies, a technique complementary to morphological analysis, is to consult a range of experts as to their insights about the possibilities and directions of research opportunities. The so-called "Delphi" technique suggests that these experts be in communication with each other and reach some consensus as to their visions of the future. The Delphi technique is a more formal manner of using expert consultants to gain consensus from such a group. Delphi groups can work on morphological analysis as a means of systematizing the consensual effort (Jantsch, 1967).

MORPHOLOGICAL
ANALYSIS AND
TECHNOLOGY STRATEGY

Morphological analysis looks for alternative structures that may provide different or improved functions and performances. However, technical change must also be evaluated in regard to whether such change is desirable for the corporation. Michael Porter suggested some tests of desirability:

> The technological change itself lowers cost or enhances differentiation, and the firm's technological lead is sustainable.
> The technological change shifts cost or uniqueness drivers in favor of a firm.
> Pioneering the technological change translates into first-mover advantages besides those inherent in the technology itself.
> The technological change improves the overall industry structure (Porter, 1985, pp. 171–172).

Since competitive advantage in products lies in either lower price or product differentiation, the alternative technical structures should first be examined as to whether they will result in lower cost or differentiated products. Moreover, if lowering costs, can the company take advantage of the lower cost; or could a competitor enter (with, say, resource advantages) and take away the competitive advantage?

Pioneering technological change is no advantage to the pioneering company if it cannot capture and sustain the advantage. Thus questions should also be asked as to whether the company will have the production or marketing capability to sustain a competitive position after the technological lead has vanished. Finally, the company should examine in what ways the potential technological change might alter the industry structure. Would such alteration be to the advantage of the company?

Morphological analysis will help in examining alternative technologies to pursue, but strategy must evaluate whether to pursue an alternative in light of potential competitive advantages.

FUNDING CORPORATE R&D

The appropriate level for funding corporate R&D is a question to which many have suggested different answers without much consensus as to the correct answer. What is certain is that R&D is an important overhead expense for the long-term future of the corporation. One way of conceptualizing the contribution of R&D to profitability is to consider first the contribution of R&D to technical progress in the corporation and then of technical progress to profits. For example, Richard Foster and others suggested trying to trace the following logic in the expression:

$$\text{return} = \frac{\text{profits}}{\text{R\&D investment}}$$

This can be expanded to read

$$\text{return} = \frac{\text{profits/technical progress}}{\text{technical progress/R\&D investment}} \qquad \text{(Foster et al., 1985)}$$

In the latter formula, the numerator, profits/technical progress, may be measured by the contribution of technical progress to (1) lowering the cost of current product lines, (2) extending the lifetimes of current product lines, or (3) introducing new product lines. The denominator, technical progress/R&D investment, may be measured by the contributions of R&D research programs to improving the technical performance of products and processes. Measuring such terms, although not impossible, is beyond the normal capabilities of most industrial accounting systems and thus requires a special information-collection effort.

Incremental R&D Budgeting

In practice, most R&D funding is set by incremental budgeting—aggregating up project budgets and incremental changes from past R&D budgets. How much change from past R&D budgets depends on many variables, such as the rate of change of technologies on which the corporate businesses depend, the size of the corporation, levels of effort in R&D by competitors, and so on. In areas of rapidly changing technology (high technology), firms tend to spend more on R&D than do firms in mature technology areas. Measured as a percent of sales, high-technology firms often spend from 6 to 15% on R&D, whereas firms in mature technology areas may spend 1% or less.

Because R&D spans the spectrum from exploratory research for long-term technical horizons to short-term research for current product and process improvement, funding criteria shift as one moves across the spectrum. For example, at the production/marketing end, R&D should be aimed at improving the quality of products produced and lowering the production costs. In addition, R&D should contribute to adequate safety of the products and processes and to conservation of energy and minimization of environmental pollution. The costs of this kind of R&D should be judged as to their marginal contribution to improvement of quality, costs, safety, and environment (EIRMA Working Group, 1982).

As an example at the other extreme, exploratory research is basic research targeted toward the creation of new technologies in the long term. The amount of such research should first be considered as a kind of overhead on the technological capability of the corporation itself. For example, in 1980, W. E. Hanford, a former vice president for R&D at Olin Corp, commented: "To me, directed basic research can be defined as those problems for which I as a research director alone take responsibility for seeing that they fit with the company's strategy" (Wolff, 1981, p. 31).

In addition to targeted basic research as a technical capability overhead on R&D, there are specific times when directed basic research should address corporate problems. In a panel on targeted basic research in industry in the 1980 annual meeting of the Industrial Research Institute, A. Fred Kerst (then vice president, R&D, Calgon Corp.) suggested three "signals" as to when directed basic research should be undertaken:

> [When] important problems . . . cannot be solved with the knowledge you currently possess. . . .
> The business has become mature. . . . How are we going to stay in business?
> Top management decides to grow through acquisitions and new ventures, in which case research must be able to assess the technological needs and potentials of those activities. (EIRMA, 1982, p. 26)

In some firms, the corporate research laboratory constitutes about 10% of the total corporate research; and of that part, only about 10 to 30% of it is basic. So that targeted basic research is often only about 1 to 3% of corporate R&D. An important consideration for R&D funding is to keep the spending relatively smooth. Jerky levels (raising, cutting, raising, cutting) of R&D funding are inefficient, since R&D effort is long term in nature. Continuity in effort is important. It has been estimated that ideas from basic research may require 10 years to be realized as commercial products.

The actual level of corporate funding is thus aggregated from the numbers and types of businesses of the firm, production-related labs, and the central research lab. Each production unit will require some research, specifically for testing, safety, and process improvement. Each business will require some research, specifically for product and process improvement and for new product development. Finally, the corporation as a whole should have a central laboratory for technological exploration, new venture development, and cross-cutting technological advance. Adding together, the sizes of the individual labs with the central lab will then create the corporate R&D budget.

In the central corporate lab, R&D funding is usually of three types: (1) an allocation from corporate headquarters, (2) internal contracts from budgets of business units, and (3) external contracts from government or other sources. The corporate allocation provides the internal flexibility of the corporate lab to explore new directions. The internal contracts from other business units provide sharply focused and near-term research, linking the central lab strongly with the business units. Probably there should be about as much funding from internal contracts as from corporate allocation to maintain a balance between technological initiatives from the central lab and close linkage to the business units. The external contracts can be run as a kind of business or as a means of exploring ranges of technology beyond current business horizons.

However funded, the bottom line of corporate research is the successful transfer of new technology from the lab into business production and products. Therefore, the measure of success of corporate research strategy is the historical marginal contributions that research has made to the creation and maintainance of the businesses of the corporation.

Example: Xerox Corporate Research Strategy

An example of corporate research strategy was the research directions in 1981 of the Xerox Palo Alto Research Center (PARC). The vice president for corporate research in Xerox was George Pake. Reporting to Pake were three research centers in Xerox:

1. Webster Research Center under M. D. Tabak
2. Xerox Research Centre Canada under R. H. Marchessault
3. Palo Alto Research Center under R. J. Spinrad

The general division of research among these centers at that time was:

1. *Marking and imaging technologies:* Webster Research Center
2. *Materials processing research:* Xerox Research Centre Canada
3. *Digital systems research:* Palo Alto Research Center

Xerox's businesses then were divided principally into reprographics and office automation systems. The Webster Research Center was primarily responsible for reprographics technology and the Palo Alto Research Center for office system technology. The Palo Alto Research Center (PARC) had been created specifically to broaden Xerox's future business from copying machines into office automation.

We can compare the research strategies of Xerox at two points in time, 1972 and 1981, before and after the addition of automated office systems to the traditional Xerox copying business. In 1972, Xerox's overall research efforts were directed at:

1. Photoreceptors—alloy and organic
2. Understanding the xerographic development process
3. Laser xerography
4. Distributed systems
5. Optical digital storage
6. Solid-state lasers for scanning and storage
7. Science base

One can see that in 1972 research efforts were focused on what was then the main business of Xerox, reproducing graphically (reprographics).

However, by 1979, the strategic business plan of Xerox had changed to broaden the product base from copying machines only to automated office systems. Accordingly, by 1981, the research efforts had broadened:

1. Marking technologies and transducers
2. Optical storage
3. Programming distributed files
4. Human–digital interface
5. Microelectronics
6. Materials
7. Science base

One can see that the emphasis on copying technology and information storage remained, but research effort had broadened to add an emphasis on programming distributed files, human–digital interface, and microelectronics.

The organization and research directions corporate research should cover both the technologies of current businesses and the technologies of future businesses.

In 1981, Xerox's stated objectives for its research were:

To search for new technological concepts
To harden a technological concept

To extend/defend a deployed technology
To develop new research or engineering tools
To improve performance/cost for materials
To inform decisions on purchase or acquisition of technology
To build a base of knowledge or expertise

These objectives illustrate the central function of corporate research to create and improve the technologies available to a company to design and produce products.

SUMMARY

The research strategy of the corporate laboratory delineates the areas of technological competitiveness of the corporation's future. Morphological analysis is a technique for systematically examining alternative combinations of structures to achieve a technological function. Research topics can be focused on exploring some of variations in structures and on the scientific phenomena behind or essential to variations.

In addition to creating new technology, the corporate research laboratory plays an informative role in determining where and how to acquire technology developed by other firms, either through licensing, hiring of people, or corporate acquisition. The actual level of corporate funding is aggregated from the numbers and types of businesses of the firm, production-related labs, and the central research lab.

REFLECTION

1. Obtain recent annual corporate reports from several companies in a research-intensive industry, and obtain material from these companies on the organization of the R&D activities. How is the research organized?
2. *Business Week* magazine annually publishes R&D expenditures of major companies. Find the most recent such issue and compare R&D expenditures across industries.

For further reading

DEAN, BURTON V., and JOEL L. GOLDHAR, eds.   *Management of Research and Innovation*. New York: North-Holland, 1980.

CHAPTER TWENTY-THREE
NATIONAL R&D SYSTEMS

CENTRAL IDEAS

1. Macro-level innovation structure

2. Performance, sponsorship, and nature of national R&D

3. R&D personnel

4. International R&D comparisons

5. National partnerships for innovation

Example: U.S. Pharmaceutical Industry

We have previously focused on the process of innovation at the level of the firm; finally, we will examine the processes of innovation at the national level. This is important to the firm, for national activities provide the scientific and technological context which facilitates innovation. As an example, consider the transformation of the American pharmaceutical industry from a low-tech to a high-tech industry.

In 1983, the National Academy of Engineering and the National Research Council (NAE/NRC) reviewed the competitive status of the industry in the 1980s:

> The U.S. pharmaceutical industry has for decades been one of the most profitable and rapidly growing sectors of the American economy. Its continuing expansions of output, productivity, and jobs have been achieved alongside price increases that have been more moderated than the general rate of inflation. Together with other high-technology industries, it has played an important role in generating exports and net trade surpluses. Additionally, new pharmaceuticals have made significant contributions to improved health and to the control of escalating medical costs. (NAE/NRC, 1983)

The technical and economic progress of the pharmaceutical industry had not always been so progressive. Until the 1930s, the pharmaceutical industry looked more like a medieval apothacary. Before then, the drug industry had manufactured only a limited number of unpatented products, marketed without prescriptions. Henry Gadsden, a pharmaceutical executive with Merck in 1983, described that earlier situation:

> You could count the basic medicines on the fingers of your two hands. Morphine, quinine, digitalis, insulin, codeine, aspirin, arsenicals, nitroglycerin, mercurials, and a few biologicals. Our own Sharp and Dohme catalog did not carry a single exclusive prescription medicine.
> We had a broad range of fluids, ointments, and extracts, as did other firms, but we placed heavy emphasis on biological medicines as well. Most of our products were sold without a prescription. And 43% of the prescription medicines were compounded by the pharmacists, as compared with 1.2 percent today. (NAE/NRC, 1983)

The change of the phamaceutical industry into a high-tech, innovative industry came about after World War II, due to the creation of new drug technologies from biology and chemistry. It began with important scientific discoveries made in the 1930s, when scientists had discovered a series of natural products important to health—vitamins and hormones. This illustrates the concept of a national R&D system. The scientific discoveries were made in universities, supported by private foundations and through government sponsorship. The newly discovered vitamins and hormones were then manufactured by the pharmaceutical industry. They conquered age-old diseases—scurvy, pernicious anemia, beri-beri, and pallagra, and other endocrine dificiencies.

Science in industry and universities also provided the basis for medical anti-infective drugs. In 1908, chemists in the laboratories of the German firm I.G. Farben synthesized a dye called sulfanilamide. Much later, in 1932, I.G. Farben scientist, Gerhard Domagk, experimented with a derivative of sulfanilamide (prontosil) to see if it could kill streptococcal infection in mice and rabbits. It did, and it was the first great breakthrough for antibacterial medicines. In 1933, it was used first in a human being for the successful treatment of blood poisoning from staphylococcal speticemia (Thomas, 1984).

A next major pharmaceutical breakthrough started also in a university, Oxford, where Alexander Fleming discovered penicillin in 1928. In 1939, pure penicillin was isolated by Howard Florey and Ernst Chain. However, the manufacture of penicillin by industry did not begin immediately in the 1930s, partly because it had not been patented, due to the considerable time lapse between its discovery and the demonstration of its therapeutic properties. Consequently, at first, there was little incentive for industry to fund the R&D necessary for large-scale production of penicillin.

Then in World War II, the demand for the drug by the Allied armies became enormous, so that the U.S. government provided $3 million to industry and universities to research penicillin and its production. Furthermore, the government encouraged private construction of penicillin manufacture through allowing accelerated depreciation for tax purposes. When the war ended, the federally sponsored penicillin plants were sold to private firms at half their costs (NAE/NRC, 1983).

The discoveries of sulfa drugs and penicillin indicated the possibilities for systematic research in finding new antibiotic drugs. This view transformed the pharmaceutical industry into a modern research-intensive, high-technology industry. The new drugs played an important role in the history of advances in medicine and public health. The 100 years from 1885 to 1985 led to a dramatic decline in infant mortality and to a doubling of the average human life span.

ECONOMIC IMPORTANCE OF TECHNOLOGICAL INNOVATION

At the national level, technological innovation is important to the economy for several reasons: (1) improving national productivity, (2) providing competitive edges in international trade, and (3) improving the quality of life. Technological change stimulates economic growth and increases productivity. New technologies create new functions or improved performance, which provide trading opportunities. New technologies improve the acquisition and utilization of natural resources and also the conservation of resources (Hill, 1979).

Technological change may, of course, bring problems along with its benefits—common problems are pollution, environmental hazards, and population displacements. Cultural or aesthetic values previously prized may be lost in the new social conditions that society constructs to use technology. Technology is a kind of tool, and all tools can be used or misused. It is important for managers to participate as citizens in national decisions that structure the safe and beneficial use of technology.

FUNDING AND PERFORMANCE OF RESEARCH

A national R&D system is the infrastructure that creates new technology and influences the directions of its use and safety. The performers of R&D are industrial research laboratories, governmental research laboratories, and universities. The sponsors of research are principally the federal government, industrial firms, and private philanthrophic foundations. The nature of the research is basic, applied, or developmental.

In the United States in the second half of the twentieth century, on a yearly average, about half of the funds for R&D came from industry and about half from the federal government (for example, in 1985, 50% from industry and 47% from the federal government). In the performance of R&D, about three-quarters was performed annually by industry, with universities and federal laboratories performing the rest (for example, in 1985, industry performed 73% of the R&D, universities 12%, and federal laboratories 12%). Overall, the character of the R&D performed nationally was about two-thirds developmental, one-fifth applied, and one-eighth basic (for example, in 1985, developmental research was 67%, applied research 21%, and basic research 12%) (NSB/NSF, 1983).

Industry performs most of the R&D, and most of the R&D industry performs is developmental (since developmental research leads directly to new products and processes). Industrial research in America was annually about four-fifths developmental, one-fifth applied, and only a little basic (for example, in 1985, it was 78% developmental, 19% applied, and 3% basic). In the industrial research setting, basic research is fairly close to being what one ordinarily means by "science," and applied and developmental research to what one means by "technology." Thus industrial research is predominantly technological.

In comparison, university research in the United States was annually about two-thirds basic and one-third applied (for example, in 1985, university research was 68% basic and 32% applied and developmental). Thus university research is predominantly science (with a third technology).

Although R&D statistics vary from year to year, this broad pattern has been characteristic of the United States since World War II. The universities have performed most of the scientific research, with industry performing most of the technological research. The federal government has funded most of the university research, and industrial research has been funded about half by industry and half by the federal government. Most of the research performed in the United States has been technological, with some (about a fifth) scientific.

Example: Industry/University Cooperative Research

A cooperative research project sponsored by the National Science Foundation illustrates how university research can be directly useful to an industrial R&D manager. The project was an engineering basic research project jointly performed by Michael Werle of United Technologies and by Professors Walker and Smith of Lehigh University. The project modeled the turbulent flow of air across turbine blades. Werle performed the experimental tasks for the project, and Walker and Smith performed the theoretical and complementary experimental tasks.

The project was initiated in 1980 by Werle as the manager of gas dynamics and thermophysics at the United Technologies Research Center at Hartford, Connecticut. United Technologies consisted then of four groups of companies, classified as (1) power, (2) helicopters, (3) building systems, and (4) electronics. In this project, Werle's technological concern was for the turbine technologies of Pratt & Whitney aircraft.

The design of turbine blades is a critical feature in the efficiency and safety of jet engines (as the blades compress the air prior to ignition with aviation fuel). The smooth flow of air over the turbine blades is necessary for fuel economy and safety. In the early days of jet aircraft, "flame-out" was a frequent and disastrous occurrence that killed many pilots. Flame-out occurred when the air flowing over the turbine blades broke into turbulence, stopping the flow of air into the jet combustion chamber and snuffing out the combustion. Planes suddenly lost power and often crashed. This turbulence problem is the same as "stalling" of an airplane by the loss of a smooth flow of air across the wings. The smooth flow of air over turbine blades thus improves blade life, fuel economy, and safety.

From a basic engineering view, the modeling of gas and liquid flows over surfaces is a fundamental problem, involving general techniques such as finite element analysis and differential equations of flow. Werhle approached Walker and Smith and suggested a joint project, combining their complementary skills. A project proposal was written and submitted to the National Science Foundation for funding. NSF reviewed the proposal, judged it outstanding, and funded it.

In the cooperative gas turbine research project, Werle's goals were to affect the product lines of gas turbines by improving the design methodology of their company. In their design process, Pratt & Whitney engineers had accumulated a simplified analysis of gas turbine operation (partly from theory and partly from experience). Their simplified analysis provided a knowledge base for the design system. Designs produced using the design system were then evaluated and hardware (constructed to such designs) were tested. These steps of design evaluation and hardware testing were the most expensive steps in new engine development.

Werle's goal as a research manager was to improve Pratt & Whitney's design methodology. Werle performed experiments and fluid dynamics calculations. The experiments were scientifically conceived and performed to address puzzling or unknown parts of the engineering correlations (used in Pratt & Whitney's design system). The cooperative project sponsored by NSF was one such experiment.

In the NSF cooperative research project, the knowledge gained not only advanced public knowledge (through scientific pubilications in fluid dynamic engineering journals) but also helped Pratt & Whitney improve their technical capability. The interests of industry and university in advancing basic engineering knowledge coincided. Although their primary purposes still differed (education as opposed to production), their interest in basic engineering knowledge was mutual.

FEDERAL SUPPORT OF SCIENCE AND TECHNOLOGY

The example shows one of the important roles the federal government has played in sponsoring basic research in universities, much of which has had direct importance to industry. Federal support of research has been organized through different mission agencies. The federal agencies with the largest programs in R&D were the Department of Defense (DOD), National Aeronautical and Space Agency (NASA), National Institutes of Health (NIH), Department of Energy (DOE), Department of Agriculture (DOA), and the National Science Foundation (NSF). In the distribution of R&D effort in federal agencies, the emphasis was on defense (for example, in 1981 50% of federal R&D funds were expended in defense, 13% in space, and 38% in civilian functions).

R&D RESEARCHERS

In 1983, there were about 1.5 million scientists employed in research and about 1.9 million engineers. Scientists in the United States were employed about one-half in industry, one-fourth in universities and colleges, and one-fourth in government and other laboratories (for example, in 1983, industry employed 51% of the scientists, academia employed 24%, and government 17%). Of the engineers, most are employed in industry (for example, in 1983, industry employed 80% of the engineers in research, academia 3%, and government 12%). The scientists were about evenly divided among the physical, life, and social sciences (for example, in 1983, 26% had Ph.D.'s in the physical sciences, 30% in the life sciences, and 34% in the social sciences, with 9% in mathematics and computers).

INTERNATIONAL COMPARISONS

Each nation structures its national research systems differently, according to differences in culture, philosophy, and political beliefs. These differences stem from the role of the government in the economy, the funding and structure of the universities, and the centralization of research policies (Betz et al., 1980). For example, the communist countries monopolize production and education, and their research is centralized in government laboratories. In the Western democracies, technological innovation is predominantly decentralized in the research of private firms, and scientific research is performed in universities (and university-related laboratories or governmental laboratories). The United States has the largest, most decentralized, and most pluralistic form of research system of the Western democracies.

Since the middle of the twentieth century, the ratio of scientists and engineers engaged in research and development to the population labor force in the United States has averaged about 55 to 65 per 10,000 (or about 0.55% to 0.65%). Since World War II, the Japanese have increased their numbers of scientists and engineers in research to nearly the same ratio as the United States (for example, it was about 0.55% in 1981). Since World War II, West Germany, the United Kingdom, and France increased their numbers of scientists and engineers from about 0.3% to 0.4%. The USSR was estimated to have more scientists and engineers as a proportion of their labor force than any of the Western countries (for example, between 0.9 and 1% in 1981) (NSB/NSF, 1983).

In terms of funding levels of R&D, the U.S. funding of R&D as a ratio to GNP (gross national product) has averaged around 2.5 to 2.7% in the 1970s and 1980s. West Germany, the United Kingdom, and Japan had increased their funding of R&D since 1950 to about these same ratios by the 1980s. When one compares R&D on nondefense research, however, in the 1980s, the United States annually expended less as a ratio of R&D to GNP than the Japanese (for example, 1.7% to 2.5% in 1983).

The broad picture of funding in the second half of the twentieth century was that the United States annually expended more on R&D than any other country in the Western world, but it was invested more heavily toward military than toward commercial applications. The importance of R&D in international competition was broadly shown by comparing the trade balance of the United States classified into research-intensive and non-research-intensive industries. Figure 25.1 shows the change in U.S. trade balance in industries classified as R&D intensive and non-R&D intensive. It clearly shows the importance of advanced technology in U.S. competitiveness in world trade. Since the industrial revolution, technological innovation has been an important factor in international competitiveness (NSB/NSF, 1983).

Example: Synthetic Rubber

The innovation of synthetic rubber shows the participation of the different sectors of university, industry, and government in innovation. Synthetic rubber was a vital governmental concern in World War II after the sources of natural rubber, for tires and other applications, had been closed to the United States by the Japanese conquest of southern Asia in 1941.

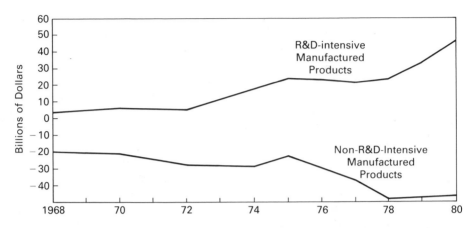

FIGURE 25.1   U.S. trade balance (exports less imports) in R&D-intensive manu-factured product groups. (From U.S. Department of Commerce).

In 1906, at a German university, Julius Nieuwland, a chemist, discovered a chemical reaction of the organic compound acetylene placed in an alkali medium. Then he worked 10 more years to try to get a higher yield of the reaction. This was the basic invention required for synthetic rubber. Later, in 1921, Nieuwland demonstrated that his new material (which he called divinylacetylene) was a polymer that could be produced in a catalytic reaction. This was the technical feasibility of a new production process for producing the new material.

The step to commercialization began in 1925 in American industry, when an American chemist, E. K. Bolton, working at E.I. du Pont de Nemours Co. in America, heard Nieuwland lecture at the American Chemical Society. Bolton reported the commercial potential to DuPont, and they reached a commercial agreement with Nieuwland to try to develop it as a new product. This began the development phase of the innovation. Then in 1932, DuPont introduced the new product under the brand name Neoprene, a synthetic rubber. It created an enormous and continuing market.

PARTNERS FOR INNOVATION—BUSINESS, UNIVERSITY, AND GOVERNMENT

Since technology is important in international competition, the common national interest between business, government, and universities should be to prepare for the national technological future. Proper relationships between industry, universities, and government can contribute to the long-term technological capability of a nation. For example, in the 1980s, several industrial sectors responded to the increased international technological competitiveness by focusing on basic research (that is, science underpinning technology). They created new research-oriented, cooperative oganizations. In 1981, the chemical industry formed the Council for Chemical Research; the electronics and computer industries formed the Semiconductor Research Corporation and the Microelectronics and Computer Technology Corporation.

The Council for Chemical Research was an industry/university organization devoted to the advancement of basic research in chemistry and chemical engineering (vital to the future of the U. S. chemical industry). The Semiconductor Research Corporation was an industrial research fund supporting basic research in universities on semiconductor materials and properties. The Microelectronics and Computer Research Corporation was an industrial research laboratory to advance computer technology (funded by an industrial consortium of 13 companies).

These examples marked a renewed industrial interest in basic research in the 1980s and a determination to maintain national leadership in technology. Some observers in the 1980s saw cooperative research efforts as important: "The research scene in the U.S. is changing rapidly. Spurred by growing international competition in various companies, many of the 'interpretations' of antitrust and related laws have significantly changed. This has led to cooperative efforts on a scale never before attempted" (Gerstenfeld and Berger, 1984).

Technology is partly prior experience, partly trial-and-error experimentation, and partly the systematic understanding of the scientific basis of technological processes. To the extent that technological development is attempted through the application of scientific methods and information, it is "scientific technology." Some scientific knowledge ordinarily precedes invention, but seldom enough scientific knowledge to fully understand, explain, or model the phenomena underlying the invention. Taking invention into commercial applications requires a great deal of research, development, and further inventions. This innovation process is lengthy and costly, requiring partnerships between universities, industries, and governments.

SUMMARY

The innovation process has a macro level (the national and international level) and a micro level (the firm and industry level). At the national level, the infrastructure that creates new technology and influences the directions of its use and safety is the R&D system of a nation. The performers of R&D are industrial research laboratories, governmental research laboratories, and universities. The sponsors of research are principally the federal and state governments, industrial firms, and philanthropic foundations.

Scientists in the United States are employed about half in industry, one-fourth in universities and colleges, and one-fourth in government and other laboratories. Most engineers are employed in industry and government. The United States has annually expended more on R&D than any other country in the Western world, but this has been heavily toward military rather than commercial R&D. Research relationships between industry, universities, and government are important in creating the long-term technological capability of the nation.

Reflection

1. Every two years (1980, 1982, 1984, etc.) the National Science Foundation publishes a statistical summary of national R&D in a volume called *Science Indicators.* Obtain a recent copy (for sale by the Superintendent of Documents, U.S. Government Printing Office, Washington D.C. 20402), and compare the different national activities in R&D and international trade. How is the United States doing? Could we be doing more or better?

FOR FURTHER READING

ROMAN, DANIEL D., *Science, Technology, and Innovation: A Systems Approach.* Columbus, Ohio: Grid Publishing, 1980.

RAMO, SIMON, *America's Technology Slip.* New York: Wiley, 1980.

CHAPTER TWENTY-FOUR
TECHNOLOGY
REVOLUTIONS

CENTRAL IDEAS

1. New technology firms in technology revolutions
2. Technology revolutions and scientific progress
3. Science bases of technology

Example: New Biotechnology Firms in the 1980s

R&D infrastructures have a major impact on the economy when technological revolutions are begun on scientific discoveries. We recall that long waves of industrial expansion have been triggered by technological revolutions. The opportunity to start new firms and the ability to position a corporation in new technology are most favorable in the early years of the technology when competition is open. In the late 1970s and early 1980s, biotechnology was created from scientific discoveries in genetics. We will describe two of the new firms that were created around genetic engineering: Genentech and Cetus.

In 1973, two professors, Stanley Cohen of Stanford University and Herbert Boyer of the University of California at San Francisco, applied for the basic patent in recombinant DNA techniques for genetic engineering. This invention was a culmination of about 100 years of prior scientific research in genetics. Subsequently, Boyer founded Genentech, and Cohen joined Cetus. Over 100 other research firms were formed in the years from 1978 to 1982 to commercialize the new technology. In 1980, Genentech and Cetus went public, and Boyer and Cohen became millionaires.

Genentech was created by Herbert Boyer and Robert A. Swanson. Swanson saw the potential for raising venture capital to start a genetic engineering firm. The story is that Swanson walked into Boyer's office, introduced himself, and proposed that they start a firm. They each put up

$500 in 1976 and started Genentech. Cetus has been founded in 1971, providing a commercial service for fast screening of microorganisms. However, by 1976, after the discovery of recombinant DNA techniques, Cetus changed its business and technology strategy toward the new genetic engineering possibilities of designing gene-engineered biological products. Cetus retained Stanley Cohen as one of its 33 scientific consultants and later as head of Cetus Palo Alto (*Business Week*, 1984b).

Early financing in Genentech was secured from venture funds and industrial sources. Lubrizol purchased 24% of Genentech in 1979, Monsanto held about 5%, and a consortium of Japanese companies owned 1.5%. In Cetus, Standard Oil of Indiana purchased 28% of their stock in 1977. In 1978, Standard Oil of California bought 22.4%, and later, National Distillers & Chemical purchased 14.2%. The corporate investors were primarily looking to learn the new technology.

Both Genentech and Cetus offered forms of stock-option plans in order to retain their key scientists. In addition, Cetus had set up three small subsidiaries, with two of them providing 40% control by the key scientists. Genentech and Cetus were the first of the biotechnology firms to offer public stock in 1980.

In its public offering, Genentech realized net proceeds of $36 million. At the end of fiscal year 1981, it had $30 million cash but required about $17 million yearly for its R&D activities. Then it had assets of $65 million, with a 1981 income of $21 million and net earnings of $503,000. In its public offering, Cetus raised $115 million at $23 a share. Of this, $27 million was intended for production and distribution of Cetus-developed products and processes, $25 million for self-funded R&D, $24 million for research and administrative facilities, $19 million for additional machinery and equipment, and $12 milion for financing of new-venture subsidiaries. For the fiscal year ending June 1981, total revenues at Cetus were $15.5 million, with a net income of $590,700.

For new firms, it is important that early products create income. For example, Genentech's product interests were in health care, industrial biocatalysis, and agriculture. In 1982, early products included genetically engineered human insulin, human growth hormone, leukocyte and fibroblast interferons, immune interferon, bovine and porcine growth hormones, and foot-and-mouth vaccine. Genentech's human insulin project was a joint venture with Eli Lilly, aimed at a world market of $300 million, served by animal insulin. Genentech's human growth hormone project was a joint venture with KabiGen (a Swedish pharmaceutical manufacturer), with a world market of $100 million yearly. The leukocyte and fibroblast inteferon was a joint venture with Hoffmann–La Roche, and the immune interferon, with Daiichi Seiyaku and Toray Industries. The bovine and porcine growth hormones were a joint venture with Monsanto, and the foot-and-mouth vaccine, with International Minerals and Chemicals.

In comparison, in 1982, Cetus was interested primarily in products in health care, chemicals, food, agribusiness, and energy. Their commercial projects included high-purity fructose, veterinary products, and human interferons. The high-purity fructose project was a joint venture with Standard Oil of California. In 1983, Cetus introduced its first genetically engineered product, a vaccine to prevent scours, a toxic diarrhea in newborn pigs. Also in 1983, a new president, Robert A. Fildes, developed a five-year projection to provide Cetus with a positive cash flow by 1987. His plan narrowed the focus to the two major health care markets, diagnostics and cancer therapeutics. Both monoclonal antibody and recombinant DNA technologies were employed. Through layoffs and attrition, Cetus reduced employment in 1983 to 480 people (with 280 scientists). The new president then hired people experienced in developing drugs and taking them to market.

Central to the creation of the genetic firms was a combination of university scientists, entrepreneurs, and venture capitalists. Successful new business ventures in new technology always require teamwork between technical and financial talents. Moreover, many of these firms began as joint ventures with established chemical and pharmaceutical firms. These joint ventures provided "windows on science" for chemical and pharmaceutical companies.

WINDOWS ON SCIENCE

In this example, we see that corporations invested heavily in the new biotechnology firms. The reason was to have a "window on science" so that they would be prepared for rapid commercial movement as the technological revolution created business opportunities.

We next review the origin of biotechnology, in order to illuminate answers to the following questions:

1. In what manner and how long does it take science to provide the knowledge base for new technologies?
2. When should investment in new technologies occur?

GENETIC RESEARCH
BEFORE BIOTECHNOLOGY

It would be nice if technology revolutions occurred all the time. They have occurred often, but perhaps not often enough. The problem is that technology revolutions depend on scientific progress, and major scientific progress can take decades to accumulate the knowledge for technological "breakthroughs." We will review the history of research in genetics to illustrate the length of time and complexity of research often required to advance a science base for new technology. It was at a scientific conference in 1972 in Hawaii that Stanley Cohen met with Herbert Boyer, and they began a research collaboration that invented the revolutionary recombinant-DNA techniques.

Where did their idea begin historically? What scientific research preceded and provided the basis for this creative invention? That story started almost 100 years earlier. Fundamental questions were being asked, by early scientists, about the origin of life. It was the new biology in the nineteenth century. Then science was a time of wonder and excitement—electricity, magnetism, atoms, cells—the new phenomena of the brand-new sciences of physics, chemistry, and biology. These disciplines provided knowledge bases for the inventions that created the electrical and chemical industries and modernized medicine and agriculture. A novelist of the time, Jules Verne, depicted the contemporary scientific and technological excitement as adventures, creating the literary genre of science fiction.

For real scientists, however, adventure begins in asking a fundamental question, such as: What is matter? What is life? In the case of genetic engineering, the fundamental question was: How does life reproduce itself? The next step of the scientific adventure is to try to answer the questions by observing nature. Scientific instrumentation provides the means of observing and experimenting with nature. Science advances with the invention and use of new instruments. In the late eighteenth century, biology was revolutionized by the invention of the microscope. It profoundly altered ideas about living beings and the origins of life because it provided the view that organisms were composed of cells.

The problem of the origin of life thus became focused on the nature of cell reproduction and growth. Research followed several directions and reached several stages of discovery before the nature of cell reproduction became understood:

1. The structure of the cell was investigated.
2. The nucleus of the cell was isolated and chemically analyzed (DNA).
3. The principles of heredity were established.
4. The function of DNA in reproduction was discovered.
5. The structure of DNA was discovered.
6. The genetic code was deciphered.
7. Recombinant DNA techniques were discovered.
8. Applications of genetic engineering were begun.

The Structure of the Cell

In biology, by the early nineteenth century, scientists looking at the cell through the microscope had focused on trying to understand the cell's structure. The cell consisted principally of a cell wall, a nucleus, and surrounding protoplasma. Studies next aimed at determining the substructure of the nucleus of the cell. In 1838, Christian Ehrenberg observed the division of the nucleus. In 1842, Karl Nageli saw the rodlike chromosomes within the nucleus of the plant cells. Thus by the middle of the nineteenth century, the biologists had seen that the key to reproduction of life involved the chromosomes which divided into pairs when the nucleus of the cell split in cell reproduction (Portugal and Cohen, 1977).

Discovery and Chemical Analysis of DNA

Attention turned next to investigating the chemical nature of chromosomes. Science is a system containing disciplines; and the techniques and knowledge in one discipline may be used in another discipline. Chemistry and physics provided tools and knowledge to the study of biological phenomena. In 1869, Friedrich Miescher, a chemist, reported the discovery of DNA, by precipitating material from the nuclear fraction of cells. He called the material nuclein. Subsequent studies showed that it was composed of two components, nucleic acid and protein.

While these studies were occurring, continual improvements were being made in microscopic techniques. The more detail one wishes to observe, the more the means of observation need to be improved. For the microscope, specific chemicals were found that could be used to selectively stain the cell. Paul Ehrlich discovered that staining cells with the new chemically derived coal-tar colors correlated with the chemical composition of the cell components. This is an example of how technology contributes to science, for the new colors were the products of the new chemical industry.

In 1873, A. Schneider described the relationships between the chromosomes and various stages of cell division. He noted two states in the process of mitosis (which is the phenomenon of chromosome division resulting in the separation of the cell nucleus into two daughter nuclei). In 1879, Walter Flemming introduced the term "chromatin" for the colored material found within the nucleus after staining. He suggested that chromatin was identical with Miescher's nuclein.

At this time, studies of nuclear division and the behavior of chromosomes were emphasizing the importance of the nucleus; but it was not yet understood how these processes were related to fertilization. In 1875, Oscar Hertwig demonstrated that fertilization was not the fusion of two cells but the fusion of two nuclei. Meanwhile, the study of nucleic acid components was progressing. In 1879, Albrecht Kossel began publishing in the literature on nuclein. Over the next decades, he (along with Miescher) was foremost in the field of nuclein research; and with them, Phoebus Levine (1869–1940) finally laid the clear basis for the determination of the chemistry of the nucleic acids.

As early as 1914, Emil Fisher had attempted the chemical synthesis of a nucleotide, but real progress was not made in synthesis until 1938. Synthesis was important to understand the chemical composition of DNA. Alexander Todd made significant progress. But it was still difficult to isolate deoxyribose from nucleic acid, and this delayed the understanding of the chemical structure of DNA for many years.

It also was not appreciated that RNA and DNA were two different kinds of nucleic acid. Finally by 1938, the distinction between RNA and DNA was understood; and the true molecular size of DNA was being determined in the 1930s. In 1949, C. E. Carter and W. Cohn found a chemical basis for the differences between RNA and DNA. By 1950, DNA was known to be a high-molecular-weight polymer with phosphate groups linking deoxyribonucleosides between the 3 and 5 positions of sugar groups. The sequence of the bases was still unknown. Thus the detailed chemical composition of DNA was finally determined by 1950, but not its molecular geometry. Almost 100 years had passed between the discovery of DNA and determination of its chemical composition.

The Principles of Heredity

While the chemistry of DNA was being sought, the foundation of modern genetics was (at the same time, from 1900 to 1930) being laid. The clarification of the nature of heredity had begun in the nineteenth century with Darwin's epic work on evolution and Mendel's pioneering work on heredity. However, modern advances in genetic research began in 1910 with Thomas Morgan's group, researching the fruit fly, *Drosophila melanogaster.* Morgan demonstrated the validity of Mendel's analysis and showed that mutations could be induced by x-rays. By 1922, Morgan's group had analyzed 2000 genes on the four *Drosophila* fly's chromosomes and attempted to calculate the size of a gene. Müller showed that ultraviolet light could also induce mutations.

The Function of DNA in Reproduction

While these geneticists showed the principles of heredity, the mechanism of heredity had not yet been shown. Was DNA the transmitter of heredity, and if so, how? Other scientists continued to study the mechanism of the gene, with early work on bacterial reproduction coming from scientists studying bacterial cultures. R. Kraus (1897), J. A. Arkwright (1920), and O. Avery and A. R. Dochez (1917) had demonstrated the secretion of toxins by infectious bacteria. This raised the question of what chemical components in the bacterium were required to produce immunological specificity. The search for the answer to this question then revealed relationships between bacterial infection and the biological activity of DNA.

Indications that viruses might also be involved in disease had occurred in 1892. In 1911, Peyton Rous had discovered that rat tumor extracts contained virus particles capable of transmitting cancer between chickens. In 1933, Max Schlesinger isolated a bacteriophage that infected a specific kind of bacteria. Next, scientists learned that viruses consisted mainly of protein and DNA. In 1935, W. M. Stanley crystallized the tobacco mosaic virus, which encouraged scientists to study further the physical and chemical properties of viruses.

Meanwhile, earlier, in 1928, Frederick Griffith had showed that a mixture of killed infectious bacterial strains and noninfectious strains could create a live, infectious strain. Then in 1935, Lional Avery showed that the transformations were due to the exchange of DNA. This was the first demonstration that DNA did, in fact, carry the genetic information. By 1940, work by George Beadle and Edward Tatum had further investigated the mechanisms of gene action by demonstrating that genes control the cellular production of substances by controlling the production of enzymes needed for their synthesis. The scientific stage was now set to understand the structure of DNA and how DNA's structure could transmit heredity.

Structure of DNA

In 1940, three scientists began studying viruses, M. Delbruck, S. Luria, and A. Hershey. They were important in training a new generation of biologists who were to concentrate on the molecular basis of genetics—the origin of molecular biology. Because viruses were then also called bacteriophages, they became known as the "phage group." A student of the phage group was James Watson. In 1953, James Watson and Francis Crick discovered the molecular model of DNA. But the success of their work had critically depended on two prior developments—the development of x-ray crystallography and Pauling's model of the helix structure of a polypeptide chain (Judson, 1979).

As the prior ability to see the cell required a new instrument, the microscope, the ability to "see" molecular structure and small particles such as viruses required more new instrumentation—x-ray crystallography and the electron microscope. X-rays had been discovered in 1985 by Wilhelm Roentgen, a physicist. The diffraction of x-rays by crystals was suggested and described theoretically by Max von Laue in 1912. Lawrence Bragg and William Henry Bragg established experimental x-ray crystallography as a technique. William Astbury applied the technique to the study of organic fibers in 1928. Dorothy Crowfoot Hodgkin published the first x-ray study of a crystalline protein in 1934.

As a fresh Ph.D. from Luria's group, Watson came to Cambridge to work at the Rutherford Lab as a postdoctoral student. A very famous research laboratory, Rutherford Laboratory was at that time directed by

Bragg. Watson then learned that the laboratory had been conducting x-ray diffraction research on DNA. Rosalind Franklin, nominally working under Maurice Wilkins, was producing the first crystallographic pictures of the DNA molecule. Watson and Crick used Franklin's pictures to help create their model. Watson and Crick also used the concept of a helix form of a molecule, derived from the work of Linus Pauling and Robert Corey on the structure of crystalline amino acids and small peptides.

Then Watson and Crick correctly modeled the DNA molecule in the form of a double helix, two strands of amino acid chains, twisting about each other like intertwined spiral staircases. This model was verified by Franklin's pictures. The model was startling because it clearly indicated the molecular action of DNA in the mitosis of cell reproduction. DNA was structured as a pair of twisted templates, complementary to one another. In reproduction, the two templates untwisted and separated from one another, providing two identical patterns for constructing proteins, that is, reproducing life. In this untwisting and chemical reproduction of proteins, life was biologically inherited.

Genetic Coding

By the early 1960s it was therefore clear that the double-helical structure of DNA was molecularly responsible for the phenomenon of heredity and life. Proteins serve as structural elements of a cell and as catalysts (enzymes) for metabolic processes in a cell. DNA provides the structural template for protein manufacture, replicating proteins through the intermediary templates of RNA. DNA structures the synthesis of RNA, and RNA structures the synthesis of proteins. What was not yet clear was exactly how the information for protein manufacture was encoded in the DNA. In 1965, Marshall Nirenberg and Philip Neder deciphered (what many researchers were working toward) the basic triplet coding of the DNA molecule. The amino acids that composed the DNA structure, taken in groups of three, provided the information for protein construction.

Thus in a 100 years, science had discovered the chemical basis for heredity and decoded its information pattern. The scientific knowledge base for a new technology was laid. What was left was to invent techniques to manipulate gene structures and to transfer manipulated genes into cells.

Recombinant DNA Techniques

All that history had to pass before the ideas were ready for manipulating genes. Then several researchers began trying to cut and splice genes. In 1965, Paul Berg at Stanford University planned to transfer DNA into *Escherichia coli* bacteria, using an animal virus (SV40 lambda phage). *E. coli* bacteria lodge normally in human intestines, and the SV40 virus is a virus of monkeys which can produce tumor cells in cultures of human cells. Because of the dangerous nature of the SV40 virus, Berg decided not to proceed with the experiment, publishing a design for hydridizing bacteria in 1972. Berg organized a historic meeting on safety, the Conference on Biohazards in Cancer Research, held at the Asilomar Conference Center, Pacific Grove, California, on January 22–24, 1973 (Olby, 1974).

Peter Lobban, a Stanford graduate student, had simultaneously been working on a similar approach to gene splicing. Lobban was studying under Dale Kaiser of the Stanford Medical School. Kaiser had been one of the "phage school" group. He studied the lambda phage virus, which attaches itself to the *E. coli* bacterium. Kaiser learned that the DNA in lambda phage was circular but opened to insert itself into the DNA of *E. coli* (with so-called sticky ends). It was this mechanism that Berg and Lobban had intended to use to create *E. coli* hybrids. However, before Berg succeeded in the bacterial approach, other scientists attained the genetic engineering goal first.

Herbert Boyer of the University of California had given Berg some EcoRI enzyme, which cleaves DNA to have sticky ends. Berg had given the enzyme to Janet Mertz to study the enzyme's behavior. Mertz noticed that when the EcoRI enzyme cleaved an SV40 DNA circlet, the free ends of the resulting linear DNA eventually re-formed back into a circle. Mertz asked Ronald Davis at Stanford to look at the action of the enzyme under the electron microscope. They learned that any two DNA molecules exposed to EcoRI could be "recombined" with the help of nothing more than the DNA ligase to form hybride DNA molecules.

Stanley Cohen, a professor in Stanford University's Medical Department, learned of Janet Mertz's results. Cohen then thought of constructing a hybrid DNA molecule from plasmids using the EcoRI enzyme. Plasmids are circles of DNA which float in the cell, outside the cell's nucleus, and control the synthesis of enzymes which the cell requires.

Thus it finally happened, after 100 years of scientific research into the nature of heredity—Cohen and Boyer planned the critical experiments that were to create genetic engineering technology. This planning occurred in November 1972 when Cohen attended the biology conference in Hawaii. After a day of meetings, Cohen went out for a late supper with some colleages: Herbert Boyer of the University of California, Stanley Falfkow of the University of Washington at Seattle, and Charles Brinton of the University of Pittsburgh. Cohen told them of his plan to create hybrid DNA molecules without the help of viruses using the enzyme EcoRI. Cohen and Boyer agreed to do this as a joint experiment. Falkow offered Cohen and Boyer a plasmid, RSF1010, to use, which confers resistance to antibiotics in bacteria.

After returning from the Hawaii conference, Boyer and Cohen began their joint experiment. By the spring of 1973, Cohen and Boyer had completed three splicings of plasmid DNAs. Boyer discussed these experiments at the 1973 Gordon Research Conference on Nucleic Acids in June 1973 (with publication occurring in the *Proceedings of the National Academy of Sciences* in November 1973). Boyer and Swanson then founded Genentech. Thus began the age of genetic engineering.

SCIENCE BASES OF TECHNOLOGY

We can generalize from this example several lessons about the relation between science and technology. Science creates phenomenal knowledge bases, used by new technologies. The knowledge bases include discovery and understanding of phenomena which technologists use to invent ways of solving human problems.

1. Scientists pursue research that asks very basic and universal questions about what things exist and how things work. In the case of genetic engineering, the science base was guided by the questions: What is life? How does life reproduce itself?

2. To answer such questions, scientists require new instrumentation to discover and study things. In the case of gene research, the microscope, chemical analysis techniques, cell culture techniques, x-ray diffraction techniques, and the electron microscope were some of the important instruments required to discover and observe the gene and its functioning.

3. These studies are carried out by different disciplinary groups specializing in different instrumental and theoretical techniques: biologists, chemists, and physicists. Even among the biologists, specialists in gene heredity research differ from specialists in viral or bacterial research. Accordingly, science is pursued in disciplinary specialties, each seeing only one aspect of the existing thing—much like the tale of the blind philosophers who never saw a whole elephant but went about feeling each part and trying to think how it all went together.

4. Major advances in science occur when sufficient parts of the puzzling object have been discovered and observed and someone imagines how to put it all together properly, as Watson and Crick modeled the DNA molecule. A model is conceptually powerful because it often not only shows structure but also implies the dynamics of a process.

5. Scientific progress takes much time, patience, continuity, and expense. Instruments need to be invented and developed. Phenomena need to be discovered and studied. Phenomenal processes are complex, subtle, multileveled, and microscopic in mechanistic detail. In the case of gene research, the instruments of the microscope and electron diffraction were critical, along with other instruments and techniques. Phenomena such as the cell structure and processes required discovery. The replication process was complex and subtle, requiring determination of a helix structure and deciphering of nature's coding.

6. Science is therefore a kind of societal investment in the possibilities of future technologies. Since time for scientific discovery is lengthy and science is complicated, science must be sponsored and performed as a kind of overhead function in society. Without the overhead of basic knowledge creation, techno-

logical innovation eventually stagnates for lack of new phenomenal knowledge for its inventive ideas.

7. Once science has created a new phenomenal knowledge base, inventions for a new technology may be made by either scientists or technologists (for example, scientists invented the recombinant DNA techniques). These radical technological inventions start a new technology curve. This is the time to begin investment in technological revolutions.

8. When the new technology is pervasive across several industries (as genetic engineering is across medicine, agriculture, and materials), the technological revolution may fuel a new industrial expansion. The long waves of economic history are thus grounded in scientific advances that create the bases for major new industrial technologies.

9. There are general implications for management. Corporations should generally be supportive of university research which focuses on fundamental questions and trains graduate in scientific techniques. Corporations should also actively perform some basic research in the science areas underlying corporate technologies, in order to prepare for long-term technological futures.

SUMMARY

Technological revolutions often arise from major scientific advances. Scientists pursue research that asks basic and universal questions about things and how things work. To answer such questions, scientists require new instrumentation to discover and study existing things. A major advance occurs in a science when sufficient parts of a puzzling object have been discovered and observed and someone puts it all together properly in a model. Science is a kind of societal investment in the possibilities of future technologies. Without the overhead of basic knowledge creation, technological innovation eventually stagnates for lack of new knowledge for its inventive ideas.

REFLECTION

1. Chose a technology and ask what scientific knowledge bases the technology rests on. When was the technology first invented? What was the state of its scientific basis then? Has it progressed?

FOR FURTHER READING

BEN-DAVID, JOSEPH, *The Scientist's Role in Society*. Englewood Cliffs, NJ: Prentice-Hall, 1971.

JUDSON, HORACE FREELAND, *The Eighth Day of Creation,* New York: Simon and Schuster, 1979.

SPIEGEL-ROSING, INA, and DEREK DE SOLLA PRICE, eds., *Science, Technology and Society*. Beverly Hills, Calif.: Sage, 1977.

CHAPTER TWENTY-FIVE
TECHNOLOGY AND
CAPITAL

CENTRAL IDEAS

1. Technological progress and the effective use of capital
2. Technological progress: an accrued economic cost
3. Patents and proprietary information
4. Patent infringement

Example: Sam Insull, an Innovative Manager

We have progressed through the the study of new ventures, innovation, and research. In these concepts, technology is managed and linked into business strategy. We conclude by emphasizing, the fundamental principle that the business function of technological progress is to improve the productivity of capital. Production, generally, is the result of integrating capital and labor through technology. Viewed from the eye of the manager, the essential objective of managing technology is to improve the productivity of capital. Since capital is the marshaling of resources for future economic action, effective use of capital often requires technological progress. Technological progress can often expand markets, lower production costs, and improve utilization of productive capacity. An innovative manager views technology with an eye on future capital.

Samuel Insull was one such example of an innovative manager who played an important role in the early expansion of the electrical power industry. Insull is sometimes remembered for an unfortunate incident at the close of his life; yet earlier, he was a widely respected manager. He innovated new technologies, new organizational structures, and new management techniques in the electrical power industry.

Samuel Insull started as Thomas Edison's secretary and was his administrative assistant from 1880 to 1892. He then became the head of Chicago

Edison (later called Commonwealth Edison). At that time, Chicago Edison was only one of about 20 electric utilities in Chicago (Hughes, 1984).

Some of Thomas Edison's inventions, such as the electric light bulb and the phonograph, are well known. He also created the first electric power system. By 1882, Edison had built and put into operation a coal-fired power plant, with an electric-light load, serving the Wall Street district of New York City. It was a major investment of Edison's capital, but the cost of electricity to customers was high. There were two principal reasons for the high unit costs: limited market and inefficient utilization of capital plant.

First, the electricity was in the form of direct current and could not be delivered to offices beyond a mile from the plant (due to the power losses from direct current heating the power lines). Second, the Wall Street business district was active only in the few, early evening hours when electricity was needed for lighting. Therefore, the power plant was underutilized most of the day.

To solve these problems in the management of capital, technology came to the rescue. First, the problem of market was solved by extending the distance electricity could be transmitted. The technological solution was to change from direct to alternating current (and at higher voltages). Alternating currents generated less heat loss in transmission wires than did direct current. Transformers also easily stepped alternating-current voltages up or down, up for transmission and down for use.

The physical reason why high-voltage alternating current was able to transmit electrical power over longer distances was that electricity in this form travels along the surface of a conducting wire rather than inside the wire as direct current does. At the surface of the wire, the transmitting electrical fields of alternating current meet fewer atoms of the wire, thereby losing less energy through heat loss in the atoms (it shakes up fewer atoms).

A young American inventor, William Stanley, helped the Westinghouse Company to begin the manufacture of alternating-current systems. By 1890, aternating-current transmission supplied electric lighting through the whole city, out to nearby towns and farms. Thus the first 10 years of electrical systems saw an exponential growth in the rate of innovations (as the first part of the technology S-curve for electrical power).

Additional technical inventions steadily improved the efficiency of alternating-current power systems. The distance a power plant could cover expanded the market for the plant. One major innovation was the use of a many-phase (polyphase) alternating-current system. This was introduced in 1910 in urban areas such as Chicago. Phase denotes the timing when alternating voltages increase or decrease. Alternating currents generated by different power plants were out of phase with one another. By using a polyphase system, one did not care which power plant generated the electricity. This made it possible to interchange power from different power plants and to different kinds of loads. As these innovations positioned the industry for rapid expansion, managerial capability became very important to effective management of the growing and complex power industry.

After these technical innovations, Samuel Insull became a major figure in introducing effective management practices into the new, expanding industry. Insull introduced cost-accounting methods to find where unit costs were high and could be reduced. He expanded his distribution system by buying and absorbing inefficient companies. In 1896 (after the introduction of the polyphase current invention), he transformed technically obsolete generating systems into substations and began increasing the size of generating units.

Technological advances in an industry often provide the opportunities for managerial advances. For example, Insull was a leader in (1) extending the distribution system, (2) rationalizing the network, and (3) increasing generating power. Insull also led in making better use of load capability in the network. He had the load factors measured and then dispatched the loading in the network in the most economically efficient manner. For peak-load hours, the network would call on different generating stations to deliver power to areas of exceptional demand.

Insull reorganized the structure of the industry so that economies of scale increased economic efficiency. For example, the new steam turbines had the great power needed to drive the large generators. In 1903, Insull installed in the Fisk Street station a 5000-kilowatt turbine, which was the largest steam turbine at that time. By 1910, 14,000-kilowatt turbogenerators were installed.

A new capital structure was then required for funding the new large-scale technologies. To finance this increase of scale, Insull (and others) altered financing concepts, adapting the concept of the holding company to utility stocks. Investors had been reluctant to invest in small companies (such as a Kansas City utility). General Electric then facilitated the funding for utilities by creating the Electric Bond & Share Company. This holding company, backed by the prestigious General Electric Company, financed the growth of small utilities by taking over their hard-to-market stock and bonds and substituting the stock of the holding company.

Unfortunately, Insull was caught in a public reaction against holding companies, brought about by the stock market collapse and depression of the 1930s. Until the depression, Insull had been greatly respected in the industrial world. In 1934, he went on trial, accused of using the mails to defraud the public. He was trying to save the Middle West Utilities Company, a holding company he had formed. He was acquitted but badly treated by the press. Four years later, he died. In 1935, the federal government passed the Public Utility Holding Company Act, which directed the dissolution of the holding-company networks. Only those companies that were electrically connected in a network could thereafter be part of a utility holding company.

TECHNOLOGY AND THE PRESERVATION OF CAPITAL

This example of growth of the electric power industry shows the kinds of interactions between technical innovations, managerial techniques, and financial mechanisms that are often required to build and develop a major new, high-tech industry. One of the measures of good management is the increase and preservation of capital. Technological advances that improve productivity, create markets, or improve capital utilization can contribute to future productivity and the preservation of capital.

For example, Peter Drucker emphasized the responsibility of management to preserve capital:

> Managing the fundamentals includes earning today the costs of staying in business tomorrow. A business that does not earn these costs is bound to fade and to disappear. These are not "future costs"; they are costs incurred now though not paid out until later. They are "accrued" or "deferred" costs—and we learned long age that these are true costs that must be shown in the current accounts of a business. A business that does not earn the accrued costs of staying in business impoverishes the economy and is untrue to its first social responsibility: to maintain the wealth-producing and employment-producing capacities of the resources entrusted to the enterprise and its management. (Drucker, 1980, p. 28)

Technological progress is one of the accrued economic costs of a nation. The wealth we currently enjoy—the technologies we currently use to produce that wealth—are benefits from previous generations, bequests from technological inventors and innovative managers. Such progress can be facilitated by industrial support of research and of governmental policies for the support of research and education.

PATENTS

Knowledge which is valuable to the firm is both proprietary and nonproprietary. The closer and more focused the knowledge is as to specific products and processes, the more proprietary the knowledge becomes. Proprietary knowledge includes trade secrets, copyrights, and patents.

An important legal connection between technology and capital is the patent. In the United States, the most common form of patent is called a "utility patent," which is granted by the U.S. government to inventors. Utility patents are legal rights to exclude anyone other than the inventor from making, selling, or using the patented invention for a specific term. The term is normally 17 years, and this legal exclusive right to use of the invention is given to the inventor, in return for the inventor disclosing full information about the invention to the public. After 17 years, the invention is thus in the public domain. In the United States, design patents are also granted on new ornamental designs, and plant patents are granted on new varieties of plants (Bell, 1984).

The steps of acquiring a patent consist of filing a disclosure and patent application with the U.S. patent office. It is essential that information about a new invention not be made public before the patent has been filed, or domestic rights may be lost and foreign patents may not be obtained. An invention includes the conception of an idea and the reducing of the idea to workable form. Workable form may be an actual device, built and working, or may be filing a patent application that meets the requirements of full disclosure.

Patent rights fall within an area of the law called intellectual property, which also includes trademarks, copyrights, and trade secrets. A trademark is any word, symbol, or device used to identify a manufacturer's good, distinguishing them from those of a competitor. A copyright is an exclusive right to authors and composers or artists, controlling use of their productions. A trade secret is any formula, pattern, device, or information used in business to provide a competitive advantage.

Inventions made by employees of an organization in the performance of their duties, while using the employer's time, material, facilities, funds, and information, belong to the employer. This ownership may be upheld by the courts, even in the absence of formal agreements between employers and employees about patent rights.

Licenses on patents are rights granted to others, including competitors, to use an invention commercially in exchange for consideration such as money or property. Licenses may be granted exclusively to one licensee or nonexclusively to several licensees. A patent owner may assign title to another, freely or in exchange for valuable consideration.

PATENT INFRINGEMENT

In the United States, it is the responsibility of the patent holder to litigate to defend against patent infringement. Defending patents can be a costly and lengthy process. For example, Eli Whitney was issued a patent in 1794 on the invention of the cotton gin, a machine to comb the seeds out of cotton before it is spun into thread. Other manufacturers copied his machine, without obtaining licenses or paying royalties. For 13 years, Whitney prosecuted infringers. Finally, he won the right as sole inventor of the cotton gin. But by that time, his factory had burned down, and he was disgusted with the long legal battle. He turned to manufacturing firearms. Whitney's experience has been shared by many others. Lloyd H. Conover had to fight from

1955 to 1982 to establish his rights to the invention of tetracycline—an important penicillin-like drug (Conover, 1984).

Example: Litigation over a Catalyst Patent

In the early 1960s, zeolite, a porous material, was used only for water softeners. By the 1980s, zeolites were applied to petroleum refining and the preparation of specialty chemicals. Then the volume of zeolite use became large. U.S. oil refineries were replenishing about 2000 tons of catalysts per day. Zeolites had become valuable properties. Holding patents in zeolites in the 1980s were Mobil Oil, Union Carbide, and Standard Oil of Indiana, and they were battling each other in the courts over patent infringements (Fox, 1985).

Zeolites are porous structures useful in holding catalysts. Catalysts help chemical reactions to occur speedily and are essential to much chemical production. At a molecular level, zeolites look sort of like sponges with tiny cagelike holes. Zeolites are loaded with catalysts which act on chemical fluids passed through them to create useful products, such as gasoline.

Mobil had pioneered zeolites, obtaining valuable patents on zeolites made from aluminosilicate materials, materials containing aluminum and silicon. Union Carbide had patents on zeolites made from silicalites, materials containing silicon but not aluminum. In 1972, Mobil received a patent on a zeolite called ZSM-5; and discussions occurred between Mobil and Union Carbide over whether Union Carbide was infringing on Mobil's patent on ZSM-5.

In 1982, Union Carbide instituted a lawsuit against Mobil, charging that the Mobil was infringing Union Carbide patents. The issue centered on whether Union Carbide's silicalite zeolites (silicon zeolites) used aluminum, since Mobile's zeolites use both silicon and aluminum. The issue was very fine, since scientific measurements (nuclear magnetic resonance) showed small amounts of aluminum in Union Carbide's silicon zeolites. Union Carbide claimed that the aluminum was merely contamination and not essential to the catalytic ability of their zeolites. Mobil claimed, on the contrary, that the aluminum was not accidental but essential to catalytic properties and therefore infringed on their rights.

Also in 1982, Mobil filed suit against another company, Amoco, alleging that Amoco infringed on Mobil's basic zeolite catalyst patents. In this case, the dispute centered around the role of another element, boron, used in silicon–boron zeolites. In 1985, both cases were still in the early stages: "These legal actions are currently bogged down in the pretrail 'discovery' phase during which the companies' scientists and lawyers pore over the documents that will either make or break their respective cases. Negotiations to find an out-of-court settlement are also taking place, according to sources who asked not to be identified. . ." (Fox, 1985, p. 35).

CONCLUSION

Technological innovation is the organizational process for creating and implementing the products and production capabilities of a company. New ventures are new products introduced into new markets. Research is the business function of creating technology. Innovative managers take the risks of creating new technologies and new markets, managing technology as a means of improving the productivity of capital.

SUMMARY

Production is the result of integrating capital with technology. One of the measures of good management is the increase and preservation of capital. Technological progress is one of the accrued economic costs of a nation. Patents are an important legal connection between technology and capital, providing limited time but exclusive production rights to the inventor, in return for the inventor disclosing full information about the invention to the public.

Licenses on patents are rights granted to others, including competitors, to use an invention commercially in exchange for a consideration such as money or property. In the United States, it is the responsibility of the patent holder to litigate to defend against patent infringement.

REFLECTION

1. **Think of a clever idea to patent. Prepare a disclosure and patent application for filing. How would you do a patent search to learn if anyone has already patented the idea?**

FOR FURTHER READING

DRUCKER, PETER, *Managing in Turbulent Times.* New York: Harper & Row, 1980.

BIBLIOGRAPHY

ABERNATHY, WILLIAM J. 1978. *The Productivity Dilemma.* Baltimore, Md.: Johns Hopkins University Press.

ABERNATHY, WILLIAM J., and K. B. CLARK. 1985. Mapping the Winds of Creative Destruction, *Research Policy,* Vol. 14, No. 1, pp. 2–22.

ABERNATHY, WILLIAM J., KIM B. CLARK, and ALAN M. KANTROW. 1983. *Industrial Renaissance.* New York: Basic Books.

ABERNATHY, W. J., and J. M. UTTERBACK. 1978. Patterns of Industrial Innovation, *Technology Review,* Vol. 80, June–July, pp. 40–47.

AHL, DAVID H., 1984. The First Decade of Personal Computing, *Creative Computing,* Vol. 10, No. 11, pp. 30–45.

ALLEN, THOMAS J., 1978. *Managing the Flow of Technology.* Cambridge, Mass.: MIT Press.

AYRES, ROBERT U. 1969. *Technological Forecasting and Long-Range Planning.* New York: McGraw-Hill.

BANKS, HOWARD. 1984. General Electric—Going with the Winners, *Forbes,* March 26, pp. 97–106.

BARDEEN, JOHN. 1984. To a Solid State, *Science 84,* November, pp. 143–145.

BARTIMO, JIM. 1984. "Smalltalk" with Alan Kay, *InfoWorld,* June 11, pp. 58–61.

BEATTIE, C. J., and R. D. READER. 1971. *Quantitative Management in R&D.* London: Chapman & Hall.

BELL, JAMES R. 1984. Patent Guidelines for Research Managers, *IEEE Transactions on Engineering Management,* Vol. EM-31, No. 3, pp. 102–104.

BEN-DAVID, JOSEPH. 1971. *The Scientist's Role in Society.* (Englewood Cliffs, N. J.: Prentice-Hall.

BERGER, A. 1975. Factors Influencing the Locus of Innovation Activity Leading to Scientific Instrument and Plastics Innovation, unpublished S.M. Thesis, MIT Sloan School of Management, Cambridge, Mass.

BETZ, FREDERICK L., VAUGHN BLANKENSHIP, CARLOS KRUYTBOSCH, and RICHARD MASON. 1980. Allocating R&D Resources in the Public Sector, in *Management of Research and Innovation,* B. V. Dean and J. L. Goldhar, eds. New York: North-Holland.

BIGGADIKE, RALPH. 1979. The Risky Business of Diversification, *Harvard Business Review,* May; reprinted in *Readings in the Management of Innovation,* M. L. Tushman and W. L. Moore, eds. (Marshfield, Mass: Pitman, 1982).

BIRNBAUM, PHILIP H. 1984. Strategic Management of Industrial Technology: A Review of the Issues, *IEEE Transactions on Engineering Management,* Vol. EM-31, No. 4, pp. 186–191.

BITONDO, DOMENIC, and ALAN FROHMAN. 1981.   Linking Technological and Business Planning, *Research Management,* Vol. XXIV, No. 6. pp. 19–23.

BOYDEN, J. 1976.   A Study of the Innovation Process in the Plastics Additives Industry, unpublished S.M. thesis, MIT Sloan School of Management, Cambridge, Mass.

BOYER, EDWARD. 1983.   Turning Glass to Plastic to Gold, *Fortune,* April 4, pp. 172–176.

BRICKLIN, DAN, and BOB FRANKSTON. 1984.   Visicalc '79, *Creative Computing,* Vol. 10, No. 11, pp. 122–123.

BRIGHT, JAMES R., and MILTON SCHOEMAN. 1973.   *A Guide to Practical Technological Forecasting.* Englewood Cliffs, N.J.: Prentice-Hall.

BRITTAIN, JAMES E. 1984.   Biographical sketch on John Mauchly, *in* Hopper and Mauchly on Computer Programming, *Proceedings of the IEEE,* September p. 1213.

BROWN, WARREN B., and ROBERT C. SCHWAB. 1984.   Boundary-Spanning Activities in Electronics Firms, *IEEE Transactions on Engineering Management,* Vol. EM-31, No. 3, pp. 105–110.

BURNS, TOM, and G. M. STALKER. 1961.   *The Management of Innovation.* London: Social Science Paperbacks.

Business Week. 1984a.   Apple Computer's Counterattack against IBM, January 16, pp. 78–82.

Business Week. 1984b.   Biotech Comes of Age, January 23, pp. 84–94.

Business Week. 1984c.   RCA's Rivals Still See Life in Videodiscs, April 23, p. 88.

Business Week. 1984d.   The Anatomy of RCA's Videodisc Failure, April 23, p. 89.

Business Week. 1984e.   How Japan Helped Spoil RCA's Plans, April 23, p. 90.

BYLINSKY, GENE. 1981a.   The Japanese Chip Challenge, *Fortune,* March 23, pp. 105–112.

BYLINSKY, GENE. 1981b.   Japan's Ominous Chip Victory, *Fortune,* December 14, pp. 52–57.

BYLINSKY, GENE. 1981c.   A New Industrial Revolution Is on the Way, *Fortune,* October 5, pp. 106–114.

BYLINSKY, GENE. 1982.   U.S. Chipmakers Are Back in the Race, *Fortune,* June 28, pp. 79–80.

BYLINSKY, GENE. 1983.   The Next Battle in Memory Chips, *Fortune,* May 16, pp. 152–156.

CERUZZI, PAUL E. 1983.   *Reckoners.* Westport, Conn.: Greenwood Press.

CHANDLER, ALFRED D., JR. 1962.   *Strategy and Structure.* Cambridge, Mass.: MIT Press.

Chemical & Engeering News. 1983.   Monsanto's Richard Mahoney: Ready to Take On the 1980's, September 26, pp. 10–13.

COLL, STEVE. 1984.   When the Magic Goes, *INC,* October pp. 83–97.

COLVIN, GEOFFREY. 1982.   The De-Geneening of ITT, *Fortune,* January 11, pp. 34–39.

CONOVER, LLOYD H. 1984.   Discovering Tetracycline, *Research Management,* Vol. XXVII, No. 5, pp. 17–22.

Creative Computing. 1984.   Vol. 10, No. 11.

DAY, GEORGE S. 1975.   A Strategic Perspective on Product Planning, *Journal of Comtemporary Business,* spring, pp. 1–34; reprinted in *Readings in the Management of Innovation,* M. L. Tushman and W. L. Moore, eds. (Marshfield, Mass: Pitman, 1982).

DEAN, B. V., and J. L. GOLDHAR. 1980.   *Management of Research and Innovation,* New York: North-Holland.

DEWHURST, HAROLD A. 1970. The Long Range Research That Produced Glass Fiber Reinforced Tires, *Research Management,* Vol. XIII, No. 3.

DIDRICHSEN, JON. 1972. The Development of Diversified and Conglomerate Firms in the United States, 1920–1970, *Business History Review,* Vol. 46, Summer, p. 210.

DRUCKER, PETER F. 1980. *Managing in Turbulent Times.* New York: Harper & Row.

DRUCKER, PETER F. 1984. Our Entrepreneurial Economy, *Harvard Business Review,* January-February, pp. 58–59.

DRUCKER, PETER F. 1985a. *Innovation and Entrepreneurship: Practice and Principles.* New York: Harper & Row.

DRUCKER, PETER F. 1985b. The Discipline of Innovation, *Harvard Business Review,* May–June, pp. 67–72.

The Economist. 1983. New Routes for New Petrochemicals, October 8, p. 77.

The Economist. 1985a. Another Turn of the Wheel: A Survey of the World's Motor Industry, March 2–8, p. 52.

The Economist. 1985b. General Motors: Survival of the Fattest, October 12, pp. 35–38.

EHRBAR, A. F. 1982. Splitting Up RCA, *Fortune,* March 22, pp. 62–76.

EIRMA WORKING GROUP. 1982. Quality Assurance: R&D and Production/Marketing, *Research Management,* Vol. XXV, No. 5, pp. 25–31.

Electronics Week. 1984. General Electric is on Target with Second Shot at Chip Making, October 29, pp. 51–53.

ENOS, J. 1962, *Petroleum Progress and Profits.* Cambridge, Mass.: MIT Press.

EVANS, CHRISTOPHER. 1981. *The Making of the Micro.* New York: Van Nostrand Reinhold.

FAGEN, M. D., ed. 1975. *A History of Engineering and Science in the Bell System: The Early Years (1875–1925).* Murray Hill, N.J.: Bell Telephone Laboratories.

FAST, NORMAN D. 1981. Pitfalls of Corporate Venturing, *Research Management,* Vol. XXIV, No. 2, pp. 21–24.

FORD, DAVID, and CHRIS RYAN. 1981. Taking Technology to Market, *Harvard Business Review,* March–April, pp. 117–126.

FORRESTER, JAY W. 1961. *Industrial Dynamics.* Cambridge, Mass.: MIT Press.

FORRESTER, JAY W. 1964. Common Foundation underlying Engineering and Management, *IEEE Spectrum,* September, pp. 66–77.

FORRESTER, JAY W. 1979. Innovation and the Economic Long Wave, *Management Review,* June, pp. 16–24.

FORRESTER, JAY W. 1983. A Longer-Term View of Current Economic Conditions, talk given at the National Association of Business Economists, March 24.

FOSTER, RICHARD N. 1982. A Call for Vision in Managing Technology, *Business Week,* May 24, pp. 24–33.

FOSTER, RICHARD N., LAWRENCE H. LINDEN, ROGER L. WHITELEY, and ALAN M. KANTROW. 1985. Improving the Return of R&D II, *Research Management,* Vol. XXVIII, No. 2, pp. 13–22.

FOX, JEFFREY L. 1985. Zeolites Catalyze Patent Dispute, *Science,* Vol. 227, January 4, pp. 35–36.

FRAKER, SUSAN. 1984. High-Speed Management for the High-Tech Age, *Fortune,* March 5, pp. 62–68.

FRAME, J. DAVIDSON. 1984. Tax Considerations in R&D Planning, *IEEE Transactions on Engineering Management,* Vol. EM-31, No. 2, pp. 50–54.

FREEMAN, C. 1967.   Chemical Process Plant: Innovations and the World Market, *National Institute Economic Review.*

FREEMAN, CHRISTOPHER. 1974.   *The Economics of Industrial Innovation.* New York: Penguin Books.

FROHMAN, ALAN L. 1982.   Technology as a Competitive Weapon, *Harvard Business Review,* January–February, pp. 97–104.

GATES, WILLIAM. 1984.   A Trend toward Softness, *Creative Computing,* Vol. 10, No. 11, pp. 121–122.

GEE, EDWIN A. 1976.   *Managing Innovation.* New York: Wiley.

GENERAL ELECTRIC. 1980.   Descriptive Material on the Corporate Research Laboratories, Schnectady, N.Y.

GERSTENFELD, ARTHUR, and PAUL D. BERGER. 1984.   Joint Research—A Wave of the Future, *Research Management,* Vol. XXVII, No. 6, pp. 9–11.

GERWIN, DONALD. 1982.   Do's and Don'ts of Computerized Manufacturing, *Harvard Business Review,* March–April, pp. 107–116.

GLUCK, FREDERICK W., STEPHEN P. KAUFMAN, and A. STEVEN WAL-LECK. 1980. Strategic Management for Competitive Advantage, *Harvard Business Review,* July–August, pp. 154–161.

GOLD, BELA. 1982.   CAM Sets New Rules for Production, *Harvard Business Review,* November–December, pp. 88–94.

GOLDBERG, ALBERT I., and YEHOUDA A. SHENHAV. 1984.   R&D Career Paths: Their Relation to Work Goals and Productivity, *IEEE Transactions on Engineering Management,* Vol. EM-31, No. 3, pp. 111–117.

GRAHAM, ALAN K., and PETER M. SENGE. 1980.   A Long-Wave Hypothesis of Innovation, *Technological Forecasting and Social Change,* Vol. 17, August, pp. 283–312.

GRAY, STEVEN B. 1984.   The Early Days of Personal Computers, *Creative Computing,* Vol. 10, No. 11, pp. 6–14.

GRUNEWALD, HANS-GUNTER, and KARLHEINZ VELLMANN. 1981.   Integrating Regional and Functional Plans at Henkel, *Long Range Planning,* Vol. 14, No. 2, pp. 19–28.

GUMPERT, DAVID E., ed. 1985.   *The Marketing Renaissance.* New York: Wiley.

HAEFFNER, ERIK. 1980.   Critical Activities of the Innovation Process, pp. 129–144, in *Current Innovation,* B. A. Vedin, ed. Stockholm: Almqvist & Wiksell.

HAMERMESH, R. G., and R. E. WHITE. 1984.   Manage beyond Portfolio Analysis, *Harvard Business Review,* January–February, pp. 103–109.

HARDYMON, G. F., M. J. DENINO, and M. S. SALTER. 1983.   When Corporate Venture Capital Doesn't Work, *Harvard Business Review,* May–June, pp. 114–121.

HAYES, ROBERT H., and WILLIAM J. ABERNATHY. 1980.   Managing Our Way to Economic Decline, *Harvard Business Review,* July–August, p. 67; reprinted in *Readings in the Management of Innovation,* M. L. Tushman and W. L. Moore, eds. (Marshfield, Mass.: Pitman, 1982).

HAYES, ROBERT, and DAVID GARVIN. 1982.   Managing As If Innovation Mattered, *Harvard Business Review,* May–June, pp. 70–79.

HAYES, ROBERT H., and STEVEN C. WHEELWRIGHT. 1979.   The Dynamics of Process-Product Life Cycles, *Harvard Business Review,* March–April, p. 127.

HENWOOD, FELICITY, and GRAHAM THOMAS. 1983.   *Science, Technology and Innovation: A Research Bibliography.* New York: St. Martin's Press.

HICKS, WAYLAND R. 1984.   A New Approach to Product Development, *High Technology,* October, pp. 11–12.

HILL, CHRISTOPHER T. 1979.   Technological Innovation: Agent of Growth and Change, in *Technological Innovation for a Dynamic Economy*, C. Hill and J. Utterback, eds. Elmsford, N.Y.: Pegamon Press, pp. 1–39.

HILL, CHRISTOPHER T., and JAMES M. UTTERBACK, eds. 1979.   *Technological Innovation for a Dynamic Economy*. Elmsford, N.Y.: Pergamon Press.

HONEYWELL CORP. 1983.   Profile, 59–4042 (Honeywell Corp. brochure).

HUGHES, THOMAS P. 1984.   The Inventive Continuum, *Science 84*, Vol. 5, No. 9, pp. 83–87.

JANTSCH, ERICH. 1967.   *Technological Forecasting in Perspective*. Paris: Organization for Economic Cooperation and Development.

JELINEK, MARIANN. 1979.   *Institutionalizing Innovation: A Study of Organizational Learning Systems*. New York: Praeger.

JUDSON, HORACE FREELAND. 1979.   *The Eighth Day of Creation. A Study of Organizational Learning Systems*. New York: Simon and Schuster.

JURGEN, RONALD K. ed. 1983.   Data Driven Automation, *IEEE Spectrum*, May.

KANTROW, ALAN M. 1980.   The Strategy-Technology Connection, *Harvard Business Review*, July–August, pp. 6–21.

KANTROW, ALAN M., ed. 1985.   *Sunrise . . . Sunset, Challenging the Myth of Industrial Obsolesance*. New York: Wiley.

KARGER, D. W., and ROBERT G. MURDICK. 1972.   *New Product Venture Management*. New York: Gordon and Breach.

KATZ, R., and M. TUSHMAN. 1979.   Communication Patterns, Project Performance and Task Characteristics: An Empirical Evaluation and Integration in an R&D Setting, *Organizational Behavior and Human Performance*, Vol. 23, pp. 139–162.

KELLER, ERIK L. 1983.   Clever Robots Set to Enter Industry En Masse, *Electronics*, November 17, pp. 116–119.

KELLEY, ALBERT J., FRANK B. CAMPANELLA, and JOHN MCKIERNAN. 1971.   *Venture Capital*. Chestnut Hill, Mass.: School of Management, Boston College.

KIDDER, TRACY. 1981.   *The Soul of a New Machine*. New York: Avon Books.

KIECHELL, WALTER, III. 1981.   The Decline of the Experience Curve, *Fortune*, October 5.

KNIGHT, K. E. 1963.   A Study of Technological Innovation: The Evolution of Digital Computers, unpublished Ph.D. dissertation, Carnegie Institute of Technology, Pittsburgh, Pa.

KORNHAUSER, WILLIAM. 1962.   *Scientists in Industry*. Berkeley, Calif.: University of California Press.

KOTKIN, JOEL. 1984.   The Third Wave, *INC*, February, pp. 57–66.

LABICH, KENNETH. 1984.   Monsanto's Brave New World, *Fortune*, April 30, pp. 57–68.

LANGRISH, J. 1971.   Innovation in Pharmaceuticals, *Research Policy*, Vol. 1, No. 1, pp. 89–98.

LARSEN, JUDITH K. 1983.   Information Exchange in Silicon Valley, *Proceedings of the 1983 Conference on Industrial Science and Technological Innovation*. Washington, D.C.: National Science Foundation, pp. 73–74.

LAYTON, CHRISTOPHER. 1972.   *Ten Innovations*. New York: Crane, Russak.

LEAR, JOHN. 1978.   *Recombinant DNA: The Untold Story*. New York: Crown Publishers.

LERNER, ERIC J. 1981.   Computer-Aided Manufacturing, *IEEE Spectrum*, November, pp. 34–39.

LEVERING, ROBERT, 1984.   Michael Katz, and Milton Moskowitz. *The Computer Entrepreneurs.* New York: New American Library.

LINDEN, EUGENE. 1984.   Let a Thousand Flowers Bloom, *INC*, April, pp. 64–74.

LIONETTA, W. G., JR. 1977.   Sources of Innovation within the Pultrusion Industry, unpublished S.M. thesis, MIT Sloan School of Management, Cambridge, Mass.

LITTLE, ROYAL. 1984.   Conglomerates Are Doing Better Than You Think, *Fortune*, May 28, pp. 50–60.

MACE, SCOTT. 1984.   A New Atari Corp., *InfoWorld*, August 6.

MADLIN, NANCY. 1985.   The Venture Survey—Sticking to Business Plans, *Venture*, April, p. 25.

MAGNET, MYRON. 1982.   Corning Glass Shapes Up, *Fortune*, December 13.

MAIDIQUE, MODESTO A. 1980.   Entrepreneurs, Champions, and Technological Innovation, *Sloan Management Review*, Vol. 21, No. 2, pp. 59–76; reprinted in *Readings in the Management of Innovation*, M. L. Tushman and W. L. Moore, eds. (Marshfield, Mass.: Pitman, 1982).

MAIDIQUE, MODESTO A., and BILLIE JO ZIRGER. 1984.   A Study of Success and Failure in Product Innovation: The Case of the U.S. Electronics Industry, *IEEE Transactions on Engineering Management*, Vol. EM-31, No. 4, pp. 192–202.

MARQUIS, DONALD G. 1969.   The Anatomy of Successful Innovations, *Innovation*, November, Reprinted in *Readings in the Management of Innovation*, M. L. Tushman and W. L. Moore, eds. (Marshfield, Mass.: Pitman, 1982).

MCDONOUGH, EDWARD F., III, and RAYMOND M. KINNUNEN. 1984.   Management Control of New Product Development Projects, *IEEE Transactions on Engineering Management*, Vol. EM-31, No. 1, pp. 18–21.

MEADOWS, EDWARD. 1981.   The Slippery Market for Videodiscs, *Fortune*, November 2, pp. 83–85.

MENSCH, GERHARD. 1979.   *Stalemate in Technology.* Cambridge, Mass.: Ballinger.

MERRIFIELD, D. BRUCE. 1981.   Selecting Projects for Commercial Success, *Research Management*, Vol. XXIV, No. 6, pp. 13–18.

MERRIFIELD, BRUCE. 1982.   Expanding the R&D Base, in *Public Policies and Strategies for U.S. High Technology Industry*, Proceedings of the SIA Long Range Planning Conference, Semiconductor Industry Association.

MIMS, FORREST M., III. 1984.   The Altair Story, *Creative Computing*, Vol. 10, No. 11, pp. 17–27.

MONTEITH, G. STUART. 1969.   *R&D Administration.* London: Iliffe Books.

MORONE, JOSEPH, and RICHARD ALBEN. 1984.   Matching R&D to Business Needs, *Research Management*, Vol. XXVII, No. 5, pp. 33–39.

MORRISON, ANN M. 1982.   Trying to Bring GE to Life, *Fortune*, January 25, pp. 51–57.

MORRISON, ANN M. 1984.   Apple Bites Back, *Fortune*, February 20, pp. 86–100.

MURPHY, SHELDON R. 1981.   Five Ways to Improve R&D Efficiency, *Research Management*, Vol. XXIV, No. 1, pp. 8–9.

NATIONAL ACADEMY OF ENGINEERING AND NATIONAL RESEARCH COUNCIL. 1982.   *The Competitive Status of the U.S. Auto Industry, 1982.* Washington, D.C.: National Academy Press.

NATIONAL ACADEMY OF ENGINEERING AND NATIONAL RESEARCH COUNCIL. 1983.   *The Competitive Status of the U.S. Pharmaceutical Industry, 1983.* Washington, D.C.: National Academy Press.

NATIONAL SCIENCE BOARD, NATIONAL SCIENCE FOUNDATION. 1983. *Science Indicators 1982.* Washington, D.C.: Superintendent of Documents, U.S. Government Printing Office.

New York Times. 1983. December 18, Sec. 3, pp. 1, 30.

New York Times. 1984. February 20, p. D1.

NOCERA, JOSEPH. 1984. Death of a Computer: TI's Price War with Commodore Dooms the 99/4A, *InfoWorld,* June 11, pp. 63–65; Reprinted from *Texas Monthly,* April 1984.

NULTY, PETER. 1981. A Peacemaker Comes to RCA, *Fortune,* May 4, pp. 140–153.

NULTY, PETER. 1984. Cool Heads Are Trying to Keep Commodore Hot, *Fortune,* July 23.

OLBY, ROBERT. 1974. *The Path to the Double Helix.* London: Macmillan; Seattle: University of Washington Press.

OSBORNE, ADAM, and JOHN DVORAK. 1984. Hypergrowth, Adam Osborne's Upcoming Book Tells His Side of the Story, *InfoWorld,* July 9, July 16, and July 23.

PERRY, TEKLA S., and PAUL WALLICH. 1985. Design Case History: The Commodore 64, *IEEE Spectrum,* March, pp. 45–58.

PORTER, MICHAEL E. 1985. *Competitive Advantage.* New York: Free Press.

PORTUGAL, FRANKLIN H., and JACK S. COHEN. 1977. *A Century of DNA.* Cambridge, Mass.: MIT Press.

PRATT, STANLEY E., and JANE K. MORRIS. 1984. *Pratt's Guide to Venture Capital Sources.* Wellesley, Mass.: Venture Economics, Inc.

PRESTON, JACK. 1985. "Vita," National Science Foundation Award, DMR 8419803.

PUTNAM, ARNOLD O. 1985. A Redesign for Engineering, *Harvard Business Review,* May–June, pp. 139–144.

PYKE, DONALD L., 1973. Mapping—A System Concept for Displaying Alternatives, in James Bright and Milton Schoeman, *A Guide to Practical Technological Forecasting.* Englewood Cliffs, N.J.: Prentice-Hall, pp. 81–91.

QUINN, JAMES BRIAN. 1979. Technological Innovation, Entrepreneurship, and Strategy, *Sloan Management Review,* Vol. 20, No. 3, pp. 19–30; reprinted in *Readings in the Management of Innovation,* M. L. Tushman and W. L. Moore, eds. (Marshfield, Mass.: Pitman, 1982).

QUINN, JAMES BRIAN. 1980. *Strategies for Change: Logical Incrementalism.* Homewood, Ill.: Dow Jones–Irwin.

QUINN, JAMES BRIAN. 1985. Managing Innovation: Controlled Chaos, *Harvard Business Review,* May-June, pp. 73–84.

RAMP, SIMON. 1980. *America's Technology Slip.* New York: Wiley.

RAY, GEORGE F. 1980. Innovation and the Long Cycle, in *Current Innovation,* Bengt-Arne Vedin, ed. Stockholm: Almqvist & Wiksell.

REID, T. R. 1985. The Chip, *Science 85,* February, pp. 32–41.

RICH, S. R., and D. E. GUMPERT. 1985a. *Business Plans That Win $$: Lessons from the MIT Enterprise Forum,* New York: Harper & Row.

RICH, S. R., and D. E. GUMPERT. 1985b. Growing Concerns, *Harvard Business Review,* May–June, pp. 156–164.

ROBERTS, EDWARD B. 1980. New Ventures for Corporate Growth, *Harvard Business Review,* July–August, pp. 134–142; (Reprinted in *Readings in the Management of Innovation,* M. L. Tushman and W. L. Moore, eds. (Marshfield, Mass.: Pitman, 1982).

ROBINSON, ARTHUR L. 1984. One Billion Transistors on a Chip?, *Science,* Vol. 223, January 20, pp. 267–268.

ROMAN, DANIEL D. 1980. *Science, Technology, and Innovation: A Systems Approach.* Columbus, Ohio: Grid Publishing.

ROSENBLOOM, RICHARD S. 1978. Technological Innovation in Firms and Industries: An Assessment of the State of the Art, in *Technological Innovation,* P. Kelly and M. Kranzberg, eds. San Francisco: San Francisco Press.

ROSENBLOOM, RICHARD S., and WILLIAM J. ABERNATHY. 1982. The Climate for Innovation in Industry, *Research Policy,* Vol. 11, No. 4, p. 218–225.

ROUSSEL, PHILIP A. 1983. Cutting Down the Guesswork in R&D, *Harvard Business Review,* September–October, pp. 154–160.

RYANS, JOHN K., JR., and WILLIAM L. SHANKLIN. 1984. Positioning and Selecting Target Markets, *Research Management,* Vol. XXVII, No. 5, pp. 28–32.

SAPPHO—REPORT ON PROJECT SAPPHO. 1972. Success and Failure in Industrial Innovation, Centre for the Study of Industrial Innovation, 162 Regent St, London, W1R 6DD 2/72.

SCHMITT, ROLAND W. 1985. Successful Corporate R&D, *Harvard Business Review,* May–June, pp. 124–129.

SCHMOOKLER, JACOB. 1966. *Invention and Economic Growth.* Cambridge, Mass.: Harvard University Press.

SCHON, D. A. 1963. Champions for Radical New Inventions, *Harvard Business Review,* March–April.

Science. 1984a. Exxon Builds on Basic Research, Vol. 225, September 7, pp. 1001–1003.

Science. 1984b. The 1984 Nobel Prize in Medicine, Vol. 226, November 30, pp. 1025–1028.

Science. 1985. Zeolites Catalyze Patent Dispute, Vol. 227, January 4, pp. 35–36.

SHACKIL, ALBERT F. 1981. Design Case History: Wang's Word Processor, *IEEE Spectrum,* Vol. 18, No. 8, pp. 29–34.

SHANKLIN, WILLIAM L. 1983. Supply-Side Marketing Can Restore "Yankee Ingenuity," *Research Management,* May–June, pp. 20–25.

SHRAYER, MICHAEL. 1984. Confessions of a Naked Programmer, *Creative Computing,* Vol. 10, No. 11, pp. 130–131.

SILVER, A. DAVID. 1985. *Venture Capital.* New York: Wiley.

SINGER, CHARLES, E. J. HOLMYARD, A. R. HALL and TREVOR I. WILLIAMS. 1958. *A History of Technology,* Vols. IV and V. New York: Oxford University Press.

SLOAN, ALFRED P. 1963. *My Years with General Motors.* New York: Macfadden-Bartell Corp.

SMITH, JOHN K. 1985. The Ten-Year Invention: Neoprene and DuPont Research, 1930–1939, *Technology and Culture,* Vol. 26, No. 1, pp. 34–55.

SMITH, J. J., et al. 1984. Lessons from 10 Case Studies in Innovation, *Research Management,* Vol. XXII, No. 5, pp. 23–27.

SMITH, LEE. 1980. The Lures and Limits of Innovation, *Fortune,* October 20, pp. 84–94.

SPIEGEL-ROSING, INA, and DEREK DE SOLLA PRICE, eds. 1977. *Science, Technology and Society.* Beverly Hills, Calif: Sage.

STEVENSON, H. H., and D. E. GUMPERT. 1985. The Heart of Entrepreneurship, *Harvard Business Review,* March–April, pp. 85–94.

SULLO, P., T. TRISCRARI, and W. WALLACE. 1985. Reliability of Communication Flow in R&D Organizations, *IEEE Transactions on Engineering Management,* July, pp. 91–97.

THAMBAIN, HANS J. 1983.   Managing Engineers Effectively, *IEEE Transactions on Engineering Management,* Vol. Em-30, No. 4, pp. 231–237.

THOMAS, LEWIS. 1984.   Medicine's Second Revolution, *Science 84,* November, pp. 93–98.

TOWNES, CHARLES H. 1984.   Harnessing Light, *Science 84,* November, pp. 153–155.

TRACY, ELEANOR JOHNSON. 1984.   Ricoh's Foray into Xerox's Heartland, *Fortune,* May 28, p. 94.

TUSHMAN, M.L., and R. KATZ. 1985.   External Communication and Project. Performance: An Investigation into the Role of Gatekeepers, *Management Science,* Vol. 26, No. 11, pp. 1071–1085.

TUSHMAN, MICHAEL L., and WILLIAM L. MOORE. 1982.   *Readings in the Management of Innovation.* Marshfield, Mass.: Pitman.

TWISS, BRIAN. 1980.   *Managing Technological Innovation.* Harlow, Essex, England: Longman Group.

UTTAL, BRO. 1981.   Xerox Xooms toward the Office of the Future, *Fortune,* May 18, pp. 44–52.

UTTAL, BRO. 1983.   Sudden Shake-Up in Home Computers, *Fortune,* July 11, pp. 105–106.

UTTAL, BRO. 1983b.   The Lab That Ran Away from Xerox, *Fortune,* September 5, pp. 97–102.

UTTERBACK, JAMES. 1974.   Innovation in Industry and the Diffusion of Technology, *Science,* Vol. 183, February 15, pp. 620–626.

UTTERBACK, JAMES. 1978.   Management of Technology, in *Studies in Operations Management,* Arnoldo C. Hax, eds., Amsterdam: North-Holland Publishing, pp. 137–160.

VESPER, KARL H. 1980.   *New Venture Strategies.* Englewood Cliffs, N.J.: Prentice-Hall.

Videography. 1984.   Conversation with John Messerschmitt: North American Philip's Disc Expert Explains Why His Company Is Moving into Industrial Video, January 1984, pp. 31–52.

VON HIPPEL, ERIC. 1976.   The Dominant Role of Users in the Scientific Instrumentation Innovation Process, *Research Policy,* Vol. 5, No. 3, pp. 212–239.

VON HIPPEL, ERIC. 1977.   The Dominant Role of the User in Semiconductor and Electronic Subassembly Process Innovation, *IEEE Transactions on Engineering Management,* May.

VON HIPPEL, ERIC. 1978.   Successful Industrial Products from Customer Ideas, *Journal of Marketing,* January, pp. 39–49.

VON HIPPEL, ERIC. 1982.   Appropriability of Innovation Benefit as a Predictor of the Source of Innovation, *Research Policy,* Vol. 11, No. 2, pp. 95–115.

WALL, WILLIAM C., JR. 1984.   Integrated Management in Matrix Organization, *IEEE Transactions on Engineering Management,* Vol. EM-31, No. 1, pp. 30–36.

Wall Street Journal. 1984.   September 21.

WALTHERS VON ALTEN, JUDITH. 1984.   Corvus Tries to Pick Itself Up, *Info-World,* July 30, pp. 44–45.

WARD, E. PETER. 1981.   Planning for Technological Innovation—Developing the Necessary Nerve, *Long Range Planning,* Vol. 14, April 1981, pp. 59–71.

WATERS, CRAIG R. 1984.   Born-Again Steel, *INC,* November, pp. 52–64.

WHEELWRIGHT, STEVEN C., and ROBERT H. HAYES. 1984.   *Restoring Our Competitive Edge: Competing through Manufacturing.* New York: Wiley.

WHEELWRIGHT, STEVEN C., and ROBERT H. HAYES. 1985.   Competing through Manufacturing, *Harvard Business Review*, January–February, pp. 99–109.

WHITE, GEORGE R., and MARGARET B. W. GRAHAM. 1978.   How to Spot a Technological Winner,   *Harvard Business Review*, March–April, pp. 146–152.

WHITEHEAD, DON. 1968.   *The Dow Story: The History of the Dow Chemical Company*. New York: McGraw-Hill.

WISE, G. 1980.   A New Role for Professional Scientists in Industry: Industrial Research at General Electric 1900–1916, *Technology and Culture*, Vol. 21, p. 408–415.

WISEMAN, P. 1983.   Patenting and Inventive Activity, *Research Policy*, Vol. 12, pp. 329–339.

WOLFF, MICHAEL. 1981.   The Why, When and How of Directed Basic Research, *Research Management*, Vol. XXIV, No. 3, pp. 29–31.

WOLFF, MICHAEL F. 1983.   Mervin J. Kelly: Manager and Motivator, *IEEE Spectrum*, December, pp. 71–75.

WOLFF, MICHAEL F. 1984.   William D. Coolidge: Shirt-Sleeves Manager, *IEEE Spectrum*, May, pp. 81–85.

YPSILANTI, DIMITRI. 1985.   The Semiconductor Industry, *The OECD Observer*, No. 132, pp. 14–20.

ZACHARY, WILLIAM B., and ROBERT M. KRONE. 1984.   Managing Creative Individuals in High-Technology Research Projects, *IEEE Transactions on Engineering Management*, Vol. EM-31, No. 1, pp. 37–40.

INDEX